The Development of American Literary Criticism

The Development of American

Literary Criticism

By

HARRY H. CLARK

RICHARD H. FOGLE

ROBERT P. FALK

JOHN H. RALEIGH

C. HUGH HOLMAN

EDITED BY

FLOYD STOVALL

The University of North Carolina Press

1955 · CHAPEL HILL

FOREWORD

THE five essays of this volume grew out of the papers read by their respective authors on the program of the American Literature Group of the Modern Language Association at its annual meeting in December, 1952. The editor was chairman of the Group for that year.

The only general histories of American literary criticism published to date are George E. De Mille's *Literary Criticism in America* (1931) and Bernard Smith's *Forces in American Criticism*, neither of which is adequate to the needs of the contemporary student of American criticism. The essays of the present volume are offered not as a complete history of American literary criticism but with the hope that they will serve usefully the needs of advanced students of American literature until a complete history shall be provided. Each essay has been read and criticized by the editor and by at least one of the contributors other than its author. The editor has not attempted to impose an arbitrary pattern for the book, and each author is solely responsible for the opinions expressed in his essay. Yet the editor and the authors have made an effort to correlate the essays, and it is to be hoped that they have succeeded in giving the book enough unity to constitute it in effect a single work.

Chapel Hill, N. C.   FLOYD STOVALL
June 1, 1954

[v]

ACKNOWLEDGMENTS

FOR permission to quote copyrighted materials, grateful acknowledgment is made to the following:

E. P. Dutton & Co., for permission to quote from *The Confident Years,* by Van Wyck Brooks, copyright 1952.

Farrar, Straus & Young, for permission to quote from *Classics and Commercials,* copyright 1950, and *The Shores of Light,* copyright 1952, by Edmund Wilson.

Harvard University Press, for permission to quote from *The Use of Poetry and the Use of Criticism,* by T. S. Eliot, copyright 1933.

Hendricks House, for permission to quote from *American Literary Criticism,* by Charles Glicksberg, copyright 1952.

The University of Illinois Press, for permission to quote from *The Bright Medusa,* by Howard Mumford Jones, copyright 1952.

Alfred A. Knopf, Inc., for permission to quote from *The Armed Vision,* by Stanley Edgar Hyman, copyright 1948.

The Macmillan Company, for permission to quote from *The Collected Poems* of W. B. Yeats, copyright 1951.

Mrs. Ellen C. Masters and the Estate of Edgar Lee Masters, for permission to quote from *The Spoon River Anthology,* by Edgar Lee Masters, copyright 1915.

Pantheon Books, Inc., for permission to quote from R. P. Blackmur's essay "A Burden for Critics" in *Lectures in Criticism,* copyright 1949.

ACKNOWLEDGMENTS

William Morrow & Co., for permission to quote from *On the Limits of Poetry,* by Allen Tate, copyright 1941, 1948 by Allen Tate; and from *In Defense of Reason,* by Yvor Winters, copyright 1937, 1947 by Yvor Winters, and copyright 1938, 1943 by New Directions.

G. P. Putnam's Sons, for permission to quote from *Shelburne Essays,* third, sixth, and seventh series, by Paul Elmer More, copyright 1906, 1909, and 1910 respectively.

Henry Regnery Company, for permission to quote from *The Forlorn Demon,* by Allen Tate, copyright 1953.

Charles Scribner's Sons, for permission to quote from *Axel's Castle,* by Edmund Wilson, copyright 1931, and *The World's Body,* by John Crowe Ransom, copyright 1938.

The Viking Press, for permission to quote from *The Liberal Imagination,* by Lionel Trilling, copyright 1950.

CONTENTS

The Development of American Literary Criticism

INTRODUCTION

THE TITLE of this book makes, in effect, two affirmations about criticism written in America: first, that it is genuinely "American," as distinguished from criticism written in Great Britain, France, or some other European country; second, that it has come to be what it is through a process of growth sustained, in part at least, by the absorption of native materials. I propose in this introduction to examine briefly the grounds on which such affirmations may be justified.

It is self-evident that criticism is an art and not a science, though it may use scientific tools. It is therefore affected by the critic's individual idiosyncrasies and by the mores of his cultural *milieu*. The American critic shares with his British or French counterpart the common heritage of European civilization, but he has also a national heritage which is different from that of a European national and which he cannot wholly escape. American civilization may be said to have grown from the scion of seventeenth-century European civilization engrafted upon the wild North American plant. Native elements, together with what has been drawn from continuing relations with the Old World, have produced a complex organism that is both like and unlike the parent plant that has flourished on other soil. The unlikeness increased while civilization moved westward across the continent, and the rate of change was accelerated after the colonial status

[3]

was exchanged for independence. At some indefinite period in the latter half of the nineteenth century the movement towards difference diminished and a strong tendency towards likeness became dominant, though both tendencies have undoubtedly coexisted from the beginning.

Out of this American culture, forming part of its growth, an American literature has been created. Some date its beginning from Anne Bradstreet, some from Irving or Cooper, and some from Whitman (Hemingway has said from Mark Twain!), but no one denies any longer that it exists. Lowell was probably mistaken in saying that we must have a criticism before we can have a literature, but in any case we have the literature. Do we also have the criticism? I think it must be acknowledged that we do. Poe, Emerson, Lowell, Whitman, Howells, Henry James, and even T. S. Eliot are widely recognized as "American" in varying degrees, and many will insist that they in large part constitute the main stream of American literature. Yet they are all critics of literature, and therefore American critics. It has been usual rather than exceptional, since Goethe at least, for great writers to be critics, often great critics; hence, having a literature, America was assured sooner or later of having a literary criticism. The close relationship of the two is indicated in the historical fact that critical activity has been greatest during or immediately following periods of creative activity.

The growing difference between eighteenth-century America and England created the desire for American independence, and pride in nationality undoubtedly went far to spur efforts to produce a literature that would be American and not merely a branch of English literature. By 1815 there were unmistakable evidences that an American literature was in process of becoming, and it was appropriate that public-spirited men of letters should desire a medium in this country for the expression of critical literary opinion. Hence the *North American Review* was established. The founders were Federalists in politics and predominantly neoclassical in their literary taste, and so it was to be expected that they would be moderate in their nationalism. The promoters of the *Democratic Review* some twenty years later, on the contrary, were Democrats with a tendency to romanticism and a vigorous nationalism. The *Whig Review,* launched in 1845, took a stand between the two extremes. All three were nationalistic, differing only in degree. The editors of the *North American Review* were better educated academically than most magazine editors of the time and probably more familiar with the traditions of European culture, and yet it must be remembered that these men were the first to feel the need for an American literary criticism.

Lesser journals followed the lead of these three, and of course, as political nationalism grew into the doctrine of "manifest destiny," there were extremists. Reviewers had a tendency to praise all literary products by Americans, regardless of intrinsic merit. This folly raised up Edgar Poe to defend the universal values and repudiate nationalism as a criterion of literary worth. The realm of art, said Poe, is international, and the principles by which it should be judged are unaffected by time or place. The critic's function is to evaluate, and neither personal nor national interests should bias his judgment. This is not to say that Poe undervalued the importance of creating an American literature. He would have been as proud as Cornelius Mathews himself to affirm that American literature is equal to any European literature, but he protested that such a literature cannot be produced by partial critical judgments. In fact, he knew better than his contemporaries that such dishonest criticism would only tend to perpetuate mediocrity and so defeat its purpose in the long run. In effect Poe supported the *North American* critics in defending the European tradition in opposition to an exaggerated emphasis on an "American" newness; but he went further and anticipated more recent criticism in his insistence that the critic must judge the work of art as something in itself and not merely the vehicle of ideas, emotions, and events. Poe stands as a bulwark against the fallacious opinion, persisting to this day in Europe, that an American writer is not genuinely American unless he breaks completely with the European tradition and renounces both its methods and its standards.

Longfellow, Holmes, Lowell, and their group followed Irving and Bryant and the early *North American* critics in their moderate nationalism. Yet they too assisted in the establishment of an American literature and criticism. Believing that American culture must be an extension of the European tradition, not in conflict with it, they undertook to stimulate American writing by translating European culture into forms easily understood by Americans. Poe disapproved of the unoriginal way in which they treated native materials while approving their moderate nationalism. Originality, Poe thought, can be achieved by conscious techniques and need not reflect the image of the artist or the *milieu* in which he works. Longfellow, Holmes, and Lowell, on the contrary, felt that American writers must use native materials as much as possible but need not present them in original forms. They believed form is conventional and is not determined by content.

Emerson urged American writers to be original in both materials and forms. If they obey their genius and are sincere, they cannot be otherwise, for the writer works organically and re-creates himself in his art, and the forms of his artistic creation will be determined by his materials. To follow the European tradition slavishly was therefore, in Emerson's opinion, to be less than a genuine American. The tradition was perhaps less authoritative for him than for Longfellow and Lowell because, though he knew it well and loved it, he also knew and valued other cultures, such as those of Persia and India. If America was a child of Europe, so was Europe, in a remoter time, the child of Asia. In fact he saw America, somewhat in the manner of Victor Cousin, as the synthesis in a process of which Asia was the thesis and Europe the antithesis. Asia is the soul, Europe the intellect, and America must somehow prove itself to be both soul and intellect. This it cannot be if it uses its past as something to be reproduced instead of something to grow from. Emerson was more conscious of the geography and character of the United States than were his Boston contemporaries. His travels in the East and Middle West as a lecturer afforded him opportunities to feel the pulse of his nation and to recognize the character of its nationality. But even Emerson found it difficult to escape altogether the New England point of view, as Poe never was able to hold clearly any but a Southern point of view.

If there was to be a genuinely national point of view in litera- ture before the Civil War, one would expect its development in New York City, and that is where it did develop in the 1850's. Walt Whitman, a native of Long Island and long identified with greater New York, had absorbed the national spirit first through politics in the Democratic Party, and later through his participa- tion in the Free Soil movement. He made himself at home in New England transcendentalism by reading Emerson, and he lovingly identified himself with certain aspects of the South and West by making in 1848 a long journey to New Orleans and back by way of the Mississippi River and the Great Lakes. He em- braced both evolutionism and Hegelianism and saw in them the justification of his belief in America's destined role as the liberator and unifier of the Oriental and Occidental worlds. Yet he was by no means indifferent to the European tradition. He read Homer, Shakespeare, and Carlyle with admiration and some thoroughness, but he also knew the Scottish common sense philosophy through the *Edinburgh Review* and the *North British Review* and the positivism of J. S. Mill and his school through the *Westminster Review*. He admired the vigor of the American actor Edwin Forrest and the polish of the English actor W. S. Macready, but he found greatest satisfaction in the acting of Junius Brutus Booth, who, he thought, exemplified the best quali- ties of both. He was like Emerson in his determination not to be mastered by the European tradition but to master it and use it effectively in the creation of a literature that should be not anti- European but genuinely American.

Melville was less radically the nationalist than Whitman, and yet he was not less certain that America must and will produce its own literature and that it will not, as he said in "Hawthorne and His Mosses," appear "in the costume of Queen Elizabeth's day." His own creative work owed something to his reading, and what he owed shows up more obviously than it would have done if he had taken the time, as Whitman did, to digest his reading and make it a part of his own mind. It may be that Whitman and

Melville are freer from the past because their minds were not at an early age subjected to the discipline of Greek, Latin, and the English classics. By the time they came under the influence of the great masters of literature their individualities had become firmly integrated with their own time and place. Besides, as I have already said, they belonged to New York City, which even then had no provincial character distinct from the character of America as a whole.

It is ironic that America produced its most truly national writers at the very moment when political disunity was about to precipitate the Civil War. Actually the contemporaries of Whitman and Melville did not recognize them as symbols of American cultural nationalism because but few of them had a clear notion of what American culture was or was to be. Most literate Americans in 1850 or 1860 believed Longfellow, Holmes, and Lowell to be the architects of American literary culture, whereas in fact the true architects were those then least acknowledged: Emerson, Whitman, Poe, Hawthorne, and Melville. Or so it seems from the vantage point of today.

It is also ironic that after the Civil War, which assured our political unity, our cultural unity began to disintegrate. Longfellow, Holmes, and Lowell, representing the continuation of European culture, lived on and gradually acquired, in the popular imagination, the stature of Olympians. They were the founders of the Genteel Tradition, and two of them lived into the last decade of the century to perpetuate it. They were supported by a younger generation of admirers, notably Aldrich, Taylor, Stedman, and Stoddard, whose lights sparkled but had small candle power. Howells, who had received the blessing of the Olympians in his youth, took a stand between Whitman and Lowell and tried in his theory of realism to relate art more immediately to the actualities of common life. Emerson, in his old age, lost some of the independence of his youth and moved closer to the Olympians, and indeed came to be thought of himself as an Olympian. Whitman staunchly adhered to the essential core of his early nationalism, but he mellowed. Even Mark Twain, having adopted New England as a place of residence, had often to assume a negative attitude to avoid being drawn into the charmed circle. The materialism of what he called the Gilded Age was attractive in his eyes, and yet he could not escape the idealism of his temperament and the Puritanism of his early teaching. He was capable, therefore, of appealing to the provincialism of America in *Innocents Abroad,* of subjecting American business and politics to the satire of *The Gilded Age,* and of apotheosizing a romantic ideal in *Personal Recollections of Joan of Arc.* In many ways Mark Twain was the epitome of America in the Gilded Age. Henry James preserved the moral idealism of the age of Emerson and Hawthorne by escaping to Europe, where he could look with detachment upon the struggle here and sublimate his own inner conflict in fiction. Henry Adams was less fortunate, and could find no better solution than to withdraw from active participation in the modern world and live in a medieval world largely of his own creation. The conclusion of this movement away from a unified national culture at the turn of the century was the bohemian cosmopolitanism of Huneker, which was continued by Mencken and Nathan, and which finally disintegrated in the smoke of Paris cafes after the First World War. Most of the expatriates returned during the depression years after 1929, but Pound and Eliot found Europe more congenial and remained.

To rebel against the conventionalized forms of American culture is not, however, to deny the culture itself. Rebellion has always been a recurring mood of the American temper, and constitutes the systolic movement in the rhythm of our national development. Emerson and Whitman were rebels in their time, and the twentieth-century rebellion against the ideals of their time was to be expected. Nevertheless it did not occur until these ideals had deteriorated, on the one hand, through an overemphasis on science and business, into a crass materialism, and, on the other, through the lapse of the Olympian traditionalists, into a lifeless aestheticism. This breach has not yet been closed, but indications are not wanting that latent forces exist which may eventually close it and restore the unity of our national culture. The career of Van Wyck Brooks is symptomatic. As a young man he was one of the rebels, but as he grew older he sought to recover part of the past which once he had rejected. Yvor Winters retains something of the moral idealism of the Puritans together with the censorious egotism of Poe. Eliot and the "New Critics" have rejected the immediate past only to revive the values of a remoter time, which, because the American nation was not then formed, appear to be universal and not national values. I believe this movement of rejection to be not a permanent tendency, and certainly not an end in itself, but a means for the correction of an overemphasis on certain aspects of American national culture in the nineteenth century, especially its materialism.

Parallel with the development of nationalism in conflict with universalism, America versus Europe, there has been a distinctively American development of the spirit of freedom in conflict with authority. This struggle is reflected in politics, in economics, in manners, and in art. It has been described in other terms, such as relativism versus absolutism, pragmatism versus idealism, and romanticism versus classicism. This is a universal condition of life, to be sure, but conditions in North America have been sufficiently different to produce features of the conflict that have special significance. Given a continent to grow upon and a people already in flight from the restrictions of European authority, the idea of freedom has had an influence on the daily lives of the inhabitants of the United States much greater than that felt by any other comparable people in modern times.

In America, perhaps more than elsewhere, freedom and security have been sought as equal and not mutually exclusive goods. Edwards was a dogmatic defender of Calvinism, but he was also an idealist and prepared the ground for Emerson's coming in the next century. The revolutionary generation subscribed to the declaration that all men are created free and equal, but they devised a government based on law. Even Whitman wrote in *Specimen Days*: "The whole Universe is absolute law. Freedom only opens entire activity and license *under the law*." How is it possible for man to be both free and under the law? Whitman's answer is that the mind that must obey the law is also the maker of the law and is therefore not inhibited. Freedom and law are phases of the same organic structure, and though they are forever in conflict, they are forever reconciled in a process of continual development. This theory of organic growth, though derived from European sources, has been peculiarly congenial to the American mind. Emerson and Whitman were thoroughgoing organicists. In their theories of art, Poe and James were also, in separate ways, organicists. Whitman conceived the poem as an organic growth and as the image of the poet, who in turn is an image of his society and grows therefrom. Poe conceived of the poem as beginning with an impression or felt experience in the poet, which he then proceeds to objectify by purely rational processes so that it will reproduce in his reader the effect first felt by himself. James's theory represents the artist as beginning with a "germ" which is somehow implanted in his mind, where, if it find congenial soil and is sufficiently fed by experience and cultivated by the artist's imagination, it grows into the finished work of art. This theory has some similarity to both the naturalism of Emerson and Whitman and the rationalism of Poe. All three types of organicism have been influential in later American criticism. Both the impressionists and the Freudian critics are organicists in one degree or another. Many of the formalist critics owe something to James's type of organic theory.

The organic theory of art as held by Whitman was democratic, transcendental, and to some extent evolutionary and Hegelian. The poem as he understood and created it is both universal and relative; it is universal as it participates in the idea of all, and it is relative in that it reflects the personality, time, and place of its creator. The theories of realism and naturalism that developed after the Civil War were imperfect expressions of organicism. Howellsian realism provided that the novelist must reflect and feed the social *milieu* in which he works so far as he can without violating good taste and a high moral tone. American life is commonplace and healthy; therefore the novel in America should be morally sound and deal with ordinary people and events. Naturalism differs chiefly in its more pessimistic philosophy of scientific determinism. The naturalists believed that American life had become unhealthy, materialistic, and sensational, and that their novels must deal realistically with diseased minds, violent events, and pessimistic moods.

The neohumanist movement was an attempt to correct the excessive freedom that characterized American literature and morals from Whitman to the end of the century. There is some justice in Babbitt's assumption that transcendentalism, realism, naturalism, and expressionism were all manifestations of romanticism, though he was mistaken in identifying the movement wholly with Rousseau. More recently, critics have emphasized a formal organicism that connects rather with the Aristotelian method than the looser, non-intellectual process of romantic organicism. The new rhetoric of criticism, the insistence that the poem shall be read as an end and not as a means, and the identification of idea with form are further evidences of the contemporary critic's impatience with the subjectivity and relativism of most nineteenth-century American criticism. The neohumanists, the neo-Aristotelians, and the formalist critics all tend to be conservative. Their "newness" is really the revived traditionalism which antedates the nineteenth and most of the eighteenth century in Europe. Romanticism, or naturalism, which was the newness of the nineteenth century, still survives in certain types of psychological criticism and here and there among academic critics. But the dominant mood in criticism, as in other phases of the American mind, is today conservative, restrictive, traditional, if not indeed authoritarian. The spirit of freedom is languid and anemic. This may be the result, in part, of our renewed and increasing dependence, in this century, upon Europe for our models of criticism. But it is also in part the reversion to the negative attitudes which have been attributed to Poe, Hawthorne, and Melville as against the optimism of Emerson and Whitman.

Thus, although the lines of development are obscure, it is apparent to one who will follow them closely that American criticism, like American literature, has a strong native element, and that its growth has been to a great extent independent of European models of the same period. There have been and continue to be internal tensions, conflicting tendencies, but these are not finally disintegrating; rather they are the means and the evidence of organic growth. During the first century of American national independence this growth was, in general, away from the European tradition and towards the establishment of a cognate but independent American tradition. Once such a tradition was established our nationalism lost its aggressiveness, and since the beginning of the present century the lines of development of American and European criticism have converged and now follow approximately parallel directions. This is not a denial of the continuing existence of a national American criticism but a proof that it has reached maturity. We can at last, as we could not in Emerson's time without arrogance, stand on our own feet.

Harry H. Clark

CHANGING ATTITUDES IN EARLY AMERICAN LITERARY CRITICISM
1800-1840

IN THE FOLLOWING SURVEY, organized on the basis of changing attitudes towards certain basic concepts and methods, criticism is understood as including a writer's comments not only on others but also on his own work and the literary theories which he strives to practice. Hawthorne remarked that if he could not "criticize his own work as fairly as another man's"[1] he would be ashamed; and often a writer's indication of the methods by which he elaborated his own ideas and secured the effects at which he aimed is especially illuminating as to creative methods and structure. For, broadly speaking, one may regard criticism as essentially comment on the ways and means by which one can read most intelligently and fruitfully. Since the subject involves changes of attitude, and the same critic often in this period evolved from one position to another quite different, as in the case of Bryant, Irving, A. H. Everett, and Prescott, it is hoped that a sense of confusion will be avoided by a careful attention to chronology and dates of the utterances cited. I have tried to subordinate my personal attitudes to an objective exposition of the logical articulation of critical ideas, and so far as the limited space permits I have tried to cite relevant scholarly studies where individual ideas are more fully elaborated and

1. Hawthorne's Preface to *Twice Told Tales*.

which help to provide a fuller contexture and to orient our critical ideas in relation to sources or parallels in foreign literatures to which our critics were responsive. It has been customary to dismiss much of the criticism of this early period as merely patriotic, moralistic, or impressionistic, but on the whole the findings here would seem to suggest that this period was at least the seed-time of ideas which are worthy of close study as foreshadowing what was to follow and which help to illuminate the development of the American mind and spirit as well as of literary taste. Needless to say, the subject involves many avenues which are greatly in need of further investigation.

To avoid having too many footnotes, I have referred in the body of the paper to *The Transcendentalists. An Anthology*, edited by Perry Miller in 1950, as *TA*; to the volumes in the "American Writers Series" as AWS; to the periodicals *American Literature, Publications of the Modern Language Association*, and the *New England Quarterly* as *AL, PMLA*, and *NEQ*; to "American Fiction Series" as AFS, and to my own edition of *Major American Poets* as *MAP*. In *TA*, Miller's introductory notes before the selections have provided exceptionally useful bibliographical information.

I. THE TURN FROM SOCIAL SOLIDARITY AND OUTWARD-NESS TO INDIVIDUALISM, SELF-REALIZATION, AND IN-WARDNESS

A. SOCIAL SOLIDARITY

The turn from the ideal of social solidarity to individualism and self-reliance, which Emerson and many others regarded as the key to the period under discussion, is reflected in literary theory and criticism. Concern for social solidarity, which will be discussed first, was encouraged by such influences as a natural recoil from the individualism of the American and French revolutions along with the need of stabilizing the social order represented by the Constitution; by the easterners' apprehension (as voiced by men such as Dwight and G. Morris) of the individualistic western frontiersmen; by appeals to philosophies such as "The Great Chain of Being" (involving "gradations") and Scottish associationalism which has been accused of making critics "watch-dogs" of the social order; by the cult of sympathetic social sanction and by the southern ideal of paternalism connected with slavery and a social hierarchy of classical origins; and by the vogue of English neoclassic writers such as Pope with their doctrine that in society "all nature's difference keeps all nature's peace," that conformity to an established social hierarchy should have literary encouragement.

Thus in *Modern Chivalry* (1792-1815) the Princeton-bred H. H. Brackenridge, trained by Witherspoon, said his chief literary aim, using the satiric devices of Cervantes, Swift, Lucian and Butler, was to convince his readers of the ridiculousness of letting the uneducated and incompetent aspire to public office in violation of his cherished ideal of the golden mean and that of the classical Polybius' checks and balances which constituted good government (AFS Introduction). Bryant's *Lectures on Poetry* (1826) stressed its "uses" in advancing the "welfare of communities," discussed its "relation to our age and country," and found the essence of the Homeric "hardy spirit" in heroic "present sacrifices, in order to insure the good for the future." He especially praised (AWS, 194 ff.; 296-7) the work "of peace and brotherhood" so "nobly performed" by Irving, who, following the Scottish associationalists devoted to sympathy, sought as an extrovert to be "useful" in arousing the "dormant good feeling [that] actually exists in each country, toward the other" (AWS). As Goldsmith's sympathetic biographer-critic (1840), Irving, following his *Animated Nature*, invoked the theory of "gradations" from the "meanest insect" to man to God to justify "society for its laws of rank and gradations,"[2] in an effort to reconcile the American Federalists and the British liberals after the bitterness of the two wars. Cooper took many a chapter-motto from the translation of Homer by Pope (whom he regretted Americans had "effectually forgotten" by 1838), and he seems, as he proceeded, to have tried in part to dignify the Leather-stocking Series as a sort of epic reflecting our national

2. Irving's "St. Mark's Eve" in *Bracebridge Hall*, p. 129, and *Reviews and Miscellanies* (Spuyten Duyvil ed.).

ideals as conditioned by the frontier. While Cooper thought Scott's Toryism "dangerous" for Americans because of his "deference to hereditary rank" and to a "mere feudal"[3] order, he himself used many of Scott's more literary devices such as "Unknown" characters dramatically identified later, and he attacked the French Revolution and used the Great Chain of Being theory to justify social gradations coupled (in books such as *The Bravo*) with the paternalism associated with his deep sense of Christian stewardship. Cooper's eleven novels of the sea often use ships as symbols of necessary social stratification. And in his novels with European settings such as *The Heidenmauer* (1832) he said (Chapter XXX) that his "object" was not to deal with the "workings of a single and a master mind" but "to represent society, under its ordinary faces, in the act of passing from the influence of one set of governing principles to that of another," in this case from Catholicism to Lutheranism as conditioned by the political and economic ambitions of different classes. In general, of course, the minor Knickerbockers shared literary aims which had strong social orientations, as Kendall Taft (AWS) has shown.

If Poe seems partly a Byronic lyricist in his poetry, his "Israfel" has the poet conditioned by his environment. And Poe perhaps reflects his southern environment in the forties in focusing his literary criticism on "The Heresy of the Didactic" which in practice involved criticizing writers such as Lowell who were chiefly didactic about freeing slaves, whose status Poe justified not only in terms of "property" but in terms of "the laws of *gradation* so visibly pervading all things in Earth and Heaven," which has "taught our race to submit to the guidance of natural laws, rather than attempt their control."[4] And he criticized Margaret Fuller's writings on feminism as "detestable," criticized the writings of reformers as representing "credulity" and even "insanity" because they attempted to interfere with the social hierarchy as then constituted, and he attacked Bentham's writings

3. James Fenimore Cooper, *Gleanings in Europe* (England), ed. R. E. Spiller (1930) pp. 153-54. See also Spiller's Introduction to AWS *Cooper*.
4. Poe's *Works* (Harrison ed. in 17 Vols.), IV, 201-03; see also "Eureka."

and regarded equalitarian democracy (as opposed to his ideal of the "sole unquestionable aristocracy—that of intellect") as "a very admirable form of government in the world—for dogs."[5]

But even in the North the neoclassicist Robert Walsh's *American Quarterly Review* (XXI, 20, March, 1837) criticized Catherine Sedgwick's *Poor Man, Rich Man* by concluding that "a full appreciation by the poorer and humbler classes . . . of their proper station in the social economy, their responsibilities and advantages, is what is needed. In them a spirit of contentment, not of ambition, should be fostered." And O. W. Holmes, spokesman of "The Brahmin Caste," admittedly schooled in "classical English verse as represented by Pope, Goldsmith, and Campbell," traces in "Poetry, a Metrical Essay" (1836) the decline of poetry from the martial and epic to the individualistic "Cowper's gloom and Chatterton's despair" as associated with "a pseudo-poetical race of invalids." Holmes also satirized many a "last leaf" or eccentric in dress to provoke society's "grin" at what was "queer" as a means of enforcing social conformity and acceptance of his view that " 'tis but the fool that loves excess," that deviates from the Golden Mean of his beloved Horace and good society.[6] One of Hawthorne's chief themes was the evil of isolation and social maladjustment. "The Artist of the Beautiful" suffers from "lack of sympathy" which Hawthorne equates with "restraint of example." And in dealing with the artist in "Prophetic Pictures" he says that "Unless there be those around him by whose example he may regulate himself, his thoughts, desires, and hopes will become extravagant, and he the semblance, perhaps the reality, of a madman."[7] "It is one great advantage of a gregarious mode of life that each person rectifies his mind by other minds, and squares his conduct to that of his neighbors, so as seldom to be lost in eccentricity,"[8] a tendency of the prophets of transcendental self-reliance which he seems to have disliked as much as the

5. *Ibid.*, XVII, 333; VIII, 265-75; on Bentham, VI, 204; XVI, 1, 70, 193; VI, 199ff; AWS, lxix ff.

6. *MAP*, 545-56. See notes and bibliography in *MAP*, pp. 882-92, and AWS Introduction.

7. AWS, 261.

8. "Peter Goldthwaite's Treasure," in *Hawthorne* (Modern Library Giant), p. 1106.

satirical "Celestial Railroad" suggests he disliked such writers' optimism and devotion to Kant.

B. TURN TO INDIVIDUALISM AND SELF-RELIANCE

However, if sympathetic social approval was for Hawthorne an important test of morality, he also represents a transition to individualism in criticism. For in his review of W. G. Simms, he speaks of the "worn out mould"[9] of Scott's external or historical pageantry; it needs to be vitalized by a writer's use of inward psychological tensions. "The artist," Hawthorne says in "Prophetic Pictures," "must look beneath the exterior . . . to see the inmost soul"; he must probe "The Interior of a Heart," later his own title for one of the key chapters in the *Scarlet Letter*. And Hawthorne's criticism of the case of the monomaniac reformer Hollingsworth and reformers' writings in general[10] accords with Emerson's attack in "Self-Reliance" on the writings of reformers which concludes, "Thy love afar is spite at home." Conversely, in "Earth's Holocaust" Hawthorne says to reformers of the outward, "Purify that inward sphere, and the many shapes of evil that haunt the outward . . . will vanish of their own accord." Indeed, as early as 1822, James Marsh, the pioneer introducer of Coleridge, concluded, "The modern mind removes the centre of its thought and feeling from the 'world without' to the 'world within.' "[11]

Emerson, summing up the transitional period from 1820 to 1840, found the key in the turn from the ideal of a "shining social prosperity" to the belief that "the nation existed for the individual," in the turn from extroversion to "introversion" represented by Goethe's *Faust* and by Kant, who made "the best analysis of the mind." "The [new] age tends to solitude," and the "enlargement and independency of the individual . . . In literature the

9. Randall Stewart, "Hawthorne's Contributions to *The Salem Advertiser,*" *AL*, V (1934), 327-341. See also C. H. Foster, "Hawthorne's Literary Theory," PMLA, LVII (1942), 241-54.

10. Arlin Turner, "Hawthorne and Reform," *NEQ*, XV (1942), 700-714; L. S. Hall, *Hawthorne: Critic of Society* (New Haven, 1944); and H. P. Miller, "Hawthorne Surveys his Contemporaries," *AL*, XII (1940), 228-35.

11. *North American Review*, XV (1822), 107. Hereafter cited as *NAR*.

effect appeared in the decided tendency toward criticism" as illustrated with "much importance" by William Ellery Channing's essays on Milton and others "which were the first specimens in this country of that large criticism which in England had given power and fame to the Edinburgh Review. They were widely read and of course immediately fruitful . . ." (*TA*, 494-500).

If one inquires what was the key to the pivotal theory of literary criticism by the Unitarian Channing, a reader of Coleridge, it seems to be his rejection of a mechanical appraisal of writing by external or merely traditional yard-sticks or rules, and his insistence that the reader try to respond individually, the divine within himself answering to what is divine in a great author, deep answering to deep. Thus, just as in viewing awesome scenes in nature, "a power within seems to respond to the omnipotence around us," Channing finds that "the same principle is seen in the delight ministered to us by works of fiction or of imaginative art, in which our own nature is set before us in more than human beauty and power." Criticism of Milton, for example, should tap the spiritual resources of "our *own* nature," of "our likeness to God" (*TA*, 24). Channing's theory of the relation of the new inwardness and of nature with her images (involving the doctrine of "correspondence") is of central significance: as critic he seeks "a poetry which pierces beneath the exterior of life to the depths of the soul, and which lays open its mysterious working, borrowing from the whole outward creation fresh images and correspondences, with which to illuminate the secrets of the world within us." Note the combination of the inward and the outward, and yet the subordination of the latter.

The early George Ripley, a "transition" (*AL*, 14:11) from the introvert Channing to the more extrovert Parker, in his 1830 essay on "DeGerando on Self-Education" struck the "keynote of that whole series which culminated in the papers of the Norton-Ripley controversy" by appealing to inward and intuitive truths as opposed to historical miracles (*AL*, 14:3). In 1835, ten years after Bancroft's essay on Herder,[12] Ripley saw in Herder the "germ" of the current "mighty revolution," for he argued that while by the "laws of literary criticism" the miracles could not be disregarded in the Bible, Herder held that Jesus relied not on miracles or on "tradition or authority" but on the inward character" of his teaching (*TA*, 94-97). While Ripley preferred Cousin for his stylistic clarity and Kant for his intellectual precision, he introduced his vastly influential fourteen-volume *Specimens of Foreign Standard Literature* (1838-1842) with the conviction that "the remarkable popularity of Mr. Coleridge as a philosophical writer" derived from his awakening man's "inward powers," and in Ripley's many appeals to the Reason over the Understanding he regards the former as "a voice within" (*TA*, 298; 138). Brownson, who later followed Ripley in social concerns, in 1839 centered his crusade in the conviction that advanced thinkers "have outgrown the material, soulless philosophy of the last century, and have turned their minds inward."[13] Bancroft also emphasized man's "internal moral sense," having pioneered as a first-hand student and interpreter of German thinkers, but he stressed the inward light of the Quakers also (*TA*, 423).

If these Americans later diverged from the inwardness of Emerson and Thoreau, F. H. Hedge, another master of German thought in the original (editor in 1848 of the influential *Prose Writers of Germany* and critical introducer of Coleridge in 1833), staunchly defended in 1840 Emerson's unsocial "self-culture" and concluded that it is to "such men that we must look for the long expected literature of this nation" (*TA*, 471-75).

12. Bancroft's "Writings of Herder," *NAR*, XX (1825), 138-49. Over 200 critical essays appearing in this periodical will be found conveniently summarized with brief quotations in H. H. Clark's "Literary Criticism in the *North American Review, 1815-1835*," *Trans. Wis. Acad.*, XXXII (1940), 299-350.

13. *TA*, 206 ff. Brownson was of course only one of many who waged war against Locke's so-called sensationalism and outwardness. See index to *TA* under Locke, index to Joseph Blau's *American Philosophic Addresses* (New York, 1946) and especially Merle Curti's "The Great Mr. Locke: America's Philosopher, 1783-1861," *Huntington Library Bulletin*, XI (1937), 107-155, a study which skillfully interrelates intellectual and political and social history but shows that Locke's vogue continued among conservative opponents of Scottish intuitionism and Transcendentalism much later than generally supposed.

In 1838 Jones Very's important essay "On Epic Poetry" argued that after the extroversion of Homer, Shakespeare's *Hamlet* and Milton were great mainly for "transferring the scene of action from the outward world to the world within," and he urged contemporary poets to center on the "introspective" and on "inwardness" (*TA*, 343-56).

There were other non-transcendental spokesmen of individualism or inwardness. Byronism was widely debated by American critics, and the introspective Percival, notable for metrical experimentation, was Byron's main American disciple in the 1820's. Poe was influenced by both Byronism and German writers, but he said that the horror I seek is not of Germany but of the soul; and Poe turned from the external world to inward psychological tensions as in "Ulalume," in his lonely quest of a melancholy "beauty which is not afforded the soul by any existing collocation of earth's forms" (AWS, 346). From another angle, the Quaker Whittier, while devoted during our period mainly to outward charity and reform, in 1840 presaged his later critical introduction to Woolman with a poetical tribute to his Journal, saying that a "soul-sufficing answer" to man's problems "hath no outward origin" or in "Nature" but only in a voice "within" (*MAP*, 107). In 1839 Samuel Ward reviewed Longfellow's *Hyperion* as defensibly "subjective," in contrast to Balzac as "objective." While Longfellow reluctantly concluded that the Germans such as Novalis were addicted to "poetic reverie," to "day-dreams only, as shadows, not as substantial things," he devoted an appreciative chapter of *Hyperion* to "Glimpses into Cloud-Land" of German introspection. And in 1839 in his "Prelude" on the poet's art and inspiration he had concluded, "The land of Song within thee lies" (*MAP*, 288; 859). And a host of American critics, culminating in Emerson and Henry Reed, were devoted in varying degrees to the later Wordsworth[14] of the "Ode on Intimations" (with its anti-Lockean gratefulness for "obstinate questionings of sense and outward things") and of *The Prelude*

14. See Annabel Newton, *Wordsworth in Early American Criticism* (Chicago, 1928), and on Emerson and Wordsworth see F. T. Thompson, "Emerson's Theory and Practice of Poetry," *PMLA*, XLIII (1928), 1170-1184. Also index to *TA*.

devoted to the creative imagination and the growth of his own poetic mind.

Among the many American critics who wrote of Carlyle,[15] who attacked Lockean and Benthamite mechanical outwardness, Thoreau is outstanding for his 1847 critical essay on the theme that "Carlyle alone, since the death of Coleridge, has kept the promise of England," albeit with a refreshingly unique and "vigorous and Titanic" humor (AWS, 186 ff.). Thoreau's critical individualism, apparent also in literary comment on Ossian and Homer in *A Week*, is of course reflected in social-political matters in his call for "Civil Disobedience" and in *Walden*, his quest amid the clutter of materialistic America of the "marrow" of a rich inward life.

II. THE TURN FROM THE UNDERSTANDING TO INTUITIVE REASON AND IMAGINATION

A. UNDERSTANDING AND THE SUBORDINATION OF THE IMAGINATION

There had been in English critics of the eighteenth century a considerable tendency either to distrust what Dr. Johnson in a chapter of *Rasselas* so entitled called "The Dangerous Prevalence of Imagination" or to limit it to a memory of past images and an admittedly strong power which needed the constant curbing of judgment and understanding, and many of the American writers in the earlier part of our period shared this partly neoclassic tendency. Despite some liberalizing cross-currents in American colleges, education in the main continued to be essentially in the neoclassic tradition before the impact of Pestalozzi and the Germans. The Presbyterian clergyman, Samuel

15. See F. W. Roe, *Thomas Carlyle as a Critic of Literature* (New York, 1910); Hill Shine, *Carlyle's Fusion of Poetry, History, and Religion by 1834* (Chapel Hill, 1938); George Kummer, "Anonymity and Carlyle's Early Reputation in America," *AL*, VIII (1937) 297-99; W. S. Vance, "Carlyle in America before *Sartor*," *AL*, VII (1936), 363-75, which gives important excerpts from our critics; and F. L. Mott, "Carlyle's American Public," *Philological Quarterly*, IV (1925), 245-64; *The Correspondence of Thomas Carlyle and R. W. Emerson, 1834-1872* (Boston, 1888), 2 vols. Also H. F. Widger, "Thomas Carlyle in America: His Reputation and Influence," the abstract of a dissertation at the U. of Illinois, 1945. See the index to *TA* and Gohdes' *Periodicals of American Transcendentalism*, 1931, which is also very useful for students of American criticism. Carlyle was one of the major provocative influences.

Miller, in his very representative *Retrospect of the Eighteenth Century* (1803) which included a long critical censure of the novel (to be repeated in essentials by many others), preferred the Scottish Common Sense philosophy to that of Locke as used by the perfectibilians whom he disliked, but he thought that the imaginative element in novels distracted readers from the sober duties of real life. He rejoiced because the rational "scientific spirit of the age had extended itself remarkably, in giving our language that precision, spirit, force, polish, and chaste ornament"[16] in which he thought his age excelled, although his expositions gave him a minor role historically in initiating American interest in the new German intuitive Reason. The Virginian William Wirt, U. S. District Attorney from 1817 to 1829, had much neoclassic influence through his *British Spy* (1803), *Rainbow* (1804), and his part in *The Old Bachelor* (1812). His theory of style, whose influence extended even to the "ratiocinative" Poe, called for the "cultivation of sound judgment" and he disparaged "imagination" as among the "lighter faculties" connected with "youthful vanity" in contrast to the "discipline" of "reason and judgment."

If most of the Knickerbockers eventually became romantic in one sense or another, many of them at first had some kinship with the neoclassic attitude. Bryant, author of *The Embargo*, 1808, in his magisterial *Lectures on Poetry*, 1826, recognized the role in poetry of emotion and imagination but stressed "the understanding also . . . To write fine poetry requires intellectual faculties of the highest order, and among these, not the least important, is the faculty of reason . . . A deficiency or want of cultivation of the reasoning power, is sure to expose the unfortunate poet to contempt and ridicule," for the "understanding" especially provides "the direct lessons of wisdom" which great poetry inculcates.[17]

16. *Retrospect*, II, 101, 234. See Gilbert Chinard, "Progress and Perfectibility in Samuel Miller's Intellectual History," in the collaborative *Studies in Intellectual History* (Johns Hopkins, 1952). See also G. H. Orians, "Censure of Fiction in American Romances and Magazines," *PMLA*, LII (1937), 195-214. Dr. Rush's view of imagination will be found in Joseph Blau, *op. cit.*, pp. 317 ff.

17. *Bryant* (AWS), pp. 191 ff; 211, 222.

And Irving's satirical *History of New York* (1809) reminded Scott of Swift, whom he edited. The American thought "the Scotch are a philosophical close-thinking people,"[18] and as Editor he helped to popularize Alison, and urged that writers such as Margaret Davidson should pursue studies which would strengthen the "judgment, calm and regulate the sensibilities, and enlarge that common sense which is the only safe foundation for all intellectual superstructure."[19] In "English Writers on America" (1819), respectful of historical "examples and models," Irving urged that the English traditions, as the embodiment of "sound deductions from ages of experience," should be winnowed by Americans in a "candid and dispassionate" spirit and with "calm and unbiased judgments" as a means wherewith to "strengthen and embellish our national character."

In 1822 W. H. Prescott, a much venerated literary critic as well as picturesque historian, attributed the "refinement of style" to the "peculiar intellectual character" of eighteenth century writers headed by Addison. "This character was not marked by the exuberant imagination, or intense feeling," but it was "a style which by its simple, conversational, and idiomatic character was well adapted to light familiar topics, or to calm, philosophical reflection, or to sober, dispassionate reasoning," a style perfected by "the Attic simplicity of Hume," the thinker devoted to mechanism. On the other hand, Dr. Johnson turned to Latin models (not so much admired by Prescott) for "a language that would afford scope for the free play of a grand and vigorous intellect." Prescott regarded the "period embellished by the pens of Hume, Johnson, Hawkesworth, Goldsmith, Burke, Robertson, Gibbon, Junius, and Mackenzie, as the Augustan age of English fine writing; . . . a period in which precision, perspicuity, copiousness, grace and vigor, in short whatever constitutes the perfection of style, were carried to a height which has not since been surpassed, and seldom been equaled" (AWS, 386-88).

18. In Irving's essay on Campbell. He selected and published a section on Alison's associationalism in *The Analectic Magazine,* IV (1814), 353-70.

19. *Margaret Davidson* (1841), p. 10. In "Stratford-on-Avon" Irving rejoices because "the imagination kindles into revery and rapture."

It is especially significant that, accepting in the early eighteen twenties the critical criteria of such Scottish associationalists as Jeffery and Gifford, Prescott (as Mr. Charvat has shown, *ibid.*, xc ff.) should gradually have come to accept, with some reservations, the criteria of the new German critics, such as Schlegel; in 1838 he finally attacked Johnsonian criticism as cold-blooded analysis in which "*impression* goes for nothing" (*ibid.*, xci).

J. K. Paulding, Irving's collaborator in the satiric *Salmagundi* (1807-8), was, as Kendall Taft (*Minor Knickerbockers,* 1947) has shown, essentially neoclassical in "his faith in reason; his lifelong preference for the heroic couplet; his emphasis on common sense; his admiration for Dryden and Pope and other older writers; and his basic anti-romanticism." In satires such as *The Lay of the Scottish Fiddle* (1813) Paulding attacked Scott. As A. L. Herold concludes (*D. A. B.*) Paulding "composed realistic tales and novels in consonance with his theory of 'rational fiction' based upon Fielding's practice[20] and expounded in 1820."

It is Poe, however, who best represents the persistence in America of certain eighteenth century tendencies, although he also combined these eventually with Coleridgean elements, to be discussed later. Having in his review of Hawthorne elaborated five laws of the short story (compression, immediacy, verisimilitude, totality of effect focused on "one pre-established design," and finality), Poe was distinguished for his ruthless "tomahawk" style, a "particular and methodical application" of these laws or rules, on the principle that the critic's primary task is one of "pointing out and analyzing defects." Poe's "Rationale of Verse" (1848), first sketched for Lowell's *Pioneer* in 1843 as "Notes on English Verse," was a highly rationalistic analysis of craftsmanship, stressing the dependence of poetic technique not on accent but on time or quantity (as in music), and including an attack on the "blending" or substitution of one metrical foot for another which many of the romanticists advocated. His emphasis on rationality, form, and unity was of the eighteenth cen-

20. See R. C. Beatty, "Criticism in Fielding's Narratives and his Estimate of Critics," *PMLA,* XLIX (1934), 1087-1100.

tury (not to mention his graveyardism), but especially neoclassic was his demand (as interpreted by Miss Margaret Alterton and Hardin Craig) that literary art should be modelled ultimately upon the symmetrical unity and harmony and mechanical design of the universe as interpreted (see his *Eureka*) by the rationalistic Newton and Laplace (AWS Introduction).

B. TURN TO INTUITIVE REASON AND IMAGINATION

The *sources* of American critics' growing allegiance to intuitive Reason and to the creative imagination are beyond our limited province, and the reader is referred to many able studies[21] devoted to the complex ideas of the Scottish associationalists, Coleridge, Wordsworth, Swedenborg, Cousin, the Germans such as Kant and Goethe, and their disciples and interrelations. Broadly speaking, it may be said that most of the early nineteenth century spokesmen of the imagination abroad transcended eighteenth century attitudes by including them in a larger synthesis with a change of emphasis: understanding and the fancy as passive were recognized but subordinated to intuitive reason and the active or creative imagination, which (as Coleridge says in Chapter XIV of the *Biographia Literaria*) is "first put in action by the will and understanding, and . . . reveals itself in the balance or reconciliation of opposite or discordant qualities" to achieve a larger "moulding into a unity." Thus to W. J. Bate Coleridge's criticism seeks "to harmonize the traditional rationalistic precepts of classicism with . . . romantic vitalism."[22] And M. H. Abrams devotes his elaborate book *The Mirror and the Lamp* (1953) to these figures as symbols of the turn from the outwardness of neoclassicism to the inwardness of romanticism, with emphasis (p. 168) on "antithetic metaphors by which Coleridge . . . discriminates his two productive faculties," the

21. The annual bibliography in *ELH* will provide data on studies of Coleridge's theory of the imagination by I. A. Richards, R. S. Crane, Irving Babbitt, C. D. Thorpe, Thomas Raysor, C. M. Bowra, Basil Willey, H. J. Muirhead, and Margaret Sherwood. Wilma Kennedy, *English Heritage of Coleridge* (Yale University Press, 1947) finds many of his ideas present in Berkeley, Hume, Blake, William Collins, and Reynolds.

22. In *Perspectives of Criticism* (ed. Harry Levin), Harvard University Press, 1950.

fanciful memory being a "mechanical" or "passive" or "associative" "mirrorment," while the imagination is "recreative" or "permeative" and a "blending, fusing power." The main idea is that the imaginative critic expects the artists to go beyond literal reality and to idealize or synthesize, to combine (as Coleridge said) "the individual, with the representative, . . . the natural and the artificial," an idea approached by a different route in the doctrine of correspondence of matter and mind (as elaborated by the followers of Swedenborg) involving a focused symbolism. In responding to Coleridge's "following nature in variety of kinds," Americans could justify diversitarianism, individuality, and the turn from appraisal by rules to an imaginative entering into each work as *sui generis*.

Bryant's "Lectures on Poetry" (1826, AWS, p. 187) reflect in part his study of Alison's associative theory that by "scenery" one's "imagination is struck" so as to lead to "trains of . . . imagery" involving "mental excellence . . . or . . . moral good" so that (as Bryant said) the poet's imagination, "by no means passive," "selects and arranges the symbols of thought . . . delightfully" so that "the imagination of the reader is guided" to the "highest conceptions of the beautiful." Bryant was doubtless also indebted to the Swedenborgian doctrine of correspondence (as sketched by Sampson Reed in his "Oration of Genius" to which he listened with Emerson and other critics in 1821) for his attention in the *Lectures* and in his artistry to those imaginative "analogies and correspondencies which it [poetry] beholds between the things of the moral and of the natural world" and so infuses "a moral sentiment into natural objects" (*MAP,* 794). For in 1826 Reed, developing Swedenborg's doctrine of correspondence, and revolting against Locke's supposedly restricted sensationalism, had argued that the "refined" imagination "will no longer lead the way to insanity and madness, by transcending the works of creation," as, for example, in Irving's frivolous fiction of "The German Student." Instead, "the imagination will be refined into a chaste and sober view of unveiled nature. It

[29]

will be confined within the bounds of reality,"[23] of probability. "Finding a resting-place in every created object, it will enter into it and explore its hidden treasures, the relation in which it stands to mind, and reveal the love it bears to its Creator" in the light of the doctrine of correspondence of matter to mind. "There is a language, not of words, but of things." Let man therefore "respect the smallest blade which grows, and permit it to speak for itself" as a symbol of God's love (*TA*, 57). (Here, of course, was a seminal doctrine which was to be used not only by Emerson but by the later author of "Leaves of Grass.")

About the same time the very influential W. E. Channing published his essay on Milton, crediting him with having the "creative imagination" lacking in Dr. Johnson, his harsh neoclassic critic. Channing thought that "poetry's idealizing power is needed to counteract the tendency of physical science, which . . . requires a new development of imagination . . . to preserve men from sinking into an earthly, material, Epicurean life." For to the imaginative poet "the universe . . . is . . . strictly bound together by infinite connections and correspondencies."

Emerson, looking back later, traced the new "large criticism" to the "powerful influence" of Channing in his essay on Milton (*TA*, 500, 496), but Emerson himself at the age of twenty in 1824 had decided that "the highest species of reasoning upon divine subjects is rather the fruit of a sort of moral imagination, than of 'reasoning Machines' such as Locke and Clarke and David Hume" (*Heart of Emerson's Journals,* 18). And, after associational influence, in *Nature*, 1836, Emerson said the "Imagination may be defined to be the use which Reason makes of the material world," by using images to body forth innate and divinely inspired ideas. He had developed the thesis in *Nature* that, since "nature is the symbol of spirit," "words are signs of natural facts," and "particular natural facts are symbols of particular spiritual facts" when the imaginative writer comprehends

23. Contrast the view of Kames, who had great influence in America: "This singular power of fabricating images without any foundation in reality, is distinguished by the name of imagination" (*Elements of Criticism*, 1762, quoted from the 1833 ed., p. 480).

that "The axioms of physics translate the laws of ethics." "This insight, . . . imagination, is a very high sort of seeing, which does not come by study, . . . but by sharing the path or circuit of things through forms, and so making them translucid to others." Hence, he concludes, "the legitimation of criticism [is] the mind's faith that poems are a corrupt version of some text in nature with which they ought to be made to tally" (*MAP*, 236).

. In 1834, when Emerson found "a philosophy itself" in "the distinction of Milton [*Paradise Lost,* V, 486], Coleridge & the Germans between Reason & Understanding" (*Letters,* ed. Rusk, I, 412-13), Bronson Alcott voiced a parallel theory involving education, language, and imagination, after being "released from the [Lockean] philosophy of sense" and praising Goethe and other Germans for blending imagination and reason in "one whole":

"Education is that process by which *thought* is opened out of the soul, and, associated with outward . . . things, is reflected back upon itself, and thus made conscious of its reality and shape. It is *Self-Realization.* As a means, therefore, of educating the soul out of itself, and mirroring forth its ideas, the external world offers the materials. This is the dim glass in which the senses are first called to display the soul, until, aided by the keener state of imagination, . . . it separates these outward types of itself from their sensual connection, in its own bright mirror recognizes again itself, as a *distinctive* object *in* space and time, but *out of it* in *existence,* and painting itself upon these, as emblems of its inner and super-sensual life which no outward things can fully portray . . . A language [based on these outward emblems] is to be instituted between [the child's] spirit and the surrounding scene of things in which he dwells. He who is seeking to know himself, should be ever seeking himself in external things, and by so doing will be best able to find, and explore his inmost light" (*TA,* 141).

In this difficult but central passage Alcott's meaning seems to be that education (which "is Self-Realization") is best achieved by instituting "a language" between one's spirit and external nature, but that images and laws of nature only give one a start—no more —in exploring our soul's "inmost light." For one can know one's soul as "*in* space and time, but *out* of it in existence," transcending physical limitations, only when "aided by the keener state of imagination."

If in the "Artist of the Beautiful" (1844) Hawthorne deplores the fact that "ideas, which grow up within the imagination and appear so lovely to it and of a value beyond whatever men call valuable, are exposed to be shattered and annihilated by contact with the practical" and the utilitarian, we should not overlook the fact that the artist's goal of "the spiritualization of matter" involves matter or nature as a starting-point, or as something to be mirrored or symbolized. Although usually labelled an anti-rationalist, in this story Hawthorne reiterates and gives climactic emphasis to his balanced view that the artist is not merely a man of imagination but one whose creation "represented the intellect, the imagination, the sensibility" in fruitful fusion. Indeed, it was the imagination unbalanced by these other faculties which misled the "artist" to suppose, wrongly, that Annie embodied sympathy: "there were no such attributes in [her] . . . as his imagination had endowed her with." He ought, rather, to "content himself with the inward enjoyment of the beautiful." Hawthorne's "mechanical" wood-carver Drowne (1846), also "kindled by love" mistaken, through his resultant "magic touch" evoked a statue (modelled on an actual woman) in which "intelligence and sensibility brightened through the features, with all the effect of light gleaming forth from within the solid oak. The face became alive." Hawthorne says the carver's "fertile imagination" unerringly added "vitalizing details" which could "have shocked none but a judgment spoiled by artistic rules," and the carver's friend Copley, the artist, adds that true genius is "entitled to transcend all rules." "It seemed," Hawthorne remarks, "as if the hamadryad of the oak had sheltered herself from the unimaginative world within her native tree, and that it was only necessary to remove the shapelessness that had incrusted her, and reveal the graces and loveliness of a divinity." When Drowne's fine statue is completed and after his love is disillusioned, "the light of imagination and sensibility, so recently illuminating" his face, had departed, and his later artistry is in a "mechanical style." The situation symbolizes to Hawthorne the "supposition that in every human spirit there is imagination, sensibility, and creative power, which, according to circumstances, may either be developed in this world, or shrouded in a mask of dullness. To "keep the imagination sane," Hawthorne said elsewhere, in 1841, "is one of the truest conditions of communion with heaven."[24]

Having praised Hawthorne's "fine imagination," Longfellow in his own theory resembled his friend. "The Imagination walks bravest, not in clouds, but on the firm green earth. It conquers by . . . thoughts that have been trained by sage reason and common sense,"[25] although Longfellow knew more than did Hawthorne of German "cloud-land," as *Hyperion* shows. Reminiscent of Hawthorne's Drowne, Longfellow thinks that, guided by an imagination in quest of the "shaped and perfect," the artist should "hew away" whatever tends to "imprison the lovely apparition" concealed in the particular and the commonplace, "in every block of marble." Selecting and re-creating, the artist strives to give us a beauty "more lovely than the real," although evoked from the real. "The highest exercise of the imagination," Longfellow concludes, "is not to devise what has no existence, but rather to perceive what really exists, though unseen by the outward eye—*not creation, but insight.*"[26]

Although Poe paid lip-service at least to the "chivalric" spirit of his region and to Ideality (a concept he derived partly from a current mechanistic Phrenology),[27] he differs from Longfellow as regards imagination chiefly in his view that "the highest order of the imaginative intellect is always preeminently mathematical." Poe centered his criticism not on "Didactic" ethical

24. Hawthorne's *Works (Amercian Notebooks)*, IX, 245.
25. Samuel Longfellow's *Life* (Boston, 1891), III, 407.
26. See Longfellow's *Works* (Standard Library ed.), VI, 167; III, 154; Samuel Longfellow's *Life*, III, 409; VIII, 174.
27. Edward Hungerford, "Poe and Phrenology," *AL*, II (1930), 209-31. Marvin Laser, "The Growth and Structure of Poe's Concept of Beauty," *ELH*, XV (1948), 69-84. See Joseph Blau, *op. cit.*, pp. 357-59, for F. Wayland on imagination, 1831. For Lowell's Coleridge-like concept of the imagination in 1847, see *The Round Table* (1913), pp. 114-16.

goodness nor on correspondence to "any existing collocation of earth's forms" (AWS, 346) but on what one might call the *internal structure* of a work of art either in terms of the logical relation of the part to the whole in plot or in terms of metrical harmony. He was devoted to the *"imagination* which Coleridge has justly styled the *soul* of all poetry," and in his review of Drake and Halleck in 1836 he tried to show, among other things, that Drake's fault lay partly in using a capricious or merely ornamental Fancy as opposed to the structurally law-observing Imagination. Poe sought "a perfect consistency" and "keeping" and the subordination of all incidents to "one preestablished design." According to his longest discussion of Imagination, its range "is unlimited" and it "chooses . . . hitherto uncombined" elements of "Beauty which is at once its sole object and its inevitable test," as contrasted to goodness. "The richness or force of the matters combined; the facility of discovering novelties worth combining; and especially the absolute 'chemical combinations' of the completeness—are the particulars to be regarded in our estimate of Imagination"[28] as underlying the "thorough harmony of an imaginative work." For "if the practice fail, it is because the theory [which centers on the "imaginative intellect"] is imperfect." If Emerson and Poe[29] have some kinship in relying on imagination as a guide to truth, in drawing on different aspects of Coleridge, they differ considerably as to what the content of truth and beauty actually are and in what they chose to emphasize as critics. If, as Foerster and Belden and Bowra have tried to demonstate, Poe's imaginative "vision oscillated between the infernal and the Arcadian" or fantastic at the expense of the ethically normal, it may be pleaded in his favor that *historically*, at a time when minor American writers especially had little beside normality and tended to dodge the difficulties of artistic design by platitudinous moralism or chauvinism, and when many critics took refuge in windy generalities, Poe's "particular and methodical application" of his rules and his precision in "pointing out frankly the errors"

28. Poe's *Works*, ed. J. H. Ingram (Edinburgh, 1890), III, 393.
29. See Stovall's "Poe's Debt to Coleridge," cited earlier, and his study of "Poe as a Poet of Ideas," University of Texas *Studies in English*, XI (1931), 56-62.

in the light of his imaginative ideal of the harmonious relation of parts to the whole was salutary.

III. FROM MORALISM TO BEAUTY

A. MORALISM

The Puritan distrust of human nature and the uncompromising inquisitorial attitude lived on in Federalists such as Timothy Dwight and Jedidiah Morse, sharpened by their desire to moralize on the outcome of the French Revolution supposedly inspired by the French writers Thomas Paine had praised. Novels were suspect as cultivating the passions. The *North American Review*, however, generally welcomed women novelists like Catherine Sedgwick as "administering the healing potion"[30] and raising moral standards. It is well known that Scott was hailed widely by Americans for his wholesome moral tone giving the novel the dignity which comes from serious and fairly authentic history teaching by examples. Goethe was scathingly attacked by conservative Unitarians such as Andrews Norton and William Ware, but the tide began to turn in 1838 with Motley's *New York Review* essay of self-reliant appreciation. Longfellow had deplored his "sensuality" and Emerson[31] his "velvet life," but the latter, doubtless encouraged by Carlyle and Margaret Fuller, came to share some of his aesthetic ideas. The main difficulty in this early period seems to be that, partly in accord with neoclassic tendencies stemming from Horace, our critics thought of what William Dunlap (in his biography of C. B. Brown, 1815, II, 38) called "moral instruction and fascinating amusement" as separate or at least mechanically parallel, rather than as organically fused. However, Ezra Sampson in 1818 in trying to improve the morally bad tendency he found in the genre suggested that the writer might "blend amusement with instruction, entertainment with the moral improvement."[32]

In 1839 Samuel Ward, a rich young New York epicure,

30. *NAR*, XXVI (1828), 410.

31. Vivian Hopkins, "The Influence of Goethe on Emerson's Aesthetic Theory," *Philological Quarterly*, XXVII (1948), 325-44.

32. *Brief Remarks on the Ways of Man* (Hudson, New York), p. 345.

heralded a change of attitude in his defence of the "objective" Balzac as helping to encourage mutual understanding between the rich and the poor classes by "showing the rich how noble a heart may beat beneath rags" while showing the poor that the rich are not without their own "misery" so that "romance may become, and often is, an impressive medium for the transmission of truth"[33] rather than a merely pleasurable escape to an illusory past. As democracy developed, this kind of argument was used to encourage the belief that novels gave readers vicarious experience and increased mutual understanding between all classes. In 1847 the magisterial J. L. Motley's sympathetic essay on "Novels of Balzac"[34] praised him for presenting the "world as it is"; indeed, Motley urged other novelists to "think less of reforming and more of amusing" their readers. Thus, among other influences, Goethe, George Sand, Eugène Sue, and Balzac helped to jolt American critics into recognizing if not fully accepting wider aesthetic horizons. But Shakespeare and Scott seem to have done most to convince American critics that literary beauty could be respectable, for as Prescott (AWS, 401) concluded regarding these authors in 1827, "as the one is the greatest poetic, so the other is the greatest prose dramatist of any age or country."

B. BEAUTY

Shakespeare gradually led our critics, as A. W. Westfall and R. B. Falk show, to an appreciation of the sublime largely denied them in the neoclassic age.[35] Not until the *First Class Book* edited in 1823 by John Pierpont (author of *Airs of Palestine*, 1816, glorifying sacred music) were selections from Shakespeare included for American school children. And so intelligent a man as J. Q. Adams[36] (author of the neoclassic *Lectures on Rhetoric* for Harvard, 1810) could moralize in 1835 that the "lesson

33. *AL*, XXIV (1952), 167-176.
34. *NAR*, LXV (July, 1847), 93.
35. See A. W. Westfall, *American Shakespearean Criticism*, especially useful for bibliography, and R. B. Falk's dissertation at the University of Wisconsin on the same subject, with longer analyses of the chief critics.
36. J. Q. Adams' comments on Shakespeare in long letters to the actor Hackett were included with Adams' permission in Hackett's *Notes . . . [on] Shakespeare.*

to be learned" from *Othello* is that "the intermarriage of black and white is a violation of the law of nature" in which Desdemona "discards all female delicacy, all filial duty." Joseph Hopkinson in a brief series of papers only to "amuse" in the *Port Folio* in 1801 suggested the historical approach to Shakespeare, which was developed in part by Hildreth, J. C. Hart (who began the "Baconian" interpretation in 1848), and the editors O. W. B. Peabody, Verplanck, and W. G. Simms. Jones Very wrote two important essays in 1839-40 excusing Shakespeare's obscenities because, with his loftiest insights, he was "almost as much a passive instrument as the material world" for voicing "nature" (*TA*, 346-56). H. N. Hudson's *Lectures on Shakespeare* (two volumes, 1848), with much "human" and moral appeal of a Whig slant, showed familiarity with critics such as Schlegel and Coleridge, and are distinctive in Hudson's rhapsodic worship of Shakespeare illustrated in his particularized psychological analyses of individual characters. E. P. Whipple, mediating between Macaulay and Coleridge, praised Hudson's work highly in *Essays and Reviews*, collected in 1848. These essays, which rank him in some ways with the early Lowell and Poe as a professional critic, showed much knowledge of the history of critical theory. "The mistake which the old order of critics made consisted in overlooking the doctrine of vital powers. They judged the form of Shakespeare's works by certain external rules, before they had interpreted the inward life which shaped the form."[37]

If Shakespeare helped to enrich our critics' sense of beauty, let us survey their more general and increasing concern with enjoyment and beauty. After Irving's "gaiety" (to use Bryant's word of tribute) in his *History of New York* (1809) in satirizing the ponderous solemnity of historical writers, the heroic style of Greek and Roman epics, and the Jeffersonian logomachy, he

---

37. From the reprint of Whipple's essay on Hudson in *One Hundred Years Ago* (ed. J. P. Wood, 1948), p. 490. See Denham Sutcliffe, " 'Our Young American Macaulay'; Edwin Percy Whipple . . . ," *NEQ*, XIX (1946), 3-18. See also H. H. Clark, "Macaulay in America," *Trans. Wis. Acad.*, XXXIV (1942), 237-92, for a full survey of American criticism of Macaulay.

prefaced his *Sketch-Book* with the admission that a writer would find America's scenic loveliness unsurpassed, but that he personally sought to "escape" to the "shadowy grandeur of the [European] past." In 1824, in summing up "what I aim at," Irving included style, "the weaving in of characters, lightly yet expressively delineated . . . the half-concealed vein of humor . . . nicety of execution," and being "continually piquant" without ever being "dull." After his neoclassic criticism of R. T. Paine and Edwin Holland, Irving's "Desultory Thoughts on Criticism" (1839) is frankly hedonistic, his ideal critic being one who "extricates honey from the humblest weed," much as did his fellow-Knickerbockers Cox, Sands, Fay, and Tuckerman, as we shall see.

Defining poetry as "the rhythmical creation of beauty" to which goodness and truth were subordinated, Poe was most sharply critical in "The Poetic Principle" of the "Heresy of the Didactic," and he did most in an analytical way to emphasize "the place of technique in the resources of creative genius" devoted to enjoyment and beauty. Believing poetry to be great in proportion as it approached music, Poe emphasized prosodic techniques (centering on time as opposed to accent) and music's "suggestive indefiniteness of meaning" and "novel moods of beauty in form, in color, in sound, in sentiment," and a unified and "elevating excitement of the soul." In narratives he sought "unity of effect," and in general he tried to devote himself to an absolutely independent criticism, applying the purest rules of art with impersonal austerity to winnow beauty and teach writers how to achieve an order sanctioned by the unity and harmony of the cosmos itself. Poe was our critical high priest of the religion of beauty.

From another angle, the increase of critical hedonism may be illustrated by the fact that most of the reviews of Melville's *Typee* (1846) and *Omoo* (1847) were favorable. For here the young Rabelaisian Melville delighted in debunking the moralistic missionaries and our so-called civilization, and in glorifying "the very perfection of female grace and beauty" in the person of Fayaway, that "child of nature" whom he said he could not resist in the "garb of Eden." As she "stood erect with upraised arms at the head of the canoe," Melville says "a prettier little mast than Fayaway made was never shipped aboard any craft." He shared the primitive people's "continual happiness . . . sprung principally from that all-pervading sensation which Rousseau has told us he at one time experienced, the mere buoyant sense of a healthful physical existence."[38] Charles Anderson,[39] who has printed excerpts from the criticism of these two books, concludes, "out of fifteen American magazine reviews . . . twelve were all favorable to both works in general," and six were "unequivocally enthusiastic." Of course some sectarian magazines sponsoring missionaries attacked Melville, but even the *United States Catholic Magazine* (VI, 569-86, Nov., 1847) found his "voluptuousness" "pardonable," and concludes that *Typee* is "sprightly, well-written, entertaining."

If critics crusading for reform and liberty seem indifferent to beauty, Whittier the abolitionist who wrote much on Milton (who had a strong and continued influence on American critics) prefaced a poem of 1830 on "The Beauty of Liberty" with a quotation from Milton himself: "In all things that have beauty, there is nothing more comely than Liberty" and many critics thought of beauty as a by-product of social justice. Thus Lowell, during his humanitarian period, says in his critical *Conversations on Some Old Poets* (1845) (p. 292), "That which alone can make men truly happy and exalted in nature is freedom; and freedom of spirit, without which mere bodily liberty is but vilest slavery, can only be achieved by cultivating men's sympathy with the beautiful." Lowell here rejects a judicial "code of criticism" (pp. 6, 47, 49, 95) and wants the past cleared of its "poisonous rottenness" (pp. 245-46) so as to winnow its beauty in terms of "those precious inner promptings of truth and love" (p. 289). Indeed, in *A Fable for Critics*, Lowell had concluded that he himself could not succeed as a poet until he learned "the distinction 'twixt singing and preaching."

38. *Typee*, Constable ed., pp. 114-115; 170.
39. "Contemporary American Opinion of *Typee* and *Omoo*," *AL*, IX (1937), 23-28.

If Lowell was outstanding in his "many musical ideas and expressions," if as a critic he included musical harmony among his criteria,[40] and in 1845 thought Poe (devoted to metrical harmony) our "most discriminating, philosophical, and fearless critic," this is symptomatic of a considerable current interest among critics in the cross-fertilization of music and poetry in the interest of beauty. Thus J. S. Dwight, who translated the lyrics of Goethe and Schiller for Ripley's *Specimens,* began his long career of relating music and transcendental criticism in "Poetry and Music for Public Worship" in 1836; and in *Aesthetic Papers* (pp. 25-36), edited by Elizabeth Peabody, he rapturously summed up their relationship in a representative way (*TA,* 411-14), correlating Beethoven and the rise of transcendentalism. In various addresses C. P. Cranch,[41] who became increasingly aesthetic, discussed music as "the heart's prayer" involving "the infinite," and W. W. Story called music "an art embodying the highest and noblest craving of our nature." Thoreau who was especially devoted to sound as "the agency of correspondence" as Sherman Paul has shown (*NEQ,* 22:511-27), said that "it is the height of art that, on the first perusal, plain common sense should appear; on the second, severe truth; and on the third, beauty; and having these warrants for its depth and reality, we enjoy the beauty for evermore."[42]

Longfellow, Hawthorne, and Emerson as critics all emphasized the primacy of beauty. Longfellow's devotion to ethical beauty is well known through such poems as "The Day Is Done" and "Nuremburg," his long critical introductions on writers such as Dante in *Poets and Poetry of Europe* (1845) and his critical befriending of Hawthorne whom he praised for his "genius and fine imagination." Hawthorne's concept of imagination permeates "The Artist of the Beautiful," in which Owen, the watch-maker, first tries "to connect a musical operation with the

40. See *MAP,* 861 ff. for data on many studies of Lowell's literary theory, including H. T. Henry's "Music in Lowell's Prose and Verse."
41. Quoted, with much other relevant evidence, by Abner W. Kelley, "Literary Theories about Program Music," *PMLA,* LII (1937), 589-92.
42. Thoreau's *Familiar Letters,* p. 112.

machinery of his watches, so that all the harsh dissonances of life might be rendered tuneful, and each flitting moment fall into the abyss of the past in golden drops of harmony," and then seeks "the spiritualization of matter" or "mechanism" in creating for his beloved a butterfly in whose "beauty—which is not merely outward, but deep as its whole system—is represented the intellect, the imagination, the sensibility, the soul of an Artist of the Beautiful!" When the butterfly perishes because of utilitarian "doubt and mockery" of the beautiful, Hawthorne thinks the artist should not despair but be mindful of the "lofty moral" that "the reward of all high performance must be sought within itself, or sought in vain." In this story (and also in "Sylph Etherege") he says the artists' creations in terms of "external reality" are "imperfectly copied from the richness of their visions," although in "The Great Stone Face" he denies that the beauty the poet sees in "the common dust" actually "existed only in the poet's fancy," and elsewhere he thinks beauty is less an illusion than is a transient ugliness. It is a testimony to Hawthorne's devotion to beauty and the technical management of the "atmospheric medium" by which it is effectively elaborated that Poe, the aesthetic enemy of "the Didactic," should have been able to deduce from Hawthorne's stories most of his own "laws" by which one secures the "preconceived effect" of narrative beauty.

Although Hawthorne was critical in "The Celestial Railroad" of Kant's obscurities ("smoke, mist, moonshine, . . . sawdust") and of the oddities of some of Emerson's followers, he concluded in the first version of "The Hall of Fantasy" that there were "few more successful finders" of truth than Emerson himself, and he and Emerson are often in accord in their ideas about beauty. At the age of twenty Emerson concluded, "Material beauty perishes or palls. Intellectual beauty . . . hath its ebbs and flows of delight . . . But moral beauty is lovely, imperishable, perfect."[43] This comprehensive hierarchy of values was elaborated in the chapter on "Beauty" in *Nature* (1836), culminating

43. *The Heart of Emerson's Journals,* ed. B. Perry, p. 16.

in the idea that "Beauty is the mark which God sets upon Virtue." If critically Emerson rated Milton above Shakespeare that was because, as Emerson noted in 1833, "Milton describes himself . . . as enamoured of moral perfection. He did not love it more than I. That . . . has been my angel until now."[44] Indeed, Emerson's remarks that "The creation of beauty is Art," that "Beauty is its own excuse for being," should be interpreted in the light of *Nature*, where he develops the view that "Truth, and goodness, and beauty, are but different faces of the same All," and of his more comprehensive statement elsewhere that they are "interchangeable" and that each has the other latent in it. Indeed, it is by this principle of organic fusion that Emerson was enabled to transcend the earlier American critical tendencies which were vulnerable in escapism, irresponsible hedonism, a minimizing of moral beauty as merely "didactic," or a mechanistic separation of "instruction" and "delight," although it must be admitted that he himself was vulnerable at times in slighting technique and "metres" in his greater concern for "metre-making arguments." In "The American Scholar" (1837), while Emerson belittles mere antiquarians and "restorers of readings, the emendators, the bibliomaniacs," he urges the "creative reading" of books as "the best type of the influence of the past." He stresses a high pleasure. "The character of the pleasure we derive from the best books" depends on our critical realization that "one nature wrote and the same reads," on the realization of "the identity of all minds" and their "pre-established harmony." Since true genius is not idiosyncratic but "a larger imbibing of the common heart," a creative reading or critical entering into the "great poet makes *us* feel our *own* wealth," makes it possible for us as individuals to be "born into the great, the universal mind," and to partake of the high enjoyment of having our own "worth" and potentialities revealed to us in proportion as we bring our lives into disciplined accord with the "beneficent tendency" or "animated law" which is the Over-Soul, one by-product of such an accord being beauty.

44. *Ibid.*, p. 80.

IV. FROM JUDICIAL TO SYMPATHETICALLY REPRODUCTIVE CRITICISM

A. JUDICIAL

It was to be expected that those who were sure their own standards were morally right should have felt it their duty to voice their judgment of departures from such standards. Joseph Dennie, the Philadelphia editor of *Port Folio*, 1801-09, was hailed by his Federalist friends as a "dread judge"[45] and executioner; his scathing stylistic analysis of "The Declaration of Independence" and of the Gothic novels (in five essays), and his vitriolic writing on Paine illustrate his sharply judicial criticism. The Boston *Monthly Anthology* (1803-11), sponsored by Brahmins such as William Tudor, Joseph S. Buckminster, George Ticknor, Edward Everett, and Emerson's father William, and dedicated to resisting our literary provincialism, colloquialism, and "vulgarity," aimed "to destroy . . . worthless weeds," and represented "the office of a reviewer . . . as that of an executioner." (IV, in "Silva," 1807.) The neoclassical Robert Walsh's *American Monthly Magazine* (Vol. I, 12, May, 1817), *apropos* of Coleridge's "Christabel," urged "guardians of morals and arbiters of taste, to interpose the authority with which they are invested" to protect readers from such "wantonness of innovation" and "violation" of taste and morals. When Walsh's reviewer McHenry in 1832 judged Bryant to be an imitator of Wordsworth, Willis Gaylord Clark, editor of the *Knickerbocker Magazine*, 1834-61, who was often in critical controversy with Poe and Simms, wrote a savage judicial essay (reprinted in his *Literary Remains*, pp. 273-289) to demolish McHenry by assembling all of his supposedly bad judgments.

Bryant as a young Federalist and neoclassicist had in 1818 mercilessly attacked[46] Solyman Brown's versified *Essay on American Poetry*, which was uncritical in its ardent Americanism. While A. H. Everett in 1808 ridiculed "the farrago of love, and

45. Quoted by Lewis Leary, "Joseph Dennie and Benjamin Franklin," *Penn. Hist. & Biog.*, LXXII (1948), 243. See Milton Ellis, *Dennie* (1915), on his criticism.
46. *NAR*, VII (1818), 198-211.

absurdity, and ignorance, commonly denominated a novel,"[47] it was not until about 1822 that such censure of the novel, very widespread in American criticism, was replaced by appreciation. Irving in his youthful neoclassical essays on R. T. Paine and E. C. Holland (1812-14) attacked them for the "hyperbole, and for the glare of extravagant images and flashing phrases . . . for gorgeous finery and violent metaphor" which "prevails throughout our country." And he regrets that even contemporary English writers are "continually wandering away into some new and corrupt fashion of writing, rather than conformity to those orders of composition which have had the sanction of time and citicism." Contrary to his later view, Irving thought in 1819 that "The Mutability of Literature" could be overcome only by giving "all possible encouragement" to the "growth of critics" as stern judges dedicated to weeding out worthless books. In *Salmagundi*, 1807-08, he thought that "a little well-applied ridicule . . . will do more with certain hard heads and obdurate hearts than all the logic or demonstrations in Longinus." Even the usually gentle Whittier in 1829 called for stern and "fearless" criticism:

The true cause of the imbecility of our poetry is found in the dangerous encouragement which is given to the light flashes of fancy . . . It is time a more independent mode of criticism was commenced in this country. Most of our literary periodicals are too timid, in fact too dependent, to give their opinions, with the firmness and regard to truth which are necessary. We are becoming effeminate in everything . . .[48]

And Whittier could be stern when he wrote judgments of the writings of the pro-slavery Carlyle, or of Webster the compromiser.

But Poe, representing contrasting southern standards, made even stronger charges against our criticism as "notorious" and "corrupt," as consisting of puffery for which the periodicals (which dictated the tone of the employee-critics) were bribed

47. *Monthly Anthology*, IV (1808), 336-9.
48. *Whittier on Writers* (ed. Cady and Clark), Syracuse, 1950, p. 25-26.

by the publishers' advertising. This is Poe's theme in his essay[49] praising L. A. Wilmer's wholesale condemnation in 1841 of the American "Quacks of Helicon." As a remedy, Poe crusaded for an absolute and disinterested attempt "to limit criticism to comment upon *Art*" (not ideas), and the extent to which the structural methods used to bring out the artist's "one preestablished design" had been aesthetically successful in making the reader responsive to the work's "totality of effect." Whether in the logic of the plot-structure of stories or in the prosodic quest of music which was a poem's chief justification, Poe was distinctive in his "particular and methodical application" of his aesthetic principles, convinced that "in excessive *generalization* lies one of the leading errors of criticism." His criticism is to be judicial and nothing else in an era when he thought moralism or patriotism distracted critics from what should be their true object, calling attention to structural errors.[50] If as a critic you find a literary "dunce to be gibbeted, . . . hang him by all means; but make no bow where you mean no obeisance."

The most sternly judicial of the many judicial critics who created what Dorothy Waples called "The Whig Myth of J. F. Cooper" was Edward S. Gould (beginning with his review as "Cassius" of Cooper's *Bravo*). Gould in 1836 charged that American criticism was "*superficial* in every particular," seldom providing much needed "*analysis* of merit and demerit, in detail." He believed that criticism should be "a high department of literature," and he glorified the Tory Johnson's harsh essay on Milton as "proof of the perfection to which criticism may attain, and of the talent it may embody."[51] Like Poe, Gould said critics should give their "*reasons*" why a given book is good or bad, and should avoid general terms. But in the way of merciless critical censure of a former friend and host, Cooper's own extended critical essay on Walter Scott as he is presented in Lockhart's

49. Poe's *Works*, ed. Ingram, IV, 518.
50. Poe's *Works*, ed. Harrison, XI, 133.
51. In the *N. Y. Mirror*, XIII, 322. Gould in the *Literary and Theological Review*, II (March, 1836), 46, conceded, like so many conservatives, that "Walter Scott by universal consent is the monarch and master of fiction."

biography sets a new record for detailed exposure, at least up to its date, 1838. Cooper also satirized the New York literati in *Home as Found*. The strife between exponents of political parties, between North and South, and between church sects, such as the Congregationalists, the Unitarians and Transcendentalists, was often reflected in sharply judicial literary criticism. In early American practice, judicial criticism was actually far from disinterested, for the standards of judgment adopted were relative to the critic's political or religious bias. And in so far as the standards were lofty, taken, for example from the Greek or Roman masters or from Shakespeare, such criticism, if rigorously applied, would almost necessarily make early American books seem insignificant.

B. TURN TO SYMPATHETIC CRITICISM

In contrast to Cooper's and Poe's ("Literati") attack on the Knickerbockers, it was natural that, in reaction, the Knickerbockers should wish to appear amiable. Thus the *Knickerbocker Magazine* (V, 261-9) in 1835 deplored the malignant "Abuser of Criticism," suggested the quiet burial of bad literature, and thought that the best method was for the critic "to enlighten the public mind, and brace it up fully with sound literature, that each may become the judge of what he reads, particularly of that which is strewed along the common paths of life, and is in his sight every day." Verplanck, who wrote early critical essays on Fisher Ames, Clifton, Barlow, Hunt, *The Sketch Book,* Bryant, and Sands, urged in 1814 that if a given work were rated it should be as a whole rather than on any one deficient part, but he declared the critic should keep in mind the end the author set for himself and the fact that literature may legitimately aim not only at instruction but at "amusement and escape."[52] William Cox, who contributed one hundred and eighty-six brief critical papers to the *New York Mirror*, from 1828 to 1848, reacted against "The Late Mr. Sneer" of criticism, and generally followed Charles Lamb, the appreciator of Shakespeare; Cox said that critics should act "rather as friendly assistants than as

52. *Analectic Magazine*, New Series, IV (1814), 243-49.

dogmatical censors," and Kendall Taft (*AL*, XVI, 11-18) concludes that Cox's criticism is "personal, sympathetic, informally
expressionistic," and reveals "the new romantic faith" as represented by Lamb. The editor of Cox's *Crayon Sketches* (1833)
was T. S. Fay, whose *Norman Leslie* was the object of Poe's
terrific attack which began the "War of the Literati,"[53] and he
argued that as opposed to the "sour undistinguishing critic" centering only on imperfections, the true critic should try to discover
the concealed beauties and encourage their "relish," a critical
aim illustrated in his collection *Dreams and Reveries* (2 vols.,
1832). And the amiable Irving, possibly as an indirect rebuke
to Edward Gould and his critical followers who excoriated
Cooper, wrote "Desultory Thoughts on Criticism" in 1839 liken-
ing the judicial critic he had once called for to a spider and now
advocating that the desirable critic should resemble "the honest
bee, that extricates honey from the humblest weed." His friend
and fellow Knickerbocker Henry T. Tuckerman illustrated most
fully the triumph of a somewhat sentimental critical impressionism in his *Italian Sketch Book* (1835), *Isabel; or Sicily* (1839),
Thoughts on the Poets (1835), and *Characteristics of Literature*
in two series, 1849 and 1851. "As a literary critic," concludes
Nelson Adkins (*D. A. B.*), "Tuckerman is best understood in
the light of his essay on Hazlitt, where he finds the function of
the critic that of feeler and sympathizer, as well as of analyst."
William A. Jones was also our critical "American Hazlitt" and
one of the leaders of the critics of the politically liberal "Young
America" group working through *The Democratic Review*,
Arcturus, and *The Literary World* (as opposed to the more
aristocratic *Whig Review*), a group which generally thought
that the critic's function where anti-democratic ideas were not
involved should be that of genial interpreter.[54]

Henry Reed, who was Professor of English at the University
of Philadelphia from 1835 to 1854, edited Wordsworth, and in

53. See S. P. Moss, "Poe and the *Norman Leslie* Incident," *AL*, XXV (1953),
293-306 with good orientation-notes on critical animosities.
54. See John Stafford's *Literary Criticism of "Young America"* (Berkeley, 1952),
useful in emphasizing the role of political biases.

1839 published a long sympathetic essay on him. Reed adopted the concept of the "sovereign" imagination whose chief duty is to invoke "moral and spiritual associations" involving "an affinity between the objects of nature and our moral being, . . . spiritualizing the senses." He contrasted Wordsworth's devotion to powers "within the soul" to the earlier "artificial school" which had "blunted" poetic feeling "by a cold (Lockean?) philosophy."[55] Professor Longfellow, who published nearly twenty critical or interpretative essays in addition to the introductions to his anthology *Poets and Poetry of Europe* (1845), thought criticism should be "benignant" instead of "malignant." Identifying iconoclasts and critics, Longfellow thought "many critics are like wood-peckers, who, instead of enjoying the fruit and shadow of a tree [as a good critic should do], hop incessantly around the trunk, pecking holes in the bark to discover some little worm or other." But the sympathetically interpretative critic could serve a great function—consider his own critical essay on Dante in 1845—for "next to being a great poet is the power of understanding one."[56] His work as critic as well as translator of poems in a dozen different languages is a heartening illustration of a method by which a literary man can advance assimilation and mutual understanding among our immigrants with diverse languages and heritages.

But Longfellow was but one of many American scholars and critics who learned much from Goethe and his disciple Carlyle. For while Goethe had seen the critic's function as three-fold, including the appraisal of a writing's intrinsic worth, most of his American followers noticed rather his more novel emphasis on finding out what an individual author had tried to do and then (as Thoreau expressed it in his essay on Carlyle in 1847) criticizing "by the German rule of referring an author to his own standard" (AWS, 214). F. A. Braun has shown Margaret

55. *New York Mirror,* IV, 1-49.
56. Longfellow's *Works* (Standard Library Ed.), VII, 403-04; VIII, 81. In *Hyperion,* referring to Jean Paul, Longfellow remarked that "If you once understand an author's character, the comprehension of his writings becomes easy" through "sympathy." See also Book III, Chapter VI, "After Dinner and After the Manner of the Best Critics."

Fuller's great interest in Goethe. In her "Short Essay on Critics" following "our German benefactors," she classifies critics first as the "subjective" or impressionist (whose "essential value is nothing"); second, as the "apprehensive" or "reproductive" who "enter fully into a foreign existence" or piece of writing and "live in its law"; and third, "the comprehensive" who include the apprehensive by transcending that class. The latter kind of critic, after having ascertained the artist's "design and the degree of his success in fulfilling it," knows how to put that design in its place, and how to estimate its relations to the "invariable principle" which regulates the universe. However, having outlined what are akin to Goethe's three aims of the critic, Miss Fuller, in the latter part of the essay on current periodical critical practice, attacks attempts at "dictatorship" and in contrast to "monotony" and "uniformity of tone" she sides with the "ever various" aspect of art and artists, and favors critics capable of enabling us to "catch the contagion of their mental activity" and their quickening appreciation of the "spontaneous." Thus, like George Allen and Emerson, she recognizes the need for judicial criticism; but in practice she seems to emphasize the reproductive kind by which we "enter into the nature of another being and judge his work by its own law," *sui generis*.[57]

In the early eighteen thirties, however, the way was prepared for such a sympathetic method of criticism by American admiration for Carlyle, who appealed to contemporary taste not only as a disciple of Goethe but in his own right especially by his earnestly moral conviction that the critic should be the interpreter (not the judge) of the writer's anti-rationalistic revelation of the Divine Idea, and that the critic's approach should be biographical in characterizing the man behind the book. And if his style infuriated the "Dryasdust" followers of Locke whom he blasted, his rhapsodies, apostrophes, bold colloquialisms, rhetorical flights, earnestness and humor, savageness and tender-

---

57. See Helen N. McMaster, "Margaret Fuller as a Literary Critic," *University of Buffalo Studies*, VII, 1928; W. R. Ebbitt, "Margaret Fuller's Ideas on Criticism," *Boston Public Library Quarterly*, III (1951), 171-87. Her "Short Essay on Critics" appeared in *The Dial* I (July, 1840), 5-11.

ness, and picturesque Germanisms delighted those who were starving on what Neal called a milk-and-water Addisonianism. In 1834 George Calvert, who also wrote an essay on Coleridge and much "biographical aesthetic" criticism, said Carlyle's *Life of Schiller* proved him "a fine critic" having "that strong sympathy so essential." Even the sprightly N. P. Willis had said in 1830 after reading Carlyle's Introduction to Goethe's *Wilhelm Meister* that he had "never seen a mind so nobly and worthily measured. It is the finest specimen of prose." The *New York Review* found that the essays from "Burns" to "Characteristics" were "so remarkable and startling, that they created a prodigious sensation." And F. H. Hedge, with a profound scholar's knowledge of Schiller at first-hand, glorified Carlyle's work on him for its happy method and just appreciation. "This biography is what the biography of a poet should always be—the history of a mind rather than the history of a person." C. A. Bartol, George Bancroft, W. H. Channing, and many others eulogized Carlyle's generally sympathetic criticism,[58] and it seems apparent that Carlyle's was one of the influences which inaugurated what was then the new criticism.

And Emerson, lifelong friendly correspondent of Carlyle even if they differed later on politics and abolition, developed in 1837 his critical theory of "creative reading" of books which "well used" were "the best of things" and our best key to the past. For the past is one of the scholar's three teachers when regarded, with present and future, as "triple blossoms from one root." History teaches that "the Mind is One," that men at their best have all been inspired by their harmony with the Over-Soul. Hence by sympathetic critical interpretation one mind could readily enter into another, genius being not idiosyncratic but merely "a larger imbibing of the *common* heart."[59] It should be noted how profoundly such a critical approach reinforced the transcendental "enlargement and independency of the individual," and the enrichment of his inward potentialities, as opposed

58. I am indebted to W. S. Vance's article on "Carlyle in America before *Sartor*" (*AL*, VII (1936), 363-75 for the quotations cited.
59. Emerson's *Works* (Centenary Ed.), I, 87 ff; II 38; II, 288; and notes in *MAP*.

to the caricature of neoclassical criticism in a merely external or almost mathematical detection of a violation of parroted "rules." " 'Tis the good reader that makes the good book . . . The light by which we see in this world comes out from the soul of the observer," just as Emerson had concluded in an early sermon that "the bible has no force but what it derives from within us."[60] It is deep answering to deep. " 'Every scripture is to be interpreted by the same spirit which gave it forth,'—is the fundamental law of criticism."[61] "Criticism should not be querulous and wasting, all knife and root-puller, but guiding, instructive, inspiring, a south wind, not an east wind." Of course Emerson is referring to the great books; he could be stern toward ephemeral novels[62] or writing which he thought had little spirituality but only form or only the "jingling serenader's art" as he said in "Merlin."

In the same year as "The American Scholar" George Allen, another follower of Coleridge as interpreted by his teacher James Marsh, developed these ideas in a more connected manner in a two-part essay entitled "Reproductive Criticism."[63] Allen rejected the anti-organic and the external. He said the critic's one great rule is sympathetically to bring his "mind into contact with the mind of the artist," to come "alongside" the work of genius "with the specific purpose of reproducing, step by step, the creative process of the artist." The critic should take the writer's "point of view, and adopt, for the time, his habits of thought and feeling." And Samuel G. Ward, to whom Emerson's *Letters to a Friend* were addressed, in 1849 published a plea for creative criticism, deploring our misfortune in so frequently having "reference to a standard from without, viz., England."

Among the master-artists, Hawthorne, in accord with his general philosophy of sympathy and the heart as opposed to the

60. R. L. Rusk, *Life of Emerson* (New York, 1949), p. 158.
61. *Works*, I, 35 (*Nature*).
62. J. T. Flanagan, "Emerson as a Critic of Fiction," *Philological Quarterly*, XV (1936), 30-45.
63. In the *New York Review*, March 1837, and Jan. 1839.

head, insisted that the requisite of criticism and intelligent reading is "the deepest and warmest sympathy" directed toward the
reproductive translating of the artist's sensuous or imagistic symbols back into the abstract archetypes or ideas which he had ex-
ternalized, without neglecting the structural design which the
aesthetic Poe had praised in this moralist's writing. And in the
South, W. G. Simms insisted that "the standards of good criticism require that the reader should glow with the same element
which inspires the writer; and it will not do . . . to pluck Goethe
by the sleeve and gravely say that the reign of faery has gone by.
The witch-beverage must be quaffed by the reader, or he will
never catch a solitary glimmer of the magic show."[64]

Thus most of the Knickerbockers (Verplanck, Cox, Fay,
Irving, Tuckerman, and Willis), the Young America group,
Reed of Philadelphia, Longfellow and followers of Goethe,
Carlyle or Coleridge (notably Margaret Fuller, Calvert, Hedge,
Follen, Bartol, Bancroft, Emerson, Allen and Ward), as well as
Hawthorne and Simms among novelists, all advocated at times
at least a criticism involving sympathy and reproducing the
creative process of the artist.

V. FROM UNIVERSAL "CONSTANTS" TO CHANGING HISTORY

A. "CONSTANTS"

Judicial criticism, from which the sympathetic revolted as we
have seen, usually involved the assumption of universal "constants" or invariables in human nature, in artistic structure, and
in ethical religion. The belief in such "constants" was reinforced
by two great traditions, ancient classicism and Christianity. Belief in the changeless laws of orderly nature, as interpreted in
the concept of the world-machine popularized by the followers
of Descartes and Newton, reinforced classical ideas of cosmic
law and structural design. And except for ingredients of individuality, the Scottish associational philosophy by revolting
from Locke's denial of innate ideas and exalting common sense
or a universal intuitive sense potentially common to everyone,

64. *Martin Faber*, I, 154.

reinforced Christian ideas of an inward moral sense above sensuous change.

Thus Bryant said in 1826 of Homer's heroes that their hardy spirit in facing danger illustrates that universal "principle which gives birth to all virtue and all greatness," and which involves present sacrifices for future good. The principles of taste which lie at the foundation of poetry "have their origin in the reason of things, and are investigated and applied by the judgment" (*MAP*, 97). In his eulogy of Irving, Bryant looked back to the time when his pages, in contrast to the period's "rapid and ceaseless mutations," taught the reader that "we are still in the same world into which we were born," and "Truth and Good and Beauty . . . are not subject to the changes which beset the inventions of men" (*Prose Works,* I, 367). As the refuter of Godwin's ideas of progress based on rational change, Malthus was widely cited by Americans as supposedly appealing to lustful or psychological elements in man which are universally constant. Irving, for example, in 1819 developed the idea that "The Mutability of Literature" (in his essay by that title) can be overcome only when a writer centers his work "in the unchanging principles of human nature"; departure from such "unchanging principles" justified destructive literary criticism, which he likens to those apparently harsh but divinely beneficent and "salutary checks on population" cited by Malthus. And the youthful Irving wrote much criticism in the guise of satire to kill off "unworthy weeds" among writers. William Tudor, first editor of the *North American Review,* some of whose judicial criticism was collected in *Miscellanies* (1821), spoke for The Anthology Club and its *Monthly Anthology* (1803-11) in calling for critical judgment based on fixed standards valid universally. Andrews Norton spoke for the conservative wing of the Unitarians in 1825 in demanding that criticism should be written in the light of "unalterable principles of taste, founded in the nature of man, and the eternal truths of morality and religion," which he thought the followers of Carlyle, Coleridge and the Germans were violating (*NAR*, XXI, 349).

Literary nationalism was often opposed as out of accord with the *consensus gentium*, the consent of *all* nations through time. Thus, for example, Richard Hildreth in 1829 admitted writers could readily be national, but in being national they invited short-lived appeal, for the great geniuses of the past "embody in their writings those great, universal and invariable principles of truth and beauty, which strike and please alike at all times and in all places." The year before, Cooper in *Notions* (II, 110-12) became sceptical of relying on distinctively American "novelties and varieties" and concluded critically that "on the whole the books which have been best received are those in which the authors have qualities that are common to the rest of the world and to human nature." In "Exordium" Poe was scornful of the literary nationalism[65] of current critics such as Cornelius Mathews as delimiting art, which should be devoted properly to the world at large. Poe was from all angles our most impressive practitioner of criticism devoted to universal aesthetic "constants."

Belief in these, however, was being undermined by many influences, not only by devotion to nationalism, but by Scottish associationalism (a transitional way-station) in so far as one aspect of it led its American disciples to emphasize the aesthetic possibilities for our own readers of the familiar American scene, the divorce by Alison of taste from the judgment of the objective design of writing, and the uniqueness of each writer's and reader's sequence of association with individual books and scenes,—a subject already well explored by modern scholars, notably Charvat and Streeter. In the parallel English transition from neoclassicism to romanticism, Francis Gallaway concludes with massive documentation (in *Reason, Rule, and Revolt in English Classicism*, 1940, p. 286) that on the whole associationalism, important as it was, was less influential than the rise of historical relativism in criticism, and to that we now turn.

65. "Exordium," *Graham's Magazine,* 1842, and in Poe's *Works,* ed. Harrison, XI, 1-8. He also discussed this subject in his review of Drake in the *Southern Literary Messenger,* April, 1836, and in "Marginalia," *ibid.,* July, 1849.

B. THE TURN TO HISTORICAL LITERARY CRITICISM

Broadly speaking, historical criticism may stress one of many things: change or growth or progress or the diversitarian as opposed to the changeless or universal or uniformitarian; a turn from the appraisal of the art or ethics of the writing itself to an impersonal attempt to explain its origin in terms of cause and effect and influences, with attention to temporal sequence and contexture or the conditioning influence of the author's life or of his time, place, and race; a turn to relativity, adaptation to new surroundings, and functionalism, including an encouragement of linguistic innovation, flexibility, and diverse levels of actual usage in a multi-racial democratic society, as opposed to British purism and linguistic standardization.

Since Perry Miller, writing of Brownson's review of Emerson in 1839, concludes that Brownson was by that date "practically alone" in thinking of literature as "an organic expression of the whole community" (*TA,* 431), something new may be contributed toward explaining how and why the historical approach arose by subjecting criticism itself to historical explanation. By what steps did our critics arrive at the most masterly and massive illustration of this kind of criticism in Ticknor's three-volume *History of Spanish Literature* in 1849? This work, for which he had formulated plans in his inaugural lecture in 1832, according to Prescott, "illustrates the works by the personal history of their authors, and this, again, by the history of the times in which they lived; affording, by the reciprocal action of one or the other, a complete record of Spanish civilization, both social and intellectual."[66]

First, the nationalism just outlined was especially important, including as it does our distinctive geography and scenery as well as the complicated debate (notably between Noah Webster and Worcester) regarding the merits of the critical approval of greater diversity of linguistic usage as illustrated in the collection of citicisms edited by M. M. Mathews and in Walter Blair's fully documented study of colloquialism in *Native Amer-*

66. Prescott's *Biographical and Critical Miscellanies* (New York, 1864), p. 728.

ican Humor. Second, consider the influence of foreign critics. In Herder's "genetic thinking" in *Ideen* (1784-91) literature was not an isolated, static mechanism but a vital "plant" growing out of a distinctive place, climate, race, and folk spirit, toward a greater "humanity," and to be explained critically in terms of these. A clergyman as well as a historian, Herder applied such criticism in *The Spirit of Hebrew Poetry,* which James Marsh translated in 1833 with an approving introduction; Ripley reviewed this (*TA,* 89-97) in 1835 as "a treasure of learning, . . . beautiful and winning," of a "pure and noble spirit." This, along with some thirty other[67] critical essays on Herder in our period, suggested that the same historical methods might be applied fruitfully to books other than the Bible. Translations of Madame de Staël's *Influence of Literature upon Society* were published in three different American cities in 1813, developing her view that literature depended upon social environment and that it improved in proportion as nations became Christian and politically free; H. M. Jones[68] has collected a multitude of American reviews illustrating the considerable vogue and influence of her organic historical criticism. Friedrich Schlegel's *Lectures on Dramatic Art and Literature* appeared in translation in Philadelphia in 1818, approaching literature as an expression of the national spirit and of "those patriotic feelings and associations peculiar to the people in whose language it is composed." He had considerable vogue among American critics as different as Legaré and Prescott, whose fine review of Ticknor reflects Schlegel's approach; Charvat shows that the very influential Prescott (*AWS,* xciii) "has more references in his reviews to Schlegel than to any other critic." Weigand claims that "Stendhal was the first man who conceived of art as the flower of an entire culture and who pointed to the climate and the moral

---

67. See bibliographical studies on German-American relations cited in *LHUS.* See also M. D. Learned, "Herder and America," *German American Annals,* N. S., II, No. 9, which includes evidence on his devotion to Franklin and to English writers; P. A. Shelley, "Crèvecoeur's Contribution to Herder's 'Neger-Idyllen,'" *JEGP,* XXXVII (1938), 48-69; G. A. Wells, "Herder's and Coleridge's Evaluation of the Historical Approach," *Modern Language Review,* XLVIII (1953), 167-75.

68. *The Theory of American Literature* (Ithaca, 1948).

customs of society as the source of origin of artists." Stendhal[69] was a special favorite of Taine, and Americans found his critical theory interpreted and praised in the *Edinburgh Quarterly Review* in 1817. The American *Analectic Review's* essay on Stendhal's *Rome, Naples, and Florence* in July 1818 may be by Washington Irving, who was of course as a critic of "English Writers on America" much interested in writers as responsible spokesmen of their people. Alexis Tocqueville's[70] *Democracy in America* (1835, translated in America 1838), with its conviction that we would have an unconventional, patriotic, anti-traditional and various literature commensurate with our political and social order, stimulated many American writers. And Michelet's literary theories should not be overlooked. Goethe's very important national and historical approach has been discussed, as popularized by men such as Motley and Bancroft.

A third great influence in awakening Americans to the possibilities of extending the historical approach from fiction to criticism and literary theory was Walter Scott, whose vogue here has been studied in detail by G. H. Orians, Grace Landrum, and others. Indeed, Scott had as a literary theorist definitely advocated that "national diversity between different countries" could profitably be treated by non-British writers, and Americans liked especially his use of the vernacular for low characters, the example he set for the use of native scenery and backgrounds, and during the twenties and thirties dozens of Americans like Cooper and Simms tried to substitute for his antiquities and ruins the American Indians and their mounds and historical memorials.[71] A few American critics, such as

69. See Wilhelm Weigand, *Stendhal* (Munich, 1925), p. 128 as cited by Matthew Josephson, *Stendhal* (New York, 1946), p. 227; see also 460-62. H. Bergholz, "Was Washington Irving Stendhal's First American Critic?" *Revue de Littérature Comparée,* XXVII (July-Sept., 1953), 328-39.

70. Reino Virtanen ("Tocqueville and W. E. Channing," *AL,* XXII, 1950, 21-28) thinks he derived suggestions from Channing's "Remarks on American Literature" of 1830. See G. W. Pierson, *Tocqueville and Beaumont in America* (New York, 1938) and Russell Kirk, "The Prescience of Tocqueville," *University of Toronto Quarterly,* XII (1953), 324-53.

71. See Margaret Ball, *Scott as a Critic of Literature* (1907) and G. E. Smock, *Scott's Theory of the Novel* (1934), an abstract of a Cornell dissertation.

Grenville Mellen[72] in 1828, charged that the Indian was too simple and mentally uninteresting to continue to appeal to grown-ups interested in psychological sophistication. Even Bryant praised the great depth and discrimination of Simms's critical essay on "Writings of James Fenimore Cooper," which was significantly coupled with Simms's suggestive and inspirational essay on "Epochs and Events of American History, as suited to the Purposes of Art in Fiction," an approach also elaborated by Rufus Choate, who at first influenced some of Hawthorne's antiquarianism. Edd Parks[73] thinks Scott may have been "partially responsible" for P. P. Cooke's critical celebration in 1834 of minstrels and makers of lays after translating *Froissart's Ballads*, for Scott in his critical essay on Froissart in 1815 had rejoiced that such "history has less the air of a narrative than of a dramatic representation," an ideal which also appealed to historian-critics such as Motley, Parkman, Prescott, and others.

Fourth, Alcott, Emerson, Bancroft, Horace Mann and others in advocating new educational ideals, reinforced in part by the influence of the Swiss Pestalozzi,[74] in turning from deductive dogmatism, authoritarianism, memorization, and the fear of discipline to the aim of evoking a child's individuality by kindly encouragement and seeming to share in the suspense of watching history unfold inductively, did much to lead critics and their audience to go through a parallel change of taste in their approach to books. The millions thus trained in elementary schools eventually created the demand which had to be supplied by writers and their critics in the way of the inductive historical approach emphasizing diversitarianism and individuality. And,

72. *NAR*, XXVII (1828), 143. Grenville Mellen's attitude in this review of *Red Rover* may have encouraged Cooper to turn to his three European romances if not his trans-national views in *Notions*.

73. E. W. Parks, *Southern Poets* (AWS), liv; see also Neal Doubleday's "Hawthorne and Literary Nationalism," *AL*, XII (1940-41), 447-53.

74. See the evidence and bibliography cited on Pestalozzi in Merle Curti's *Social Ideas of American Educators* (1935), pp. 29-30; 65-66; 99; 123-4; and W. H. Monroe's *History of the Pestalozzian Movement in the U. S.* (Syracuse, 1907). Edward Reisman (in *Encyclopedia of Social Sciences*, ed. Seligman) under Pestalozzi concludes that "Modern elementary education in the western world rests largely upon Pestalozzian principles."

as Merle Curti shows, "the essence of phrenology was its insistence on the unique differences in the propensities of individuals," and phrenology[75] "attracted, at least for a time, such persons as William Ellery Channing, Ralph Waldo Emerson, Walt Whitman" before 1850, Isaac Ray (*TA*, 75-78), Theodore Parker (*TA*, 487), and especially Horace Mann, who did much from 1837 to 1848 to mould Massachusetts' common school education.

Fifth, while the Scottish associationalists such as Alison (whose works were widely used as school texts) called for "*Common* Sense," they were "truly revolutionary" (as Francis Gallaway and Gordon McKenzie[76] have shown) in undermining supposedly universally valid aesthetic principles by tending to divorce judgment from taste and by the critical quest of beauty not so much in the objective design of the book criticized as in the subjective response of the individual. And since each man's *sequence* of association with specific scenery or books was different from that of his fellows, associationalism often led in critical practice to diversitarianism. W. P. Hudson has shown how Alison prepared Bryant to appreciate the Hartleian Wordsworth critically, and Robert Streeter has shown how much of the very influential criticism of the *North American Review* was permeated by the assumptions of the associationalists in regard to either the American scene or the European, thus involving relativism and nationalism. Enormously influential in America, Dugald Stewart, who recommended his pupil Alison's "ingenuity and elegance," also emphasized the relativity of nationalisms: "From the remarks which have been made on the association of ideas on our judgments in matters of taste, it is obvious (Stewart said) how much the opinions of a nation with respect to merits in the fine arts, are likely to be influenced by the form of their government, and the state of their manners." "National

75. See Riegel, "Early Phrenology in the U. S.," *Medical Life*, XXXVI (1930), 361-76.

76. Francis Gallaway, *Reason, Rule, and Revolt in English Classicism* (New York, 1940), p. 242, and Gordon McKenzie's *Critical Responsiveness* (Berkeley, 1949), a very valuable background study for our period.

associations," Alison agreed, "will have a similar effect in increasing the emotions of sublimity and beauty as they very obviously increase the number of images presented to the mind." Critics such as Tudor, Knapp, Verplanck, Gilman, the young Longfellow, and Bryant said American settings, other things being equal, would lead to the reader's more aesthetic response; Walter Channing, Jared Sparks, George Bancroft, Irving, and Cooper (at least in 1828 and 1838) thought associations with European scenes and history were more promising. But both groups used associational criteria which involved historical relativism.[77]

Sixth, the thirties and forties witnessed a cross-fertilization of "straight" history and literary history, or historical criticism. Scott and Carlyle had encouraged a "transition" (as Peardon[78] calls it) in historical writing from the school of Voltaire, Hume, and Gibbon in quest of universals and invariable laws to a concern with colorful and dramatic change. After various historical societies were founded and collections made, Jared Sparks, Bancroft, Hildreth, and Motley all wrote not only history but historical literary criticism, emphasizing change and relativity. Thus Bancroft in 1824, in his essay on Goethe, follows him in his thesis that "the literature of each nation is national, and the true critic must endeavor to regard it from the same point of view with the nation in which it was designed to produce an effect." And Motley,[79] who wrote two fine essays on Goethe in 1838, revolted like him from "narrow systems of criticism, which would bring all men to one standard," and quoted with high praise Goethe's doctrine that the biographical critic should deal not only with an author's individuality but should also represent man in relation to the age and his reactions to the epoch. W. G.

77. The evidence will be found cited by R. E. Streeter: "Association Psychology and Literary Nationalism in the *North American Review*, 1815-1825," *AL*, XVII (1945), 243-54.

78. T. P. Peardon, *The Transition in English Historical Writing, 1760-1830* (New York, 1933).

79. Bancroft's "Life and Genius of Goethe," *NAR*, XIX (1824), 304 ff., and Motley's review of Goethe's *Autobiography* in *N. Y. Review*, III (Oct. 1838). See C. P. Higby and B. T. Schantz, *Motley* (AWS, Introduction) for his literary theory.

Simms in 1842 argued that desirable literature "asserts the character of its people, speaks to their wants and represents their honorable interests," including their social and political ideas. He and others repeated this aim often.[80]

Seventh, in the forties American critics of Shakespeare also illustrate the historical diversitarianism. The voluminous critic W. B. O. Peabody's[81] earlier neoclassicism was modified, not only by his respect for the dignity which the Tory Scott gave to fiction by the use of history, but by his admiration for the sublimities of Shakespeare whom he edited, pioneering in his recourse to the basic earlier texts. Verplanck's edition of Shakespeare was also distinctive in his critical introduction, which sought to interpret text and the meaning of his words in the historical light of the dramatist's own age. Even Jones Very's "Epic Poetry" (1838) (*TA*, 343-46) managed to combine historicism and transcendentalism by arguing that Homer reflected his age's outwardness and Shakespeare his age's inwardness. And by 1848 Emerson himself with all his respect for self-reliant individuality, delivered his famous lecture on Shakespeare as having the greatest debts to others and as illustrating how the poet must be "in unison with his time and country," and needs "a ground in popular tradition" which has "a certain excellence which no single genius, however extraordinary, can hope to create."[82]

Eighth, the turn from critical uniformitarianism to diversitarianism was greatly advanced by a widening of acquaintance with other national or racial literatures. In 1838 Brownson glorified the collaborative *Specimens of Foreign Standard Literature*, edited by Ripley, which was to run to fourteen volumes with important critical introductions, as partly filling the great need for Americans to turn from the British to German and

80. *Magnolia*, IV, 251, 1842, as quoted by B. T. Spencer in "Regionalism in American Literature," in *Regionalism in America*, ed. Merrill Jensen (Madison, Wis., 1952). Spencer in this essay cites many similar theories by others.

81. W. B. O. Peabody and O. W. B. Peabody's multitude of critical essays will be found summarized in H. H. Clark's "Literary Criticism in the *NAR*," already cited.

82. *Works* (*Representative Men*) Cent. Ed., IV, 189, 194, 195.

French writers such as Cousin (*TA,* 189-91). Brownson, revolting from the eighteenth century English spokesmen of "materialism," glorified Asiatic spokesmen of "the old Braminical or spiritual world" (*TA,* 114-123), paving the way for sympathetic critical reaction to "The Orient" as chronicled by Arthur Christy, F. I. Carpenter, and others. Translator of Menzel's biography of Goethe, C. C. Felton, Professor of Greek and later president of Harvard, in his inaugural lecture of 1834 and in many other influential critical lectures sought "the widening out of this purely linguistic approach to include the whole life of the people whose language is studied, its geography, its philosophy, its political structure, and every form of its artistic expression" (*D. A. B.*). Simms and others, in attempting to justify slavery against northern anti-traditional humanitarianism, turned to glorifying their model, "*Greek* democracy" at a time when all things Greek were popular. Legaré wrote very able critical appraisals not only of Byron (two essays) but of "Classical Literature" and "Cicero." Richard Wilde did a volume on Tasso (1842), and his unfinished Dante study shows that the south partly shared Longfellow's critical devotion to Dante[83] and mediaeval writers. Our critics' treatment of French writers and critics is well known, as is the immense interest in German writers beginning with Samuel Miller and William Bentley. After 1828 critics such as Henry Wheaton, Longfellow, G. P. Marsh[84] and others did much to interpret Scandinavian and "Gothic" literature and the hardy Viking spirit. This critical recognition of diversities in national literatures and points of view was often related to the diverse strains in our immigrant population; linguistics and criticism were used partly to advance assimilation and brotherhood.

Ninth, as scientific[85] interests shifted from a mechanistic or

83. See T. W. Koch, *Dante in America* (1896), and Emilio Goggio's many studies.

84. See A. B. Benson, "Henry Wheaton's Writings on Scandinavia," *JEGP,* XXIX (1930), 546-61; Samuel Kliger, "G. P. Marsh and the Gothic Tradition in America," *NEQ,* XIX (1946), 524-31; and Andrew Hilen, *Longfellow and Scandinavia* (1947). Benson has many other relevant studies.

85. See H. H. Clark, "The Influence of Science on American Ideas, from 1775 to 1809," *Trans. Wis. Academy,* XXXV (1944), 305-49; W. Smallwood, *Natural History*

static Newtonianism (mathematics and astronomy) to a more vitalistic botany and zoology (as illustrated in the varying vogue of Erasmus Darwin, Lamarck, popularized by Lyell along with his own evolutionary *Geology*, 1830-33, Linnaeus, Robert Chambers, and the early Agassiz), American critics increasingly reflected an interest in the ways in which environment and heredity (racism) in all their manifold phases had entered into literature. Roy Pearce[86] has ably shown how much of our writers' elaborate concern with and criticism of the Indian and "savagism" derived from the semi-scientific idea of Scottish philosophers such as Adam Ferguson involving environmentalism and constant social laws of progress toward sociality. Crèvecoeur, in proving that by transplantation from a European environment the American became regenerate as a "new man" if he had a farm, explained the change, following Raynal and Locke, on the vitalistic theory that "Men are like plants; the goodness and flavor of the fruit proceeds from the peculiar soil and exposition in which they grow." The seminal idea is that man is not static and doomed to depravity, but that human nature can be changed. Jefferson, who inspired much democratic writing and criticism, said in 1814 that "briars and brambles" cannot become fruitful vines, but that environmental nurture and "culture" can do much to soften "asperities" of men; indeed, Daniel Boorstin's closely documented book[87] finds the semi-scientific philosophy of environmentalism central in Jefferson's whole circle. The idea, popularized by Montesquieu, Adam Ferguson, and Hugh Blair, that climatic *milieu* strongly conditions literary creation was well known and often linked with associational American criticism. The difference between "the tendency of a tropical climate to enervate a people" and a temperate climate was especially used in 1824 by the influential

---

and the American Mind (New York, 1941); and Merle Curti, *Growth of the American Mind* (New York, 1943).

86. Pearce, *The Savages of America* (Baltimore, 1953).

87. Jefferson's *Works* (ed. Bergh), XIV, 399-400, and Boorstin, *The Lost World of Thomas Jefferson* (New York, 1948).

Edward Everett[88] to explain "The Circumstances Favorable to the Progress of Literature" and "the formation of individual character" as well as national character. Basing his philosophic radicalism on faith in a benevolent modification of environment, Bentham (as well as the *Westminster Review*[89] which he founded in 1823) was widely read in America and had many critical followers such as John Neal and Hildreth. Early evolutionists influenced critics such as Emerson,[90] who looking back thought that among all the many influences (including Germany) on the "revolution" of the thirties "the paramount source" was "Modern Science" (*TA*, 499). Linnaeus had many American followers from the days of the Bartrams on; and even Hawthorne[91] in 1836 discussed his ideas of development and later suggested them in *The Marble Faun*. In 1846 E. P. Whipple, whom Hawthorne regarded as our greatest critic, began his pivotal work; he showed that organicism and historical relativism are right because they are sanctioned by nature as interpreted by science. Distinguishing between "mechanical regularity and organic form" in the light of "vital powers," he followed Coleridge who "was the first who made criticism interpretative." He insisted that the true critic "must pass into the mysterious depths of the mind in which it [a book] was matured, see the fountain springs of its thoughts and emotions, and discern its own laws of growth and production." Coleridge was "not content with judging it from his own point of view, but looked at it from its author's position, . . . knowing that ideas and principles varied their forms with variations in the circumstances of mankind." And, Whipple concludes,

88. Cited from *American Philosophic Addresses, 1700-1900*, ed. with introductions by Joseph Blau (New York, 1946), pp. 64-66.

89. See Granville Hicks, "Literary Opposition to Utilitarianism," *Science and Society*, I (1937), 454-72, and for the variety of comment often sympathetic to American liberalism, see *Benthamite Reviewing: Twelve Years of the Westminster Review, 1824-1836*, by G. L. Nesbitt, 1934.

90. See H. H. Clark, Emerson and Science," *Philological Quarterly*, X (1931), 225-60.

91. Cited in Arlin Turner's edition of *Hawthorne as Editor* (University, La., 1941)

If criticism be a science, if it assumes to convey any real knowledge, it deals not with individual impressions or arbitrary rules, but with laws; and its progress will be determined by its success in employing a right method to discover the laws to which it refers. [Coleridge stated the "true method": "'Follow nature in variety of kinds.'"] As the philosopher is content to investigate and establish the laws of the human mind and the phenomena of nature, . . . so the critic is bound to pursue a similar method with regard to a work of art, and to interpret, if he can, its inward meaning and significance. This, at least, is the process in all other sciences. If a plant, insect, fish, or other animal, is to undergo a scientific examination, a *savan* is not welcomed with a shower of honorary degrees because he has felicitously ridiculed its external form, or shown its want to agreement with some other natural object, but because he has investigated its inward mechanism, indicated its purpose, and shown that its form is physiognomical of its peculiar life. Now we think that Hamlet or Lear are as worthy of this tolerant treatment as a bird or a fish; at least, we are confident that no scientific knowledge of either can be obtained in any other way.[92]

VI. TURN FROM THE MECHANISTIC TO THE ORGANIC

A. THE MECHANISTIC

Since Lovejoy's *Great Chain of Being* (1936) it has been generally agreed that one of the central aspects of the turn from neoclassicism to romanticism was the turn from the idea that the universe is a machine to the idea that it is a growing organism. And this change can be traced in American literary criticism. Following his close friend Hume who saw the universe as "one great machine," Franklin said that "As Man is a Part of this great Machine, the Universe, his regular Acting is requisite to the regular moving of the whole," and he urged that writers need to govern imagination or fancy "with Judgment."[93]

92. From Whipple's very important essays on "Coleridge as a Philosophical Critic" and "Shakespeare's Critics" in *Essays and Reviews* (New York, 1848), II, pp. 183-6; 256-7. John W. Rathbun's dissertation now in progress, The Genesis and Development of Historical Literary Criticism in America, 1800-1860 (University of Wisconsin), should cast further light on this very important subject here tentatively outlined.

93. *Franklin,* ed. by F. L. Mott and C. E. Jorgenson (New York, 1936), pp. 117-118; Franklin's *Writings*, ed. A. H. Smyth (New York, 1905-07), II, 24; V, 182; II, 43; VIII, 128, 163, 604.

His well-known letter to Vaughan in which he advises him to write by successive operations such as assembling evidence, arranging its sequence so as to "proceed regularly from things known to things unknown,"[94] and then attending to stylistic polish and ease, is a typical expression of literary theory in terms of mechanism. According to Thomas Paine in his criticism of the Scriptures, since "the Almighty is the great mechanic of the creation," whose will is revealed in "the great machine and structure of the universe," the critical test of even the Scriptures is that "harmonious, magnificent order that reigns throughout the visible universe," an order which is "the standard to which everything must be brought that pretends to be the work or word of God." Paine's mechanistic aesthetic assumption (in his critical essay on Raynal) is also illustrated by his idea that the writer's "mainspring which puts all in motion, corresponds to the imagination; the pendulum which corrects and regulates that motion, corresponds to the judgment." Such regulation (the neoclassic or mechanistic ideal) enables the writer to "make a reader feel, fancy, and understand justly at the same time."[95]

Despite C. B. Brown's earlier political liberalism, most of his literary criticism, which was written late in his life, was essentially in line with neoclassic or mechanistic theories, as Ernest Marchand's study has shown.[96] John Blair Linn, like Trumbull[97] earlier, held that the greatest works of genius "were all written without attention to the rules or directions of any critic," and he occasionally glorified the escapist imagination. But he also glorified "sweet Pope" and attacked the " 'batwing wheelings' of Wordsworth" who reminded him of a "vacant-headed" girl; his *Powers of Genius* (1801), given unprecedented praise by contemporary critics, sought a "reconciliation" (as Lewis Leary has shown) between the new taste for Ossian and

94. Franklin's *Writings*, II, 24.

95. *Thomas Paine*, ed. by H. H. Clark (New York, 1944), pp. cxvi, cxiii. These ideas are more fully documented in Clark's study of "Thomas Paine's Theories of Rhetoric," *Transactions of the Wisconsin Academy*, XXVIII (1933), 307-339.

96. "Literary Opinions of C. B. Brown," *Studies in Philology*, XXXI (1934), 541-66.

97. See Alexander Cowie, "John Trumbull as a Critic of Poetry," *NEQ*, XI (1938), 773-93.

Burns and the common sense ideas of Kames and especially Hugh Blair who, "has taught us all the critic's rage."[98]

Following the Scottish school, Samuel Miller in his elaborate *Retrospect* (1803) urged correctness and refinement in place of unpolished writings.[99] A. W. Reed has illustrated the interest in regulation in the several "American Projects for an Academy to Regulate Speech,"[100] notably by John Pickering in 1815 and S. L. Mitchell[101] in 1821 (opposed by Noah Webster and others). Kames "the Mechanist," as Gordon McKenzie[102] calls him, had many American disciples, notably Jefferson, as Eleanor Berman[103] has shown; and when Bryant advocated greater prosodic flexibility in 1811-19 he was revolting, he said, from "the precepts of Lord Kames and other writers, who framed their rules of versification chiefly from the writings of Pope."[104] The majority of textbooks on grammar and rhetoric at least up to Joseph Buchanan's *Practical Grammar* of 1826 based on Pestalozzi, were in the neoclassic or Scottish tradition, emphasizing mechanistic concepts. The powerful conservative wing of the New England Unitarians is represented by Timothy Walker's critical attack in 1831 on the early Carlyle who had charged that "the whole doctrine of Locke is mechanical"; Walker said, "we deny the evil tendencies of Mechanism, and we doubt the good influence of his Mysticism . . . Give us Locke's Mechanism."[105] Indeed, if the associational ideas appeared liberal to extreme Lockeans, it should be recalled that such ideas had their roots in the mechanistic doctrines of Hartley and Newton; thus, writ-

98. Lewis Leary, "John Blair Linn, 1777-1805," *William and Mary Quarterly,* Third Series, IV (1947), 148-176.

99. In his chapter entitled, "Nations Lately become Literate." See G. Chinard, "A Landmark in American Intellectual History: Samuel Miller's *A Brief Retrospect,*" *Princeton U. Library Chronicle,* XIV (1952-53), 55-71.

100. *PLMA,* LI, 1141-79, which cites much relevant data.

101. Mitchell's *Discourse on the State and Prospects of American Literature* (Albany, New York, 1821), a Phi Beta Kappa address at Union College.

102. Gordon McKenzie, "Lord Kames and the Mechanist Tradition," University of California *Publications in English,* XIV (1943), 93-122.

103. Eleanor D. Berman, *Jefferson among the Arts* (New York, 1947).

104. *Bryant,* ed. by T. McDowell (New York, 1935), p. 410, in his essay "On the Use of Trisyllabic Feet in Iambic Verse," *NAR,* IX (Sept. 1819), 426-31.

105. *TA,* 40, from Walker's essay on Carlyle in the *NAR,* XXXIII (July, 1831), 122-26.

ing of the 1830's, J. F. Clarke says (in turning to Coleridge) that he revolted from such "deducing mind from matter, or tracing the origin of ideas to nerves, vibrations, and vibratiuncles."[106] The manner in which the transcendentalists centered their massed arguments against mechanism is ample proof of how pervasive and weighty an obstacle to their own ends the concept of mechanism actually was, especially as constituting the semi-official concept taught in our universities by spokesmen of the Scottish "Common Sense" philosophy.

To maintain historical perspective it is well to view the mechanistic-rationalistic point of view not from the prejudiced angle of the romantics but from the view of its own sponsors according to which (as A. H. Everett could say as late as 1829) the "new method" of Newton and Locke had "splendor."[107] For in place of the unpredictable "Illustrious Providences" of the Puritan Mathers' deity, the concept of the "world-machine" and God as its divine mechanic promised regularity and predictability, guaranteed man's happiness if he obeyed intelligible laws, and encouraged writers to communicate truth by an orderliness and lucidity modelled on those of the visible and ordered universe. In the eyes of men such as Franklin and Paine and even John Adams (who criticized Condorcet's book on *Progress* for being deductive instead of inductive and empirical), the mechanistic-rationalistic view as compared to that of Calvinism offered expansiveness, optimism, and exciting possibilities by which writers by free debate could advance governmental harmony and social justice. John Adams said "Newton's science is empirical,"[108] and Adams' theory of checks and balances of which he was ardently hopeful rested on mechanistic assumptions, as Dr. Hornberger has shown; indeed, it is generally

106. *TA,* 47-48. F. H. Hedge in 1834 in writing of Schiller claimed that the dominant note of modernism is a "fierce disquietude" and "dissatisfaction with the whole mechanism of society," as Perry Miller notes. *TA,* 78.

107. *TA,* 29, from A. H. Everett's essay on "The History of Intellectual Philosophy," *NAR,* XXIX (July, 1829), 67-123.

108. See Adams' criticism of Condorcet's book as quoted by Zoltan Haraszti, "John Adams Flays Condorcet's *Progress* . . . ," *William and Mary Quarterly,* Third Series, VII (1950), 238.

agreed (as Woodrow Wilson said) that the basic concept of the Federal Constitution was mechanistic or Newtonian, partly conditioned by the ideas of Montesquieu.[109] In literary theory the mechanistic-rationalistic concept promised much: the subordination of undue mysticism and the intrusion into argument of capricious individuality; the emphasis on the quest of immutable laws or "constants" comparable to those of the Newtonian universe; the possibility of improving writing by conscious revision and planning on the analogy that the parts of the literary machine are interchangeable and improvable; and the possibility of critical appraisal on the basis of rules which are but "nature methodiz'd" and the *consensus gentium.*

Cooper is of course romantic in many external ways, but he also has an important and often disregarded kinship with the mechanistic-rationalistic neoclassicists in such elements as the following: his glorification of the Newtonian-Laplace mechanistic design of the universe proving a divine designer (see *Gleanings in France* and *Crater*); his aversion (in *The Pilot*) to a literature involving spooks and witchery; his praise (in *Mercedes* and *Heidenmauer*) of rationalistic science as triumphing over superstition, and his devotion to utilitarian science (such as his friend Morse's invention of the telegraph) so long as it did not pretend to eradicate basic evil in man's heart; his use of the mechanistic Great Chain of Being to sanction a social-political hierarchy as in *The Bravo* as opposed to equalitarianism; his insistence after 1828 on a writer's devotion to qualities that are common to the rest of the world (as opposed to nationalistic uniqueness); and his stress on "characters in their classes"[110] as opposed to a too rigid adherence to truth; his satire on evolutionary or organic change as in his Swiftian *Monikins,* 1838; and his use of satire (in *Home as Found*) to effect conformity and to ridicule the literati; and his exaltation above "vraisemblance" of the power of inventing plots and characters with such devices as the mechanical revelation of the identity of an "Un-

109. See Hornberger's essay in *The American Writer and the European Tradition,* ed. by Margaret Denny and W. H. Gilman (Minneapolis, 1950), p. 22.
110. Preface to *The Pioneers,* 1823.

known" character at the end. His review[111] of Lockhart's *Scott* in 1838 is a good example of mechanistic rationalism in its detection of discrepancies and contradictions.

In 1836 in his critical essay on Drake and Halleck Poe makes his appeal to "design" as a criterion of art. He attributed design to "Nature even to Nature's God."[112] Such cosmic mechanism provided a grandiose model and sanction for his quest, as a critic, of the extent to which in the short story a given plot was focused on one pre-established design. No doubt he owed something to Coleridge and Schlegel, yet he eventually disparaged both;[113] and Poe thought that the Germans' critiques "differ from those of Kames, of Johnson, and of Blair in principle not at all . . . but solely in their more careful elaboration,"[114] while Poe also paraphrased some of his critical passages glorifying "ideality" directly from the pages of the phrenologists, who were pseudo-scientific mechanists. Indeed, Poe's "Philosophy of Composition" (1846), purporting to show how he wrote "The Raven," shows how late mechanist views lingered, for here he ridicules the poets' pretense of "ecstatic intuition" and gives us a "peep behind the scenes" at his mechanical procedures involving not only over-all design but "painful erasures and interpolations" and devices he likens to "wheels and pinions," "scene-shifting," the quest of a "pivot," etc.[115] The sixteen or seventeen revisions of "The Raven" would seem to testify to the fact that mechanistic-rationalist views were conducive to highly self-conscious craftsmanship, vitally needed during this era when moralistic or patriotic concerns tended to make our writers indifferent to technique and form. Poe's special distinction lies in what one might call structural criticism. He gets inside the form of a story and ascertains to what extent the parts are

111. *Knickerbocker Magazine,* Oct., 1838.

112. In the *Southern Literary Messenger,* April, 1836; *Works,* ed. Harrison (New York, 1902), VIII, 281.

113. See Floyd Stovall, *op. cit.,* p. 111, and A. J. Lubell, "Poe and Schlegel," *Journal of English and Germanic Philology,* LII (1953), 1-12.

114. *Works,* XI, 5. Granting the Germans "brilliant bubbles of suggestion," he also finds them "laughable," and says "I prefer even Voltaire to Goethe" (XVI, 117).

115. *Major American Poets,* ed. by H. H. Clark (New York, 1936), pp. 266-67.

adapted to the whole and to its pre-established design, and how the observance of certain rules (such as totality of effect, verisimilitude, and finality) insure artistic success. In an impersonal way he dissects the works he criticizes with the conviction that parts could be re-grouped and order more effectively imposed. This critical method is closely connected with the assumptions of rationalistic mechanism. Harsh as he often was, Poe's criticism showed with refreshing precision *how* literary art could be changed and improved, in contrast to the essentially fatalistic assumptions of organicism.

B. THE ORGANIC

M. H. Abrams may be right in concluding that Coleridge's concept of the imagination "was the first important channel for the flow of organicism into the hitherto clear . . . stream of English aesthetics."[116] Yet it should be remembered that in American criticism Thomas Carlyle also had considerable influence; that Swedenborg's idea of the "correspondence" of mind and matter gave Sampson Reed a full-bodied concept of organicism (*TA,* 53), and may through this intermediary have greatly influenced Emerson, Bryant, Whittier,[117] and others; that Edmund Spenser's semi-Platonic idea that "soul is form, and doth the body make" (*MAP,* 233) admittedly influenced Emerson, who embodied the organic theory in 1839 in "The Problem" in which the architect, "passive" to the over-soul, derived his plans for cathedral "wonders" directly "out of Thought's interior sphere" (*MAP,* 197); that some Americans (such as F. H. Hedge, Bancroft, and Margaret Fuller) may have derived the idea of organicism directly from independent German sources from glimmerings in Herder and Goethe; that some (such as Ripley and Brownson) may have been influenced by Cousin and other French sources; and that others (such as Horatio Greenough who glorified our clipper ships and characteristic New England farm houses) may have gotten their ideas of functionalism and adaptation from the

---

116. *The Mirror and the Lamp* (Oxford, 1953), p. 168. This is the most incisive study of the shift to English organic theory.

117. Whittier's essay on Swedenborg stresses the idea of correspondence.

long tradition in America (from the days of fighting Indians) of survival growing out of our adaptation to our unique physical conditions.

Broadly speaking, there were at least five different varieties of organicism recognized by Americans. First, the great American vogue of Milton, as part of our early Puritan heritage, encouraged acceptance of his well-known idea that whoever would write a great poem must first make his own life a true poem and achieve virtue, a theory of the organic relation of literary creation and creator which encouraged biographical criticism. This idea is illustrated in Hawthorne's "The Great Stone Face," in which the poet fails because his life does not correspond with his thought, whereas Ernest, the preacher, succeeds because his life is wholly consonant with his words. Second, the vogue of Herder helped to inspire the beginnings of a literary criticism which stressed the organic mutual relation between literature and its authors' time, place, and race, as we have seen in connection with the rise of historical criticism. Third, Coleridge's theory that the organic form is innate in the germ of the author's material, and that it shapes itself as it develops from within, led to a critical revolt against rules and uniformity, and hence to great diversity of literary forms. Fourth, associated with Coleridge's idea that the fullness of the innate organic form is one with the perfection of the outward form, Americans, including Lowell, Emerson, Melville, and Whitman, argued that the parts of a work of art are interrelated and consonant with the whole in a manner analogous to the way in which the branches and roots of a tree are interrelated, interdependent, and consonant with its organic life. Fifth, as Lorch and Matthiessen have shown,[118] Thoreau led the way in requiring that the style of individual sentences should draw vitality and muscularity from the writer's own reports of his five senses. This biological or-

118. F. W. Lorch, "Thoreau and the Organic Principle, in Poetry," *PMLA* (1938), LIII, 286-302. Matthiessen, *American Renaissance*, see index. In Walden (Modern Library ed., 1940, p. 42) Thoreau says, "What of architectural beauty I now see, I know has gradually grown from within outward, out of the necessities and character of the indweller."

ganicism, characteristic of American criticism from 1840 to the latter part of the century, is outside the province of this essay, but will be considered in detail in the essay immediately following. [119]

119. I am indebted to Professor Stovall for his kindness in checking my references and in helping to condense this essay at a time when my residence as visiting professor in Sweden made this work difficult. Much evidence supplementing this study will be found in *Transitions in American Literary History* (Durham, 1954), ed. by H. H. Clark, especially in the essays by Professors Heiser, Kern, and Orians.

Richard H. Fogle

ORGANIC FORM IN AMERICAN CRITICISM
1840-1870

THERE ARE HARDLY five critics in America; and several of them are asleep," said Herman Melville in 1850, in his review of Hawthorne's *Mosses*.[1] This, however, was a dim view of the situation. If we number among the critics all the creative thinkers about literature, then the period from 1840 to 1870 can point at the least to Emerson, Thoreau, Hawthorne, Melville, Poe, Whitman, Lowell, and E. P. Whipple. And to these can be added a substantial group of respectable critics of the second rank—some, of course, more respectable than others: for instance, Margaret Fuller, William Gilmore Simms, W. A. Jones, E. A. Duyckinck, Cornelius Mathews, Parke Godwin, H. N. Hudson, J. D. Whelpley, H. T. Tuckerman, C. A. Bristed, C. H. Webber, and the industrious George Washington Peck. Among the magazines of the time four are especially significant for the purposes of this study: the *Dial*, the *Democratic Review*, the *Whig Review*, and the *North American Review*. Others are noteworthy, but these are particularly consistent and representative. The later journals, *Putnam's, Harper's,* and the *Atlantic*, add little that is new. *Harper's* is negligible because of its reprint policy.[2] *Putnam's Monthly Magazine* has mainly its brief re-

1. "Hawthorne and His Mosses," *Herman Melville: Representative Selections*, ed. Willard Thorp (New York: American Book Co., 1938), p. 338.
2. With exceptions like the notable review of *Moby Dick*. See *Harper's New Monthly Magazine*, IV (Dec. 1851), 137.

views, and even the great *Atlantic Monthly* offers only some competent reviewing and practical criticism. The chief literary impulse of the period was Romanticism, and by the late 'Fifties it was beginning to lose its impetus.

Against the prevailing Romanticism of the mid-century was the staunch and enduring neoclassicism of the *North American Review*. In practice neoclassicism has seldom been as pure or as rigid as it sounds in theory. It is basically traditional, absolutist, deductive, analytic, and judicial, but by 1840 it had long been alloyed with Longinian enthusiasm, the balance of beauties and faults, and doctrines of taste; and in its American version it was filtered as well through the Scottish empiricists. Its aesthetic and psychological assumptions generally went back to Locke through Addison. Neoclassicism is anti-nationalist or internationalist because it believes in absolute universal standards of judgment, and it has the fewest possible dealings with the Time Spirit. Thus a *North American Review* essay of 1840, which incidentally finds Campbell the most satisfying poet of his time, maintains that "One age, or, what is the same thing, man in one age, is much more like man in another, than we are always willing to allow."[3] A very unfavorable review of Simms's fiction and criticism correspondingly lashes out at Simms's enthusiastic Americanism. "A petty nationality of spirit is incompatible with true cultivation. An intense national self-consciousness, though the shallow may misname it patriotism, is the worst foe to the true and generous unfolding of national genius."[4] An 1845 article on "The British Critics" shows decided respect for Wordsworth and Coleridge, and praises Shelley while it attacks Jeffrey—but the critics are Macaulay, Sir James Mackintosh, and Sir William Hamilton. Hazlitt and Hunt are temperately commended for their gusto and taste.[5] A review of Cottle's reminiscences of Coleridge and the second edition of the *Biographia Literaria* plays up Coleridge's drug-taking, and raises the charge of plagiarism

3. "The Poetical Works of Thomas Campbell," *North American Review*, L (Apr. 1840), 491.
4. "Simms's Stories and Reviews," *ibid.*, LXIII (Oct. 1846), 376-77.
5. *Ibid.*, LXI (Oct. 1845), 468-97.

in the two sentences it devotes to the *Biographia.*[6] A survey of "Nine New Poets" denounces the gnomic Emerson: "this volume of professed poetry contains the most prosaic and unintelligible stuff that it has ever been our fortune to encounter"[7]— a verdict, it must be confessed, which was far from unique at the time.

Romanticism, however, was the positive movement of the time, transcendental in the *Dial,* expansively nationalist in the *Democratic Review,* complex and conservative in the *Whig Review,* chivalric and sentimental in the *Southern Literary Messenger,* and to some extent idealist and organicist in all. Its critical criteria were unity and life; its sources were the Germans and Coleridge. Emerson and Margaret Fuller set the tone for the *Dial,* transcendental, cosmopolitan but vigorously American, democratic but exacting in its literary standards. In the third number Theodore Parker vigorously asserted the claims of German literature, Romantic and transcendental. Kant, Fichte, Schelling, and Hegel were among the world's great thinkers, the German writers had produced a literature finer than anything since Sophocles. The philosophers, indeed, might have soared too high, but they were greatly superior to the British and Scotch materialists.[8]

The *Dial* has other stigmata of Romantic organicism. Emerson displays the unfortunate preference of "life" to "art," the man to his work, by praising the imperfections of Ellery Channing's poems, which "had a worth beyond that of a high finish; for they testified that the writer was more man than artist, more earnest than vain."[9] Margaret Fuller accuses Menzel of judging Goethe as a Philistine, inasmuch as he does not enter into Canaan, "and read the prophet by the light of his own law, but looks at him from without, and tries him by a rule beneath which he never lived."[10] Thus she is following the organic doctrine that a writer must be judged by what he is rather than what he is not. This observation, however, does not imply critical relativism, as it does

6. "Reminiscences of Coleridge," *ibid.,* LXV (Oct. 1847), 400-40.
7. "Nine New Poets," *ibid.,* LXIV (Apr. 1847), 407.
8. "German Literature," *Dial,* I (Jan. 1841), 315-39.
9. "New Poetry," *ibid.,* I (Oct. 1840), 220-32.
10. "Menzel's View of Goethe," *ibid.,* I (Jan. 1841), 340.

not in Emerson. For Margaret Fuller the best critics are the comprehensive critics. "They enter into the nature of another being and judge his work by its own law," but having done so they can also estimate the work in its relations. "And this the critic can only do who perceives the analogies of the universe, and how they are regulated by an absolute, invariable principle."[11]

One finds in the *Dial* also the transcendental and Romantic conception of the ideal poet, in an article on Shelley. Shelley was one of those who are unfit for the ordinary business of life, but are divinely inspired with the highest wisdom. These "execute a divine behest in . . . tracing the mystic analogies that so closely ally the worlds of matter and spirit . . . and in uttering from the depths of their divinely moved souls the sublime truths often revealed to those who are poorest in the wisdom of the world, and the most unfit for the marshalling of its affairs." The fool of genius whom Melville was later to portray in *Moby Dick* in the cabin boy Pip, goes back at least to Plato's *Ion;* but more immediately he derives from the transcendental distinction of reason and understanding, as Coleridge used it in distinguishing the mad wisdom of Don Quixote from the sane stupidity of Sancho Panza. Shelley was, it is remarked, "unfamiliar with all the processes of the practical understanding," but he was richly endowed with imagination and reason.[12] The distinction between talent and genius, made in these years very frequently, is roughly analagous. So in 1846 the *Southern Literary Messenger* remarked that Shelley possessed genius but no talent. It viewed the question in another light than had the *Dial,* however: it concluded bluntly that Shelley was a fool.[13]

The *Democratic Review* is in its criticism much akin to the *Dial;* there is the same exhilarating confidence, there are the same prophecies of future greatness. Only the *Review* is more overtly political and nationalistic. The idealism of the *Dial* is directed upward at the stars, the idealism of the *Review* horizontally toward the physical and social expansion of American democracy.

11. "A Short Essay on Critics," *Art, Literature, and the Drama* (Boston: Roberts Brothers, 1874), p. 15.
12. "Shelley," *Dial*, I (Apr. 1841), 493.
13. "Shelley," *Southern Literary Messenger*, XII (Dec. 1846), 737-42.

The clarion note is sounded in the introduction to the opening number: "The vital principle of an American national literature must be democracy. Our mind is enslaved to the past and present literature of England."[14] Park Benjamin indignantly repudiates the notion that the United States are lacking in material for romance. The nation has largeness, diversity, a "poetical" history. The time is ripe, the place propitious. "Shall there not be one great poet—that man whose eye can roam over the borders of our land, and see these things of which we have spoken? Needs not the spirit of prophecy answer, 'Yes'?"[15] One recalls that Hawthorne, who was associated with the *Democratic Review,* was asking the same question in his less expansive way in "The Great Stone Face," and that Melville, who also had ties with the *Review* through Evert Duyckinck, was to find Hawthorne himself the prophecy's fulfillment. Perhaps the young Whitman cocked an ear; he was certainly the answer to the *Democratic* prayer.

Parke Godwin praises Bryant because "his poems are strictly American." "They breathe the spirit of that new order of things in which we are cast." Significantly, he praises Bryant also for relinquishing his poetic solitude to enter the political arena;[16] as with the *Dial,* though not quite with the same reasoning, the man is superior to the artist. Correspondingly, a favorable review of *Two Years Before the Mast* avows, "For our own part, we acknowledge that nothing in this book has given us more pleasure than the evidences of the strong sympathy and brotherhood which grew up between the author and the class of which he was for a time one."[17] The *Democratic Review* diligently strove to foster an indigenous American literature and assiduously heralded the American genius to come. Consequently there is a frightful irony in its reception of *Moby Dick,* certainly a reasonable facsimile of the Great American Novel: "Mr. Melville is evidently trying to ascertain how far the public will consent to be imposed upon. . . .

---

14. *The United States Magazine and Democratic Review,* I (Oct. 1837), 14.
15. "Recent American Poetry," *ibid.,* V (June 1839), 541.
16. "Bryant's Poems," *ibid.,* VI (Oct. 1839), 273-86.
17. *Ibid.,* VIII (Oct. 1840), 319.

The truth is, Mr. Melville has survived his reputation."[18] But of course these things seldom come in the form in which they are expected, and *Two Years Before the Mast* was much closer to what the *Democratic Review* was looking for: a common-sense, not-too-radical American realism, tinged with the proper social sentiments.

The Romantic organicism of the rival *Whig Review* was more complex, more elaborate, and more cautious. H. N. Hudson, E. P. Whipple, J. D. Whelpley, and Lowell attained a high professional competence, beyond which American organicism has seldom reached. These critics were for the most part directly influenced by Coleridge, above all by the *Biographia Literaria,* as is indicated by frequent quotations and references. Thus Hudson's "Thoughts on Reading" in the first number is a thoroughly Coleridgean essay. It cites the *Biographia Literaria,* from which all of it could have been drawn. It recommends judging books according to the mental faculties to which they are addressed; it concerns itself with classes of books rather than individual works. The essay concludes with a discussion of the distinction between genius and talent. Genius reveals, talent proves; genius creates, talent combines; genius is organic and alive, talent is mechanical; genius involves its end in the means it uses, talent separates its ends and means. Macaulay is an instance of talent, Carlyle of genius.[19]

Whipple, in an essay on Coleridge's criticism, makes a frontal attack upon criticism that is over-analytical and judicial, and holds up Jeffrey as a bad example. Coleridge is "the true exponent of the philosophical criticism of the century." This essay is perhaps as good a brief summary of Coleridge's critical thought as has ever been made.[20] George Washington Peck, reviewing *Evangeline,* quotes copiously from the *Biographia Literaria,* and holds up

18. *Ibid.,* XXX (Jan. 1952), 93. For a full study of the *Democratic Review* see John Stafford, *The Literary Criticism of Young America:* Berkeley and Los Angeles, University of California Press, 1952.

19. *The American Review: A Whig Journal of Politics, Literature, Art and Science,* I (May 1845), 483-496. I am indebted to Professor Floyd Stovall for the suggestion that this article influenced Whitman.

20. "Criticism: Coleridge," *ibid.,* III (June 1846), 581-87. Reprinted as "Coleridge as a Philosophical Critic" in Whipple's *Essays and Reviews,* 1889.

Coleridge as the best of critics. He then condemns *Evangeline* on the Coleridgean grounds that it lacks living unity and "keeping," that the dactylic hexameter meter is arbitrary and not organic to the poem.[21] J. D. Whelpley calls Coleridge the reviver of philosophy in England, vindicates the unity of his work, gives an authoritative exposition of his idealism, and compares him favorably with the Germans.[22] H. N. Hudson's notable essays on *Hamlet* and *Macbeth* are influenced by Coleridge's Shakespeare criticism, as no doubt by Schlegel. He interprets character in terms of idealist faculty psychology; Hamlet, for example, is reason and imagination, Polonius is the understanding. It should be said that he does not accept Coleridge's famous conclusion about Hamlet's character—he is in fact rather closer to Goethe.[23] In writing on *Macbeth* he asserts the principle of life as the first criterion; the arts are to be judged not by the understanding but by more appropriate faculties. Art is neither unreal nor actual, but ideal.[24]

In general, American criticism from 1840 to 1870 widely accepts the English Romantic poets. Coleridge is the Romantic magician; Wordsworth is universally but a little unenthusiastically respected; Shelley and Keats are early recognized, and quickly settled in their stereotypes. Shelley is often deified as the archetypal poet, while Keats is enjoyed as the sensuous poet of *The Eve of St. Agnes.* Tennyson and Browning are generously praised and sympathetically understood before 1850. Bailey's *Festus* is vigorously discussed, and becomes a kind of shibboleth. Among Americans Bryant and (at least in the 1840's) the older R. H. Dana receive consistent respect as elder statesmen; Emerson is dismissed for the most part as a poet; Longfellow gets sectarian treatment which seems to follow region and politics; Lowell is very widely reviewed, with varying results. Among English novelists Thackeray appears to be most highly regarded; he is inventive, realistic, gentlemanly, but regrettably a little too cyni-

21. *Ibid.,* VII (Feb. 1848), 155-70.
22. "Life and Writings of Coleridge," *ibid.,* X (Nov. and Dec. 1849), 532-39, 632-36.
23. "Hamlet," *ibid.,* VII (Jan. and Feb. 1848), 94-99, 121-34.
24. "Macbeth," *ibid.,* VI (Dec. 1847), 581-98.

cal. Dickens is a genius with no artistic principles. The Brontës are interesting but not quite ladylike, or alternatively ladies who are meddling with themes unsuited to their ladylike experience. In the United States Irving is venerated but no longer discussed as a lively topic; Cooper is a fine novelist with serious weaknesses. Hawthorne, when he gets a hearing, is generally praised, one suspects first of all because his prose style is a model of eighteenth century purity. Yet more than Longfellow objected to the "old dull pain" which pervaded his books. Melville after his first popular successes was in the main shabbily treated, and often with a surprising personal viciousness. The strangeness of his experience, and his somewhat arrogant literary personality, apparently jarred the average reviewer. The malice of G. W. Peck's review of *Omoo* seems actuated mainly by sheer envy of the sexual experiences the reviewer thought he was reading between the lines, but when he objects to "the cool sneering wit and the perfect want of *heart* everywhere manifested"[25] he is indicating, however unfairly, a quality which really exists in Melville's strangely aloof sailor heroes.

Poetry received more serious attention than did prose fiction. Despite much good reviewing, the general attitude toward the novel fully justifies the later strictures of Henry James in *The Art of Fiction*. Writing in the *Whig Review* on Charles Brockden Brown, J. H. Barrett remarked that the novel might usefully fit into "Little intervals of business—odd ends and fragments of time."[26] Fiction was to be judged on its morality; its function was to furnish wholesome amusement to idle hours by exciting proper feelings and sympathies. A novel is "an epitome of philosophy, dramatized and made popular. . . . Its main object is to convey instruction through the channels of amusement."[27]

William Gilmore Simms, however, as a novelist himself, took higher and more serious ground. Like Scott before him, and Henry James after him, he viewed the novel as a kind of history. In fact, he went somewhat beyond Aristotle by affirming that the

25. *Ibid.*, VI (July 1847), 36-46.
26 *Ibid.*, VII (Mar. 1848), 260-74.
27. Carl Benson, "Bulwer as Novelist," *ibid.*, XII (Sept. 1850), 313.

only real history is art. His affirmation is couched in organicist and idealist terms.

Hence, it is the artist only who is the true historian. It is he who gives shape to the unhewn fact,—who yields relation to the scattered fragments,—who unites the parts in coherent dependency, and endows, with life and action, the otherwise motionless automata of history.... For what is the philosophy of history but a happy conjecturing of what might have been from the imperfect skeleton of what we know.[28]

Reviewing Cooper, Simms finds in him a serious lack of unity. "Conceiving some few scenes, or even a single one, with great beauty and boldness, he discards from his mind all serious concern for the rest." He goes on to describe the movement of a proper novel as a day's walk through a varied landscape, with progress, development, and diversity.[29] Simms was an organicist, though without the philosophical background and belief which generally goes along with literary organicism.

In the 1840's the idea of organicism could be inhaled from the atmosphere; as a method for literary criticism it derives from the general change in man's vision of reality. The world was no longer a mechanism, but a living organism; no longer a smoothly running watch, but now a growing tree. The Romantic organicism of the nineteenth century, however, was basically transcendental, whatever it owed to biological or other science. It firmly believed in spiritual truth. Thus the life which is the root idea of organicism is generally imaged as light, and the life principle is also a principle of the spirit. The notion of organic form can be pantheistic, as it often is in Whitman, rather than exactly and literally transcendental; in other words the light which infuses and unifies a natural landscape may itself be thought of as deity and final truth. Usually, however, and I think in the fullest versions of the theory, this light is the symbol of a still higher reality.

Literature imitates this higher reality. "Organic form" is both an imitation and a creation theory, for it reconciles these

28. "History for the Purposes of Art," *Views and Reviews in American Literature,* First Series (New York: Wiley and Putnam, 1845), p. 25.
29. "The Writings of James Fenimore Cooper," *ibid.,* pp. 214-16.

apparent oppositions by its peculiar concept of *imitation* as distinguished from literal *copy*.[30] It proposes to reconcile art with Nature and the mind of man. The notion of organic form envisages the work of art as a unique principle of life which permeates and vitalizes external form, or conversely as a form embodying life, identical with and inseparable from it. William Butler Yeats expresses its enigma in "Among School Children":

> O chestnut tree, great rooted blossomer,
> Are you the leaf, the blossom, or the bole?
> O body swayed to music, O brightening glance,
> How can we know the dancer from the dance?

Thus the ideas of natural growth and inseparable relationship are closely allied in organic form to the root idea of life.

Two recent interesting articles, by Morse Peckham on the nature of Romanticism[31] and by Richard P. Adams on the American Renaissance,[32] have emphasized the idea of growth in organicism. Organic form will be looked at here, however, in a different perspective, not as the origin of a critical doctrine but as the doctrine itself, insofar as I am capable of seeing and describing its wholeness. If one accepts the single notion of natural growth as a theory of literary creation one is perhaps over-committed to expansion without a compensating contraction, relationship too lacking in definite form. This was the weakness of Whitman's theory of art, and is a fault in most American organicism.

Organic form is more valuable when seen as a comprehensive reconciler of opposites, as an attempt to account for the literary act and the fact in all its complexities and contradictions. It is capable, for instance, of reconciling sympathy with judgment, historical relativism with critical absolutism by its distinction between *copy* and *imitation*. Copy is literal, mechanical reproduction of the superficial form, and in consequence worthless.

30. See S. T. Coleridge, "On Poesy or Art," *Biographia Literaria*, 2 vols., ed. J. Shawcross (London: Oxford University Press, 1907), II, 255 f. Coleridge has a number of passages on the imitation-copy distinction.

31. "Toward a Theory of Romanticism," *PMLA*, LXVI (March, 1951), 5-23.

32. "Romanticism and the American Renaissance," *American Literature*, XXIII (January, 1952), 419-432.

Imitation, on the other hand, lays bare the permanent principles of reality; a work of art must indeed pay homage to the Time Spirit, and wear the livery of its age, but it still can possess unique and lasting life and value. Correspondingly organic form reconciles the universal or general with the particular in the idea of individuation,[33] by means of which an image, circumstance, action, or character may be conceived ideal and concrete, unique and representative at the same time. (Individuation in one point of view is simply classification. A man is universal as life, general as a mammal, special as a human, and unique as himself. A machine, of course, does not possess these attributes.) Organic form also reconciles the part and the whole by declaring that means and ends can be identical. A thing or entity is capable of being a means to some larger end and simultaneously an end in itself. Coleridge embodies this reconciliation as the bicentrality of organic nature, in which each living thing possesses at once a center in itself and out of itself in a more extensive system.[34]

Organicism reconciles in literary creation the active with the passive mind, the immediate and spontaneous with the discursive and voluntary, by proclaiming the vitally indivisible unity of mental processes. Thus Coleridge's famous account of imagination in the *Biographia Literaria* unites synthesis and analysis by specifying the unity of "the whole soul of man," and *also* the elements which are unified. He recognizes both the imaginative wholeness and the mental necessity to treat parts discursively as real things. The fullest and best organic theories do not depend for their criteria of value solely upon the distinction of organic from mechanical form, which by itself is likely to become an arbitrary two-handed engine at the door, summarily dividing the blessed and the damned. Organic form is also capable of subsuming the ideas of order and hierarchy, according to which a whole or structure is thought of as parts arranged in their proper order, according to their relative value, complexity, and fullness. "The poet, described in *ideal* perfection, brings the whole soul of man

33. See John H. Muirhead, *Coleridge as Philosopher* (London: Allen and Unwin, Ltd., 1930), p. 127.
34. *Ibid.*, pp. 122-23.

into activity, with the subordination of its faculties to each other, according to their relative worth and dignity."[35]

The ideal organic theory could be finely calculated to encourage art and criticism by presenting them to themselves both as wholes and as parts, in themselves and in their relationships, as symbols of reality and as real in themselves. It should stimulate the artist to think deep, and yet to lavish all care upon technique and form with no fear that his pains will be wasted. Form and idea justify each other, bear each other up.

Break this union, destroy this balance, and you get unformed thought or sterile technique, didacticism or art for art's sake, a cloddish realism or an empty elegance. So one finds a disastrous cleavage in American literature after the Civil War. On the one hand is a realism which leaves too little room for the shaping, creative mind of the artist. Reality is projected outwards, the organic light vanishes in opaque mass. Lionel Trilling's remarks upon the weaknesses of the liberal imagination are instructive on this tendency.[36] On the other hand is an empty and lifeless formalism, such as is suggested by Edgar Lee Masters' "Petit the Poet":

> Triolets, villanelles, rondels, rondeaus,
> Seeds in a dry pod, tick, tick, tick
> Tick, tick, tick, what little iambics,
> While Homer and Whitman roared in the pines.

Henry James, for example, great novelist and theorist as he was, retrogressed from as much as he advanced upon his predecessor Hawthorne. His gain in technique is balanced, despite his insistence upon *life,* by his loss in vigor. His critical theory discloses one reason why. James, a thoroughgoing organicist—how often the words *germ, seed,* and *organism* recur in his Prefaces— has stripped organicism of a dimension.[37] His organic unity refers wholly to the work, it lacks the height and breadth of philosophic speculation. James did a disservice to American

35. *Biographia Literaria,* II, 12.
36. See *The Liberal Imagination* (New York: Viking Press, 1950), pp. 3-21.
37. See *The Art of the Novel: Critical Prefaces by Henry James,* ed. R. P. Blackmur (New York: Charles Scribner's Sons, 1934).

literature by provoking that prejudice which confuses form with dullness, beauty with sentimentality, and brains with bloodlessness. Emerson and Poe, however, are the true architects of the American breakdown of organic form, from their opposite distortions of the doctrine.

Because of its capaciousness, the theory of organic form is peculiarly liable to fallacies of over-simplification. These fallacies are usually statements in themselves valid, but potentially dangerous in application. Emerson expresses a truth when he says "it is not metres, but a metre-making argument, that makes a poem."[38] This truth, however, easily leads to an absolute predominance of content, which leaves the form no status in reality. More particularly, it can lead to a doctrine of purely expressive metre which destroys the identity of metre as an element in design.

In general, the organicism of Emerson is overbalanced toward Nature, inspiration, immediate insight. As Professor Vivian C. Hopkins has recently remarked,[39] his theory of imagination is a theory of perception. It represents Coleridge's primary imagination, which is common to all mankind, but lacks the specifically poetic secondary imagination, which is the faculty of artistic creation. Indeed, Emerson's progress up the spires of form[40] is usually jet-propelled. Emerson, Thoreau, and Whitman are all possessed of the liveliest feeling for variety, as well as for unity. They are not merely undiscriminating monists. Yet none of them has an adequate notion of process, the process by which variety becomes unity. They have fully grasped the great organic principle of All in Each, by which the life of the whole exists entire in every part. They can see the world in a grain of sand; they are aware that a robin redbreast in a cage sets all heaven in a rage. This fine sensitivity to the vision of the microcosm has, however, some disadvantages for literary criticism. If a grain contains the cosmos, why look beyond it? If all reality is held within one metaphor, why bother with the completed structure

38. "The Poet," *Essays; Second Series.*
39. *Spires of Form* (Cambridge, Mass.: Harvard University Press, 1951), p. 23 f.
40. "And, striving to be man, the worm
Mounts through all the spires of form." (Motto to *Nature,* 1849.)

of the poem? The heaven of imagination is close overhead, and one jump will attain it; conversely, the poles of unity and variety are set too far apart to have intelligible connections between them.

Emerson's own literary structures exemplify this habit of mind. His wonderful sentences—"gold nails in temples to hang trophies on"—are microcosms of the whole, small worlds in themselves. There is, however, little relation between them, too little connection between part and part, or combination into larger parts, such as should gradually evolve into the unity of a total work. Emerson's prose is deficient in gradation, variety, and proportioning. He keeps hammering his nails of gold.

In Emerson, as in Thoreau and Whitman, the vision of the All in Each is a tremendous strength and also a grave defect. It leads to an astonishing eloquence, which is almost a hallmark of the period, but the power and fluency of Emerson, Thoreau, Whitman, Melville, Whipple, and even Poe, is a difficult virtuosity, with a tinge of exaggeration, a sense of straining. It comes for the most part from the gift which Coleridge saw in Wordsworth,[41] of discerning the unusual in the usual, or the whole in the part. Reality as organic form is alive, and possesses the infinite potentiality, the rich elusive mystery of the living body. Its ultimate principle is everywhere and nowhere, since it is diffused throughout—"Are you the leaf, the blossom, or the bole?" Emerson's principle of Beauty is thus, like Shelley's Intellectual Beauty, an "eternal fugitive":

> Thee gliding through the sea of form,
> Like the lightning through the storm,
> Somewhat not to be possessed,
> Somewhat not to be caressed,
> No feet so fleet could ever find,
> No perfect form could ever bind.[42]

Strangely, this problem still dogs the anti-Shelley, anti-Emerson organic theory of our contemporaries the New Critics.[43]

41. *Biographia Literaria*, I, 59-60 (quoted from *The Friend*).

42. "Ode to Beauty," *Selected Poems*, 1876.

43. See especially Cleanth Brooks, "The Poem as Organism," in *English Institute Annual: 1940*; "Irony as a Principle of Structure," *College English*, IX (February, 1948), 231-237.

Wherein resides the final principle of beauty, truth, and value? The organic theory often makes the pursuit of it a shell game, where the hand of the operator is quicker than the eye of the watcher, and the sought-for pea is always somewhere else. Its problem is the riddle of the Sphinx, who takes a thousand forms:

> She melted into purple cloud,
> She silvered in the moon;
> She spired into a yellow flame;
> She flowered in blossoms red;
> She flowed into a foaming wave:
> She stood Monadnoc's head.

Emerson's answer to the problem is,

> 'Who telleth one of my meanings
> Is master of all I am.'[44]

But part and whole cannot presumably be literally identical, though the part can implicate the whole. The sparrow, the shells, and the maid of "Each and All" represent at once too little and too much, as microcosm everything, as part nothing. The eternal Brahma is omnipresent to the point of nullity:

> They reckon ill who leave me out;
> When me they fly, I am the wings;
> I am the doubter and the doubt,
> And I the hymn the Brahmin sings.[45]

Emerson's theory of organic form is overbalanced toward Nature. All Romantic organicism places more importance in Nature than in Art, emphasizes the life more than the form, but there is a decided difference between Coleridge's "and while it blends and harmonizes the natural and the artificial, still subordinates art to nature; the manner to the matter; and our admiration of the poet to our sympathy with the poetry":[46] and the gospel of Nature according to Emerson, in which Art is merely the expression of Nature and the Oversoul within and above it, while the artist is a passive instrument.

44. "The Sphinx," *Selected Poems*, 1876.
45. "Brahma," *Selected Poems*.
46. *Biographia Literaria*, II, 12.

These temples grew as grows the grass;
Art might obey, but not surpass.
The passive Master lent his hand
To the vast soul that o'er him planned . . .[47]

"From within or from behind, a light shines through us upon things, and makes us aware that we are nothing, but the light is all."[48] Language itself is immediately dependent upon nature, and "It is this which gives that piquancy to the conversation of a strong-natured farmer or back-woodsman, which all men relish."[49] In one of Emerson's most fully achieved poems, "The Snow-Storm," nature in the north wind is art's despair and mockery; it

Leaves, when the sun appears, astonished Art
To mimic in slow structures, stone by stone,
Built in an age, the mad wind's night-work,
The frolic architecture of the snow.

The logical end to this aesthetics of Nature is the supersession and eventual discarding of art when it has served its purpose. When man shall at length grow into full maturity he will turn from art, like Shaw's ancients in *Back to Methuselah,* as a kind of beneficent child's play. Just as Romantic organicism leans toward Nature, so it is also liable, if it is pushed too hard, to fall into this denial of art. John Crowe Ransom among contemporary critics has rejected organicism for this very reason. Equating Romantic organicism with the aesthetics of Hegel, he concludes that the Hegelian concrete universal is a cheat, and the Hegelian theory of art a means of quietly destroying its own subject-matter.[50] Certainly Emerson has no such intention, and certainly his poetic sense of beauty is always in competition with the excesses of his thinking; but some of his utterances might well dismay the lover of literature.

Whitman is the most extreme, the most expansively daring of vital organicists. He goes furthest in identifying art with life and nature in organic form. His organicism means literally the word

47. "The Problem," *Selected Poems.*
48. "The Over-Soul," *Essays,* 1847.
49. *Nature,* Chapter IV.
50. "Art Needs a Little Separating," *Kenyon Review,* VI (Winter, 1944), 114-22.

made flesh, or as some Victorians would have it the word made fleshly. The human body is his symbol of organic life and unity; and in Whitman body and soul are interchangeable and identical.

> Of physiology from top to toe I sing,
> Not physiognomy alone nor brain alone is worthy
>   for the Muse,
>   I say the Form complete is worthier far,
> The Female equally with the Male I sing.[51]

The poetic imagination is fitly imaged in the receptive and sexual "body electric."[52]

Whitman carries organicism to its furthest extreme in other respects as well. Organic form is "intrinsic": it is the embodiment of an inner creative impulse. He interprets it as a doctrine of absolute functionalism, which justifies free verse, which renders art the product and consequence of the human mind and body. Therefore the poet must be serene, and full of health; therefore he should immerse himself in rich and complex physical existence, should expose himself to his whole society, excluding nobody and nothing.

The rhyme and uniformity of perfect poems show the free growth of metrical laws and bud from them as unerringly and loosely as lilacs or roses on a bush, and take shapes as compact as the shapes of chestnuts and oranges and melons and pears, and shed the perfume impalpable to form. The fluency and ornaments of the finest poems or music or orations or recitations are not independent but dependent. All beauty comes from beautiful blood and a beautiful brain. If the greatnesses are in conjunction in a man or woman it is enough . . . the fact will prevail through the universe . . . but the gaggery and gilt of a million years will not prevail. Who troubles himself about his ornaments or fluency is lost. This is what you shall do: Love the earth and sun and the animals, despise riches, give alms to everyone that asks, stand up for the stupid and crazy, devote your income and labor to others, hate tyrants, argue not concerning God, have patience and indulgence toward the people, take off your hat to nothing known or unknown or to any man or number of men, go freely with powerful

51. "One's-Self I Sing," *Leaves of Grass.*
52. Cf. "I Sing the Body Electric," *Children of Adam.*

uneducated persons and with the young and with the mothers of families . . . re-examine all you have been told at school or church or in any book, dismiss whatever insults your own soul, and your very flesh shall be a great poem and have the richest fluency not only in its words but in the silent lines of its lips and face and between the lashes of your eyes and in every motion and joint of your body.[53] ·

Whitman confidently accepts the organic idea of growth. The United States "need never be bankrupt while corn grows from the ground or the orchards drop apples or the bays contain fish or men beget children upon women."[54] Unrestrained and unmodified the concept of growth contains within it at least potentially the doctrine of inevitable progress, with its corollary "whatever is, is right": consequently it focusses attention primarily upon the future. Present evils are merely illusions, which the fullness of time will destroy.

Do we not, amid a general malaria of fogs and vapors, our day, unmistakably see two pillars of promise, with grandest, indestructible indications—one, that the morbid facts of American politics and society everywhere are but passing incidents and flanges of our unbounded impetus of growth? weeds, annuals of the rank, rich soil—not central, enduring, perennial things? The other, that all the hitherto experience of the States, their first century has been but preparation, adolescence . . . ?[55]

In art is a like beneficent determinism. "The fruition of beauty is no chance of hit or miss . . . it is inevitable as life . . . it is exact and plumb as gravitation."[56]

The values which naturally evolve from the notion of limitless growth are complexity, largeness, movement, and energy. (The complexity is probably superficial, since Whitman can so easily find a way of resolving it back to simplicity.) He carries furthest after Herder the relativist tendencies of organicism, since growth discards the old and leaves its shell behind. "Plenty of songs had been sung—beautiful, matchless songs—adjusted to other lands than these—another spirit and stage of evolution; but I would

53. Preface to 1855 Edition of *Leaves of Grass.*
54. *Ibid.*
55. Preface to 1876 *Leaves of Grass.*
56. Preface to 1855 *Leaves of Grass.*

sing, and leave out or put in, quite solely with reference to America and to-day. Modern science and democracy seem'd to be throwing out their challenge to poetry to put them in its statements in contradistinction to the songs and myths of the past."[57] More than others, as Norman Foerster demonstrates, he is preoccupied with time and change.[58] "Whatever comprehends less than . . . vast stretches of time or the slow formation of density or the patient upheaving of strata—is of no account."[59] It is easy to see, of course, how time and change become values, when assimilated to unlimited growth. For Whitman literature at any given period is the organic expression of its time, its nation, and its society.

Whitman is most fully the American critic and writer. Most of the critics with whom this essay is concerned are vitally interested in creating a literature which shall be proper to the United States of America as a growing and potentially a perfect democracy. Whitman's relativism, however, and his utter commitment to the principles of growth and progress, combine into a conscious and uncompromising nationalism. The archetypal organic body of Whitman's vision is America. "The United States themselves are essentially the greatest poem."[60] "His [the bard's] spirit responds to his country's spirit . . . he incarnates its geography and natural life and rivers and lakes."[61] His organic problem is to solve the relationship of the states to the nation. ". . . the vital political mission of the United States is . . . the fusion, through compatibility and junction of individual State prerogatives, with the indispensable necessity of centrality and Oneness. . . ."[62] His solution is organic dogma: that the whole is greater than the sum of its parts. Shifted in context, this problem becomes the relation between the democracy as social mass and the democrat as individual. The individual integrity must be preserved, while the mass exerts a dangerous pressure on it.

Welcome as are equality's and fraternity's doctrines and popular education, a certain liability accompanies them all, as we see. That primal

---

57. *A Backward Glance O'er Travel'd Roads.*
58. "Whitman," *American Criticism*, p. 179.
59. Preface to 1855 *Leaves of Grass.*   60. *Ibid.*
61. *Ibid.*   62. Preface to 1876 *Leaves of Grass.*

and interior something in man, in his soul's abysms, coloring all, and, by exceptional fruitions, giving the last majesty to him—something continually touch'd upon and attain'd by the the old poems and ballads of feudalism . . . —modern science and democracy appear to be endangering, perhaps eliminating.[63]

The American poet must aid by honoring the private individual:

> One's-self I sing, a simple separate person,
> Yet utter the word Democratic, the word En-Masse.[64]

An answer, however, lies close at hand in the concepts of organic growth and inevitable progress. The problem is merely momentary and illusory, to be discarded with further development. The apparent antinomy will be resolved in time. "But that forms an appearance only; the reality is quite different. The new influences, upon the whole, are surely preparing the way for grander individualities than ever."[65] Among our critics Whitman most fully admires sheer size (with Melville next), in his American version of the physical sublime. He is not, however, for that reason false to the organic union of part and whole, of body and informing spirit. "The largeness of nature or the nation were monstrous without a corresponding largeness and generosity of the spirit of the citizen."[66]

In his confident acceptance of democracy and science, in his rejection of poetic diction, in his feeling for the common man, Whitman is very like the early Wordsworth of the 1800 Preface to the *Lyrical Ballads*. His faults correspond with Wordsworth's, too—an almost excessive courage of his convictions, which sometimes betrays him into flat literalism; an inadequate doctrine of metre and poetic form, which defeats its own intention of creating an organic unity of form and content; a confusion of abstract and concrete from an uncompromising impulse toward truth-telling by the shortest path; in fact, a general inclination to throw out the baby with the bath. Likewise Whitman shows the same deficiencies in his notions of unity and structure as do Emerson and

63. *A Backward Glance O'er Travel'd Roads.*
64. "One's-Self I Sing."
65. *A Backward Glance O'er Travel'd Roads.*
66. Preface to 1855 *Leaves of Grass.*

Thoreau. He does not adequately grasp the possibility of progressive development; in his theory and in his practice there is too great a gap between the part and the whole, which alternates with too absolute an identification of the part and the whole. *Song of Myself* says the same thing over and over, monotonously because the answer is always evident—all is one, and too simply one. Always and everywhere Whitman is struggling to realize the immense theme of unity, the organic oneness of spirit and matter, form and content. Even the wonderfully appropriate symbol of "leaves of grass" has its evident shortcomings in the indistinguishable anonymity of the parts, and their failure to form a whole which is larger than the sum of its parts, in a new creation.

Finally, Whitman's idea of organic form is too relaxed. Professor Foerster well defines the reconciliation of opposites in his poetry as a union of power and delicacy,[67] but Whitman fails to see organic form, as Coleridge saw it, as an equilibrium achieved by effort and struggle. His reconciliation lacks tension, his form lacks design. In keeping with his value for suggestiveness, he leaves his poems unfinished, to be completed by the reader, thus anticipating the more solipsistic moments of I. A. Richards and William Empson in later criticism. He does not see that freedom and variety are possible only in relation to the limits of form and of uniformity.

A discussion of organic form is obliged to point out these weaknesses of Whitman's organicism, and in so doing it is driven to underrate his self-knowledge and his conscious purpose. No other American critic conveys more unmistakably the sense of genius, of absolute originality, of genuine breadth of mind. It has been objected that Whitman confuses actuality with the ideal, in vague magniloquence. And this is true; his monism is a bewildering process of shifts, too fast for the eye to follow. One must qualify, however. Whitman understood completely the difference between the actual and the ideal America, between actual and ideal poets and poetry. Like Emerson, like Thoreau, like Melville, he is trying to create a great American literature by dint of sheer eloquence, itself the product of supreme imaginative

67. "Whitman," *American Criticism,* p. 174 f.

[95]

effort, stimulated to action by a sense of destiny, by the vision of an American society *in posse* perfect, and by the strong intimation that the moment to strike had come. Like them he cast fear aside, perhaps more easily than they as carrying less impedimenta than they, in order to take a tremendous but still a calculated risk. Whitman might be thought of, as he uttered his barbarous yawp, as a cock crowing loudly on his own dunghill. If so, however, the dunghill was at any rate spacious, and the cock was genuinely persuaded that dawn had arrived.

Thoreau, like Emerson and Whitman, did not achieve an adequate theory of organic unity. Even *Walden* is not fully satisfactory when it is appraised as a structure. The source of the trouble, as with Emerson, is the principle of All in Each. *Walden* is essentially static, despite its careful organization by the changing seasons and Thoreau's skill in interweaving appropriate topics. There is no place to go: Thoreau knows the answers to begin with, and he tells us in every sentence. What is unintelligible paradox to the worldling presents no difficulty to him. The spirit is the reality. His task is to realize this truth in words, to evoke it in the reader's imagination. This is a great feat, but Thoreau can do it, and unfortunately he does it too early and too easily. He permits of no anticipation, no suspense, no gradual progression: in short, of no dynamic structure.

Emerson, Whitman, and Thoreau, then, accent the organism but slight the form. They wish to convey the flashing imaginative insight, the meaning, the light and the life. When that is done they feel their work is done. Consequently their organicism generally envisages a gap between conception and execution: it looks for sparks amid the ashes, it contents itself with a little life, amid much that is conventional and dead. They make use of the organic-mechanical distinction of the German and the English Romantics, and like Carlyle they use it indiscriminately. Organic comes to signify good art, mechanical bad. One thinks of that other distinction we have inherited from the Romantics, the distinction between allegory and symbol, which we have misshaped in the same fashion.[68] On the whole, their conception of

68. E.g., in F. O. Matthiessen, "Allegory and Symbolism," *American Renaissance*

imagination as insight leaves too little room for man's powers as maker and as shaper, though it does ample justice to man as mental voyager, as seeker and finder.

Whatever he may have said of transcendentalists, Poe too was transcendental in his fashion. "Inspired by an ecstatic prescience of the glories beyond the grave, we struggle, by multiform combinations among the things and thoughts of Time, to attain a portion of that Loveliness whose very elements, perhaps, appertain to eternity alone."[69] He shatters, however, the organic synthesis of art and life, of truth, and beauty, by his special interpretation of organic unity. Accepting, as he does, the unity or totality of interest and effect, which he might have found either in Schlegel or in Coleridge, he places his emphasis almost wholly upon effect:

If any literary work is too long to be read at one sitting, we must be content to dispense with the immensely important effect derivable from unity of impression—for, if two sittings be required, the affairs of the world interfere, and every thing like totality is at once destroyed. . . .[70]

Now I designate Beauty as the province of the poem, merely because it is an obvious rule of Art that effects should be made to spring from direct causes . . .[71]

It is to be hoped that common sense, in the time to come, will prefer deciding upon a work of art, rather by the impression it makes, by the effect it produces, than by the time it took to impress the effect or by the amount of 'sustained effort' which had been found necessary in effecting the impression. . . .[72]

A skilful artist has constructed a tale. He has not fashioned his thoughts to accommodate his incidents, but having deliberately conceived a certain *single effect* to be wrought, he then invents such incidents, he then combines such events, and discusses them in such tone as may best serve him in establishing this preconceived effect.[73]

Thus Poe reduces the objective reality or content of literature to nothing, and fixes his attention on the psychological response of

---

(New York: Oxford University Press, 1941), pp. 242-315. It is possible that I misunderstand Professor Matthiessen's contentions.

69. *The Poetic Principle.*
70. *The Philosophy of Composition.*
71. *Ibid.* Cf. *The Poetic Principle.*
72. *The Poetic Principle.*
73. "Hawthorne's Twice-Told Tales."

the reader. Beauty in his theory is a shadow; the effect of beauty is the substance. There is *something* in the work, some cause behind the effect, but it remains in itself undefinable. One sees the results of this doctrine in two interesting passages from "The Philosophy of Composition." The first refers to "the wheels and pinions—the tackle for scene-shifting—the step-ladders and demon-traps—the cock's feathers, the red paint and the black patches, which, in ninety-nine cases out of the hundred, constitute the properties of the literary histrio." The work, in other words, is merely a stage illusion, whose reality consists in its reception by the audience. Again, Poe remarks that a poem requires

some amount of complexity, or more properly, adaptation; and, secondly, some amount of suggestiveness—some under-current, however indefinite, of meaning. It is this latter, in especial, which imparts to a work of art so much of that *richness* which we are too fond of confounding with *the ideal*. It is the *excess* of the suggested meaning—it is the rendering this the upper instead of the under current of the theme—which turns into prose (and that of the very flattest kind) the so called poetry of the so called transcendentalists.[74]

The very shrewdness of these observations helps to emphasize that in making them Poe has deprived organicism of a dimension. He is talking not of meaning but of creating an illusion of meaning. Complexity, according to organic theory, is at once a legitimate value and an interesting problem. It is a guarantee of depth and substance in the work, and it exists to be resolved into—not simplicity, but unity. Likewise, Poe's canon of suggestiveness corresponds to the organic and Romantic doctrine of symbol, but strips this doctrine of its real life. A symbol for Coleridge is a part of the whole which it represents, an image which stands for and is implicated in an idea. Nature is itself and also a symbol of God; *The Ancient Mariner* is real in itself and also in its larger meanings. The creation of symbol is an act of imagination in its quest for totality of relationship. For Poe, however, suggestiveness itself is the absolute, without reference to what is suggested. Using, as he does, ideas and emotions as counters in a game of skill or as properties to produce an illusion, his immediate in-

74. *The Philosophy of Composition.*

fluence is toward the genteel tradition of form without content. At long range one sees in it the extremes of contemporary positivist aesthetics: *The Foundations of Aesthetics,* for instance, by Richards, Ogden, and Woods, which demonstrates that aesthetics has no foundations.

Poe's solipsism, however, is more a matter of emphasis than of belief. Indeed, almost alone among his contemporaries he has something worthwhile to say of the problems of literary development and organization, of the relationship of part to part, of progression and subordination as elements of artistic totality.

It by no means follows, however, that the incitements of Passion, or the precepts of Duty, or even the lessons of Truth, may not be introduced into a poem, and with advantage; for they may subserve, incidentally, in various ways, the general purposes of the work:—but the true artist will always contrive to tone them down in proper subjection to that *Beauty* which is the atmosphere and the real essence of the poem. . . .[75]

He comes closest after Coleridge to framing a poetics for the lyric, and in some matters of practice he is more helpful and concrete than Coleridge. On lyric poetry he is in the general tradition of *Longinus On the Sublime*: the manifestation of the poetic principle "is always found in *an elevating excitement of the Soul.* . . ." His interest in particular effects and devices of heightening and of emphasis is also akin to Longinus. Yet the genuine conception of an ultimate life and sublimity, that central idea which in Longinus justifies and unifies his elaborate analyses of rhetorical devices, is missing in Poe. The treatise *On the Sublime* contains a real synthesis and a solution of the form and content problem, which Poe lacks. He is a philosopher without a philosophy, who gives us rules without at the same time explaining where in the world or out of it resides the principle behind them.

Thus the famous *Eureka* is neither a piece of profound wisdom, as some have held, nor on the other hand sheer nonsense, as others would have it. It is a brilliant exercise in sustained reasoning, but reasoning ungrounded in intelligible premises.

75. *The Poetic Principle.* Cf. *The Philosophy of Composition.*

We see the conclusions, and respect the process which has led to them, but we cannot tell where the process started. The argument itself of *Eureka* reveals why this is so, for in it Poe establishes "consistency" as the criterion of truth and beauty, which he thus reconciles, while he denies the possibility of determining the value of premises. "I offer this Book of Truths, not in its character of Truth-Teller, but for the Beauty that abounds in its Truth; constituting it true. To these I present the composition as an Art-Product alone:—let us say as a Romance; or, if I be not urging too lofty a claim, as a Poem." *Eureka* satisfies one conception of organicism, that which is concerned only with establishing organic unity by a strict monism. In it Poe reconciles beauty and truth; he asserts the correspondence of material and ideal, making electricity the fundamental spirit and life; and he employs a dialectic of the reconciliation of opposites in the fundamental concepts of attraction and repulsion. Since the universe of *Eureka* is pantheistic, he avoids the problem of transcendence and consequently dualism in organic unity. The system, however, is wholly devoid of any real life, or any central Intelligence to make it genuinely organic.

Poe is so fine a critic that his faults are all the more glaring by contrast. He is a heretic who upsets the balance of organic doctrine by exaggerating and misapplying truth. And like most heretics, he talks too much about heresy; his Heresy of the Didactic carves away the life, not only the superficial covering. Poe is an early New Critic in his efforts to provide a fit poetics for lyric poetry, in his somewhat Draconic judicial criticism (judgment is only a subsidiary consideration to organicists), and in his professional hardheadedness. He has, it is true, been little acknowledged by his descendants because of his doctrine of Pure Poetry,[76] which calls for a kind of purity quite foreign to contemporary taste; but his ends are finally the same as theirs. In his critical attitude, though obviously not in his beliefs, he is much like his present critic Allen Tate.

Hawthorne, like the transcendentalists, takes spirit as reality,

76. See Robert Penn Warren, "Pure and Impure Poetry," *Kenyon Review*, V (Spring, 1943), 228-254.

but he places in opposition to it the actual as reality. He lacks the instinct of synthesizing. He inclines, certainly, toward identifying beauty with spiritual truth, but both his Puritanism and his skepticism prevent him from doing so fully. The Peter Hovenden, the American practical man, is usually there to shake his head. Nevertheless Hawthorne is more a Romantic organicist than is generally supposed. His theory of organic form appears most explicitly in his tale "The Artist of the Beautiful," in which a mechanical butterfly, vitalized by the imagination of Owen Warland the artist, becomes a living organism. *The Marble Faun* also proposes an organic theory of art, but in a dwindled Victorian version of his earlier Romantic conception. Perhaps Hawthorne had seen too much of Browning in his Italian travels. At any rate, the aesthetics of *The Marble Faun* possesses too much reach and not enough grasp; it praises suggestion overmuch, at the expense of realization.

In his Prefaces Hawthorne generally discusses his art by the analogy of the *picturesque*. This is basically the traditional *ut pictura poesis* of neoclassicism from Horace on, but rendered organic by a special attitude toward unity, which is conceived as a blending and fusing process, achieved by a subtle use of light and shadow. Light itself, however, is the creative and unifying agent, when combined with a certain idealizing distance of viewpoint. "He [the writer] may so manage his atmospherical medium as to bring out or mellow the lights and deepen and enrich the shadows of the picture."[77] *The House of the Seven Gables* "is a legend prolonging itself, from an epoch now gray in the distance, down into our own broad daylight, and bringing along with it some of its legendary mist, which the reader, according to his pleasure, may either disregard, or allow it to float almost imperceptibly about the characters and events for the sake of a picturesque effect."[78]

Hawthorne's treatment of the prose Romance is organic as Coleridge's account of Romantic drama and poetry is organic, that is, it subordinates surface realism to a spiritual truth and insight

77. Preface to *The House of the Seven Gables*.
78. *Ibid*.

which unifies by infusing and shaping its materials. Hawthorne, however, is much less confident than Coleridge of the validity of his unifying insight, which is to justify improbability. "The reader, *according to his pleasure, may* either disregard, *or* allow it to float almost imperceptibly about the characters and events. . . ."[79] He prefers to keep a foot in each world, rather than assert that these worlds are one. This suspension of judgment between actual and imaginary explains the ambiguity,[80] or "formula of alternative possibilities,"[81] so all-pervasive in Hawthorne's fiction.

Hawthorne deals in his Prefaces with the problem of moral content in organic form, with the organicist distinction between imagination and understanding, and with the corollary problem of the use of the marvellous. Affirmatively his insight and his judgment are perfect, but his confidence is small. He will not solve the opposition of "fancy" and reality. His criticism possesses all the essentials for a full organicist theory, but these essentials are not fully utilized. Hawthorne, it might be said, walked a strait way between skepticism and faith. On one hand he saw light and life, on the other the brute mass of an intractable reality. For long he could leaven the mass with the life, till the life and light failed him. The failure was unnecessary, had he more trusted his gifts, and been less oppressed by the weight of the matter-of-fact present. Easily a master of form, in the end he lost his confidence in the formal.

Herman Melville accepted the doctrine of organic form more easily and completely than did Hawthorne. His 1850 review of Hawthorne's *Mosses* is in the vein of Emerson and Whitman, and like their criticism it has affinities with Wordsworth's 1800 Preface to the *Lyrical Ballads*. Perhaps the earlier Melville most resembles Whitman in his exuberance, and in a certain precarious assurance of the self-educated man. The monism of Melville, however, differs from the monism of Whitman in its emphasis; whereas Whitman looks on good and evil alike in his faith in an ultimate goodness, Melville sees only an ultimate *oneness* in

79. *Ibid.*
80. See R. H. Fogle, *Hawthorne's Fiction* (Norman: University of Oklahoma Press, 1952), pp. 9-13.
81. Yvor Winters, *Maule's Curse* (Norfolk, Conn.: New Directions, 1938), p. 18.

which good and evil coexist as counterparts of each other.[82] The immediate critical result is a juster perception in Melville of the literary possibilities of contrast. Thus in the *Mosses* essay, which has not been bettered in its insight, he notes alike the humor and the "blackness" of Hawthorne's writing, and the artistic effect of their opposition.

For spite of all the Indian-summer sunlight on the hither side of Hawthorne's soul, the other side—like the dark half of the physical sphere—is shrouded in a blackness, ten times black. But this darkness but gives more effect to the ever-moving dawn, that for ever advances through it, and circumnavigates his world. Whether Hawthorne has simply availed himself of this mystical blackness as a means to the wondrous effects he makes it to produce in his lights and shades; or whether there really lurks in him, perhaps unknown to himself, a touch of Puritanic gloom,—this, I cannot altogether tell.

Melville is acute in noticing the alternative possibilities of Hawthorne's blackness, but he lacks here the final organic perception that *both* must be true, that here the belief and the artistry are organically one.

The earlier Melville shows the same overbalance as other American organicists in his preference for the life above the form, the spirit above the spirit's realization. Thus he remarks that "In Shakspeare's tomb lies infinitely more than Shakspeare ever wrote,"[83] and praises the grand unfinished. "But I now leave my Cetological System standing thus unfinished, even as the great Cathedral of Cologne was left, with the crane still standing upon the top of the uncompleted tower. For small erections may be finished by their first architects; grand ones, true ones, ever leave the copestone to posterity. God keep me from ever completing anything."[84]

Like Whitman the earlier Melville is expansive. Frequently he makes use of the metaphor of growth, and he expresses a confidence in America's destiny which does not fall short of the doctrine of inevitable progress. Like Whitman, too, he conceives

82. On Melville's monism see Mary E. Dichmann, "Absolutism in Melville's *Pierre*," *PMLA*, LXVII (September, 1952), 702-715.

83. "Hawthorne and His Mosses," Thorp, *Representative Selections*, p. 334.

84. "Cetology," *Moby Dick* (ch. 32).

of organic form as the word made flesh, and experiments daringly with sensuous effects. He complains that Hawthorne "doesn't patronize the butcher—he needs roast-beef, done rare."[85] Like Whitman, and like Emerson, however, his extravagance is conscious and dramatic, deliberately adapted to the particular needs and circumstances of a national literature. Only self-confidence and independence of spirit can create a genuinely American expression. Melville deliberately condones American brag, to counterbalance American timorousness.

And if any of our authors fail, or seem to fail, then . . . let us clap him on the shoulder, and back him against all Europe for his second round. The truth is, that in one point of view, this matter of a national literature has come to such a pass with us, that in some sense we must turn bullies, else the day is lost, or superiority so far beyond us, that we can hardly say it will be ours.[86]

There is a great difference, of course, between this expansive and affirmative critic and the Melville of *Pierre* (1852) and after. This difference, however, is not at all inexplicable; the seeds of change were present from the first. Melville's powerful absolutism could equally manifest itself in affirmation and denial, as he turned up the two sides of the same coin. Action and counteraction were laws of life; when sunlight ceased to image his experience he turned to darkness instead. "The tortoise is both black and bright."[87] Having trumpeted hope, he also could say no in thunder.[88] Thus, with the turn of the coin he satirizes American provincialism and fatuity in the uncritical adulation of Pierre, author of "That world-famed production. 'The Tropical Summer: a Sonnet.' 'The Weather: a Thought.' 'The late Reverend Mark Graceman: an Obituary.' 'Honor: a Stanza.' 'Beauty: an Acrostic.' 'Edgar: an Anagram.' 'The Pippin: a Paragraph.' "[89]

Melville vigorously affirms, but then he turns to the difficulties

85. Letter to Evert Duyckinck, *Representative Selections,* p. 386.
86. "Hawthorne and His Mosses," p. 339.
87. Sketch Second, "Two Sides to a Tortoise," *The Encantadas.*
88. "There is the grand truth about Nathaniel Hawthorne. He says No! in thunder; but the Devil himself cannot make him say *yes*" (Letter to Hawthorne, *Representative Selections,* P. 388).
89. "Young America in Literature," *Pierre* (Bk. XVII).

which the affirmation evokes. His affirmation, again like Whitman, proclaimed an ideal democratic literature of America. An American is "a man who is bound to carry republican progressiveness into Literature as well as into Life";[90] even Shakespeare might be improved upon. But the difficulties and responsibilities of democracy are as great as its opportunities, and the never uncritical Melville increasingly felt their weight. Whitman's creed of organic growth ceased to serve him. If I may speak tentatively from incomplete knowledge and thinking, the crucial problem in Melville is an unresolved conflict between his concept of form and his concept of organic expansivism: a conflict which in art is a problem of structure, and in the United States of America is the problem of reconciling democracy with order. It is at least implicitly an issue even in the earlier novels,—in *Typee, Mardi,* and *Whitejacket;* in *Redburn* and in *Moby Dick;* and certainly in *Benito Cereno* and the culminating *Billy Budd.*

Melville had his reservations about the goodness of men in the mass, whereas it was precisely the crowd of men who awakened Whitman's enthusiasm. Melville repudiated rank and all artificial distinction, but his attitude was delicately balanced. Consistently one finds in his fiction the hero who is among but not of—Melville among the Typees, Taji aboard the *Arcturus,* Whitejacket on the *Neversink,* Ishmael amid the wild crew of the *Pequod.* Even the Handsome Sailor[91] is set apart from his fellows, partly by the rumor of his noble birth. Melville's reconciliation of the issues of democracy comes through the organic doctrine of the human heart, the great leveller of men. It was through the heart that Hawthorne and Melville, haughty recluses, were Jacksonian Democrats, just as Coleridge saved himself from subjection to rigid notions of hierarchy by means of the transcendental reason, a faculty and quality independent of education, tradition, and understanding. The heart transcends all claims and requirements of form and order, for it is the life and the source, the ultimate reality, and form is properly its manifestation, at most its fruitful opposer. Only once, however, to my knowl-

90. "Hawthorne and His Mosses," pp. 335-36.
91. Billy Budd.

edge, did Melville clearly enunciate the full and ideal theory of organic form achieved by the reconciliation of opposites:

> In placid hours well-pleased we dream
> Of many a brave unbodied scheme.
> But form to lend, pulsed life create,
> What unlike things must meet and mate;
> A flame to melt—a wind to freeze;
> Sad patience—joyous energies;
> Humility—yet pride and scorn;
> Instinct and study; love and hate;
> Audacity—reverence. These must mate
> And fuse with Jacob's mystic heart,
> To wrestle with the angel—Art.[92]

Edwin P. Whipple is worthy of more attention than scholars have granted to him. At the time of his death in 1886, Whittier declared that "With the possible exception of Lowell and Matthew Arnold, he was the ablest critical essayist of his time"; and in fact he was a genuine critic, of power, learning, and insight. Only, his work was a little vitiated by journalism and the lecture platform. His professional duty, as with Poe, sometimes took him into strange literary neighborhoods. Thus toward the end of his centennial survey of American literature one finds such passages as this:

Mrs. Mary J. Holmes, the author of "Lena Rivers," Mrs. Terhune (Marian Harland), the author of "Hidden Path," Mrs. Augusta Evans Wilson, the author of "St. Elmo," are novelists very different from Dr. Holland, yet whose works have obtained a circulation corresponding in extent. We pause here in reading the list, not for want of subjects, but for want of space, and also, it must be confessed, for want of epithets.[93]

Whipple is of special interest to an essay on organic form, for his criticism may be the purest example extant of the Victorian development of Romantic organicism. To Whipple literature is

92. "Art" (from *Timoleon*), *Collected Poems of Herman Melville,* ed. H. P. Vincent (Chicago: Packard and Co., 1947), p. 231.

93. "American Literature," *American Literature and Other Papers* (Boston: Ticknor and Co., 1887), p. 127.

an organic expression of human character, as are social institutions, politics, and action itself. Character is the whole mind of man, a synthesis of the head and the heart, the heart however predominating as is usual in organic theory. In his essays upon "Character" Whipple consistently draws De Quincey's distinction between knowledge and power, which like the transcendental distinction of understanding and reason is calculated to divide mechanical from organic mental processes. Burke, Webster, and Lord Chatham, for example, are men of organic character, in whom action, nature, and intellect are one.[94]

Whipple considers all active or creative processes to begin with a dimly perceived *sentiment,* which corresponds to Coleridge's germ or core of feeling. He distinguishes vital activity of mind from abstract understanding. He asserts the primacy of mind over object or objective circumstances, but reconciles subject and object (more convincingly than most organicists manage), by the metaphor of *assimilation*: character is "the embodiment of things in persons."[95] Like Coleridge, he specifies a difference between sight and insight; what a man is capable of seeing is determined by the prior direction and quality of his mind. Gibbon is an instance of mind in reconciliation with the mind's materials. The product of his vast research is organically altered by the prevailing color of his character.

In his practical criticism Whipple seeks out the basic *characteristic,* the life-principle and organic unity. He is in quest of fundamental personality, but he does not commit the "personal heresy" as it is today conceived and attacked. He looks for the man in his works, and not in the facts of his life, which he considers to be superficial and misleading evidence. "As the inmost individuality of a man of genius inevitably escapes in his writings, and as the multitude of readers judge of him by the general impression his works have left on their minds, their intelligent verdict in regard to his real disposition and nature carries with it more authority than the testimony of his chance companions."[96] The life-principle of Thackeray, for instance, is a pervasive skepticism. Thackeray's

94. *Character and Characteristic Men.* Boston: Houghton Mifflin and Co., 1894.
95. *Ibid.,* p. 8.
96. *Ibid.,* pp. 197-98.

vision of life is essentially mechanical; his sight is sharp, but devoid of insight. "The form rather than the substance is what is new, and the superficiality of thought underlying the whole presentation is often painfully evident."[97] Correspondingly, Whipple praises Hawthorne's insight into spiritual truth and law.[98] In dealing with the fiction of both men he commences with the characters of the authors, then proceeds to the characters in their books, but he succeeds in keeping in sight the problems of structure and language. Whipple, in general, provides a good and enlightened Victorian version of the theory of organic form.[99] The one significant weakness in his critical system is contained in the word "character" itself. Whipple could not wholly control its ethical implications, and the results of vulgarizing it are obviously disastrous. One consequence is our present cant phrase "character-building," especially as it is used by educators and football coaches.

Many men, including himself, have denied to James Russell Lowell any firm central identity. Professor Foerster and Professor Clark, on the other hand, have vigorously defended his claims to centrality.[100] Where lies the truth? It shifts, perhaps, according to one's views on the location of the center. In Lowell it is less within himself, and more outside himself in the main stream of European and American culture. He has the chameleon quality which is proper to an academic and a professional critic, the shape-changing sensitivity and the caution which faithfully register the work as it is, within a broad context of its cultural surroundings. The conservatism for which Lowell has been taxed, his inhospitality to new writers, has perhaps two causes, which are at bottom one. He comes at the end of a great tradition, which at the last failed in energy to revitalize itself; and there really was much in the new generations which Lowell did well to reject.

97. *Ibid.*, p. 204.

98. *Ibid.*, pp. 238-242.

99. The only contemporary estimate of Whipple which I have heard of is Denham Sutcliffe, " 'Our Young American Macaulay,' Edwin Percy Whipple, 1819-1886," *New England Quarterly*, XIX (March, 1946), 3-18.

100. Norman Foerster, *American Criticism* (Boston: Houghton Mifflin Co., 1928), pp. 111-156; Clark and Foerster, *James Russell Lowell: Representative Selections* (New York: American Book Co., 1947), pp. c-cxxxix.

Lowell is in the organic tradition of Herder, Goethe, and Coleridge in seeking the life principle of a man or work intrinsically, within themselves. His early criticism of Emerson's poetry in *A Fable for Critics* has almost all of the organicist ideas:

> Some poems have welled
> From those rare depths of soul that have ne'er been excelled;
> They're not epics, but that doesn't matter a pin,
> In creating, the only hard thing's to begin;
> A grass-blade's no easier to make than an oak;
> If you've once found the way, you've achieved the grand
>   stroke;
> In the worst of his poems are mines of rich matter,
> But thrown in a heap with a crash and a clatter;
> Now it is not one thing or another alone
> Makes a poem, but rather the general tone,
> The something pervading, uniting the whole,
> The before unconceived, unconceivable soul,
> So that just in removing this trifle or that, you
> Take away, as it were, a chief limb of the statue;
> Roots, wood, bark, and leaves singly perfect may be,
> But, clapt hodge-podge together, they don't make a tree.

A poem, then, should be an organic expression of the soul ("Some poems have welled / From those rare depths of soul. . . ."). It is to be judged from within, through the critic's intuition of its vital impulse. Consequently the problem of genre is only superficial at most ("A grass-blade's no easier to make than an oak"), and the old neoclassical ranking by kinds no longer has validity. Instead the criterion is the genuineness of the creative urge (the organic life of the work). If form and content are truly one, this organic unity will be manifested in unity of tone, which is the outward evidence of the inner life ("The something pervading, uniting the whole"). A genuinely organic work must be judged as a whole ("Now it is not one thing nor another alone / Makes a poem"), since its parts are organically inseparable; insofar as any part of it can be without harm abstracted, so far the work is imperfect. Finally, the work should be not the sum of its parts (mechanical unity by arrangement or aggregation), but more than the sum of its parts (organic unity by fusion).

> Roots, wood, bark, and leaves singly perfect may be,
> But, clapt hodge-podge together, they don't make a tree.

Lowell's criticism is eclectic, but organicist in its very eclecticism, since its method is determined by the requirements of his subject. He shows the organicist willingness to sympathize, to assimilate, to absorb before he passes judgment. And his judgments generally stand up well. His essay on Keats, for example, written in 1854, contains in the germ all that modern scholarship has fathomed of Keats's identity, his unique fusion of experience and thought, his sensuous power and his idealism. Although less well-known, his essay is better than Arnold's on Keats. The organicist Lowell, unlike the judicial Arnold, is not led astray by his own social and moral prejudices.

His criticism is most completely organic when it deals with established, unshakeable masters. In treating of Dante and Shakespeare he is expounding on the foundation of the organic principle of life and unity, the presence of which he is able to assume.

In the fine arts the vehicle makes part of the thought, coalesces with it. The living conception shapes itself a body in marble, color, or modulated sound, and henceforth the two are inseparable. The results of the moralist pass into the intellectual atmosphere of mankind, it matters little by what mode of conveyance. But where, as in Dante, the religious sentiment and the imagination are both organic, something interfused with the whole being of the man, so that they work in kindly sympathy, the moral will insensibly suffuse itself with beauty as a cloud with light.[101]

He varies his approach, however, according to his subject. For Wordsworth he uses a beauties-and-faults, credit-and-debit system, such as might have been employed by Addison or Johnson. He first discusses Wordsworth's faults, then proceeds to praise his compensating, or over-compensating virtues. Finally, however, he returns to organicism and modifies this balancing of the books

101. *Lowell's Prose Works* (Boston: Houghton, Mifflin and Co., 1898), IV, 165-166.

by evoking the organic doctrine of the inseparability of virtues and defects to define the poet's unique and distinguishing quality.

The normal condition of many poets would seem to approach that temperature to which Wordsworth's mind could be raised only by the white heat of profoundly inward passion. And in proportion to the intensity needful to make his nature thoroughly aglow is the very high quality of his best verses. They seem rather the production of nature than of man, and have the lastingness of such, delighting our age with the same startle of newness and beauty that pleased our youth.[102]

Wordsworth's power is in part his weakness. His gift of concentration is at times unaccompanied by the artistic judgment which would realize it in form. He is therefore an "inorganic" poet in whom life is not everywhere diffused, who is great primarily in isolated passages, who lacks the sense of wholeness and proportion, whose means and ends are only occasionally adapted to each other. It is interesting that Coleridge, greatest of organic critics, also partially forsook the organic method in dealing with Wordsworth. Perhaps the reason is the same in both instances. The critical method of organic form is calculated to perceive and to define the virtues of unity and proportionateness; where such unity is felt to be absent the method is inappropriate.

Lowell, and doubtless Hawthorne, do not share the great strength and weakness of the other American organicists, their tremendous eloquence and energy. Emerson and Whitman and Thoreau and Melville and Whipple all said, "If there is no American literature it will be necessary for us to invent one." Poe, on the other hand, was equally vigorous in his contrariness. Probably it required such supernal drum-beatings as theirs to awaken American self-confidence, as Melville said, but the net result was overstraining. The inevitable exaggerations of a spell-binder like Emerson could make a doubtful case sound all too specious; to combat his persuasiveness it took the opposite exaggerations of a Poe. Strained by such stresses as these, the organic synthesis was broken by the 1860's, although it partially survived in Whitman, Whipple, and Lowell.

102. *Ibid.*, pp. 404-05.

Robert P. Falk

THE LITERARY CRITICISM OF THE
GENTEEL DECADES
1870-1900

IN THE DEVELOPMENT of American criticism, as in other
areas of intellectual or cultural history, the genteel decades
between 1870 and 1900 have not fared well among interpreters
and critics of American literature. The liberal intellectuals of
the twenties and thirties coined many of their best adverse epithets
in reference to the cultural tone of American life in The Gilded
Age. "The Age of Innocence" came to signify social and moral
hypocrisy; "The Genteel Tradition" suggested the imposition of
false and decadent values upon an industrial society; "Chromo-
civilization" meant outward glitter and inward indifference; "The
Pragmatic Acquiescence" was an equally patronizing phrase;
"New England: Indian Summer" expressed an attitude that after
the Civil War there was a broadening down of cultural standards
to lower, workaday levels. Literary criticism in those decades,
said Bernard Smith, belonged to "Academy and Drawing
Room"; or it was, as Sinclair Lewis put it, "a chill and insignificant activity pursued by jealous spinsters, ex-baseball reporters
and acid professors."[1] It is hard now to discuss the closing decades of the last century without falling into one or the other of
these well-worn epithets—"Robber Baron," "Tragic Era," "Great
Barbecue," "Chaos."

1. "The American Fear of Literature," *Why Sinclair Lewis Got the Nobel Prize,*
ed. E. A. Karlfeldt (New York, 1930), p. 20.

[113]

The reasons for this concerted devaluation of an epoch of American cultural history are complex, but it has become increasingly apparent that it was in part due to the impulse of critics of the 1920's to express their own feelings of liberation by revolting against the underlying assumptions of the preceding generation. The strong anti-Victorianism of Sinclair Lewis, Mencken, Van Wyck Brooks, Parrington, and other disparagers of the genteel decades was, to some extent, a self-justification. On the other hand, it would be useless to deny that the struggle to preserve the older securities and traditions in an increasingly industrialized and urbanized society brought about many strains and paradoxes which marked those years as confusing and uncertain of aim. Criticism and critical theory, like other avenues of thought and expression in the Age of Decorum, came to be judged by a growing feeling on the part of the newer generation that 1900 had marked the end of an era. Thus Santayana, defining with irony "The Genteel Tradition," said that a fundamental orthodoxy had existed among American highbrows down to 1900, dissent from which was felt to be scandalous. "It consisted in holding that the universe exists and is governed for the sake of man or of the human spirit."[2]

The student of critical theory and practice in the genteel decades must inevitably come to some terms with this formidable body of opinion, for criticism with its academic flavor was especially subject to the attack. That there was no easy blending of ideality and reality during those years is undeniable, yet it does not follow that critical theory suffered irreparably from such intellectual conflicts as those between religious orthodoxy and evolution or between ideal and material interpretations of the universe. Practical criticism in the seventies and eighties no doubt showed a leavening down to more utilitarian standards; nevertheless individual critics and theorists of literature sought a new vision of reality with a seriousness and enthusiasm equal to that of the leading critics of the mid-century. When one is dealing with the work of an individual critic of major stature like

2. George Santayana, *Character and Opinion in the United States* (New York, 1920), pp. 16-17.

Henry James or one more representative of his age like Stedman or Woodberry, it is a mistake to allow broad cultural generalizations to outweigh other considerations. It is not the social tendency nor even the intellectual character of an era that makes a critic, though in varying degrees such influences are present. An infinite variety of intangible qualities of mind are likewise significant—grace, verbal fluency, subtlety, seriousness, devotion to the task—all must be accounted for by him who ventures upon criticism of criticism.

With James as its leading practitioner and Howells, Garland, Norris, Higginson, Lanier, Stedman, T. S. Perry, Lathrop, Woodberry and others of less intrinsic but considerable historical importance, the cavalcade of criticism during the Age of Decorum may be watched with more than passing interest by the student of American literature and thought. We have come increasingly in recent years to comprehend and admire the major literary figures of the Howells-James era and to study the work of a number of the minor ones. The time seems opportune to make a more generous estimate of that underrated age, and one way to do this is to survey the literary criticism, in theory and (as far as possible) in practice, and to reappraise it both as to its ultimate value and as a reflection of those currents of thought and expression which we have come to associate with the pattern of late Victorian realism.

Realism, as the word was used during the genteel decades, had many meanings and associations—so many, indeed, as to make it (like other such broad classifications) nearly meaningless. In one sense, it was associated with the novel as distinct from the "romance" in prose fiction. In another, it implied a closer adherence of the artist to the claims of empirical or literal reality. A later perspective suggested that realism signalized a declaration of independence on the part of the younger generation from the intellectual dominance of its elders. There were various "realisms" in the decades following 1870—realism of the commonplace, urban realism, the realism of science and positivism, the realism of local color. But in the more limited realm of critical theory the term came gradually to characterize a method and a loose rationale for the rapidly growing, amorphous child of literature, the novel.

In the best hands, moreover, the word did not signify a complete break with the literary ideals of the past. Those who thought seriously about realism were both unwilling and unable to jettison the entire cargo of Coleridgean principles and the language of transcendental criticism. The romantic elevation of the artist, the organic theory of art, the moral function of literature, the responsibility of the writer in a democratic society—even the very terms "imagination," "idealism," and such—were retained with certain qualifications and reservations. James, for instance, preserved something of Emerson's belief in the essential morality of aesthetics and much of Poe's insistence upon unity and the necessity of craftsmanship. Lanier envisioned a new ideality which carried over much of the romantic fervor. Howells and Garland sought to revive in a different sense the broad democratic humanitarianism of Whitman. In short, the earlier realism, far from abandoning the literary ideals of the New England renaissance, sought instead to harmonize this inheritance with the claims of Darwinian science and industrial democracy and to bring about a new artistic revival through the medium of the novel.

When one turns from literary theory to practical criticism he must enter into the heated battles of the bookmen which were fought out in the columns of the newly flourishing monthlies. Here the historian of this late Victorian *Sturm und Drang* in criticism can learn much of the relation of art and society in America when the nation was seeking some new orientation between the fading ideals of an earlier day and the increasing social tensions of the reconstruction decades. These were years of intellectual cleavage and social change. Older democratic hopes were leavened by the political opportunism and acquisitive materialism of The Great Barbecue. Ethical integrity was blunted by the lowered moral tone of Boss Tweedism and the exploitation of natural resources by a few irresponsible railroad barons and lobbyists. The arts, especially poetry, were challenged in the general Mammonism of the Grant era, and religious orthodoxy increasingly found itself on the defensive against the materialism implicit in the new evolutionary science. Prudery and gentility were sometimes the only recognizable remnants of a loftier and more dignified intellectual idealism. Although American criticism suffered somewhat from the weaknesses of a genteel outlook, at its best it transcended them. Critics were conscious of both the old and the new; they strove to define the term "realism," especially as it was applied to the novel, to learn the extent to which it could be used as a conscious aesthetic philosophy, and to adjust it to the changing social scene without losing the traditional literary values of the past.

Intellectual America after the Civil War was groping for a new basis and a new justification. Poets, philosophers, editors, "romancers," and critics anxiously strove to discover fresh and vital intellectual patterns or nostalgically recalled older and established ones. The younger generation of the seventies hoped to find in realism a philosophy of letters which could supersede declining romantic ideals and express the rising age of science and empiricism. Older and wiser heads, however, feared the specter of scientific determinism and clung to the lofty principles which had informed the work of the earlier New England literary masters. The battle lines gradually formed in the periodicals of the 1870's between the progressive spirits whose watchwords were "science" and "reality," and the traditionalists who deplored the trend toward literalism and actuality and sought a neo-romantic ideal of ethics and broad universal truths in which the artist was free to explore the world of imagination and romance.

In the eighties and early nineties the disciples of Howells became increasingly militant. Realism, through discussion and experiment, took shape as a literary movement with certain recognizable aims and principles, while the proponents of "romance," still very much alive, sniped at them from the strongholds of traditionalism. Finally, in the closing years of the century, the pendulum swung back, and for the moment the realists were eclipsed by the return of historical romance, popular adventure, and the domestic proprieties in fiction. Viewing the thirty-year period as a whole, one may justifiably study the literary controversy over realism in four distinct phases, roughly parallel to the social and intellectual trends of late Victorian America. *First,* from the appearance of *Democratic Vistas* in 1871 to approximately 1880, the prevailing literary temper may be described as a kind of "post-Darwinian idealism" in which intellectuals fervidly tied their hopes to the twin balloons of Spencerian evolutionary optimism and Comtean Positivism. The seventies belonged to "The Afterglow of Transcendentalism," hesitating between old dreams and new science, timidly provincial and loudly nationalistic by turns. *Second,* the years from 1880 to approximately 1887 witnessed a literary renaissance of prose fiction, "The Triumph of Realism," in which the forces of realism and those of romance seemed, for the time, to merge in a kind of synthesis, and the more strident tones of the 1870's mellowed to produce some of the best work of Howells, James, Mark Twain and others of the first generation of realists. *Third,* "The Years of Protest" from 1887 to 1894 brought a closer alignment of literary principles with collectivist tendencies, Utopian ambitions, and sociological probings of the weak spots of urban democracy. Howells, from his Editor's Study of *Harper's Magazine,* became the champion of a new realism of humanitarian aims and social protest. *Fourth,* there took place a revival of romance after 1894 when labor strikes and the Populist Revolt of the early nineties subsided and a period of complacency and optimism preceded the war against Spain. In this rosy interlude of *"Fin de siècle* romanticism" Marion Crawford, Stevenson, Lew Wallace, and Conan Doyle reigned popular favorites, while Ibsen and Tolstoi were regarded by right-thinking Americans as the satanic idols of Bohemianism.

In studying the literary criticism of the period against the background of Victorian America one is struck by certain broad differences from the theories and speculations of the romantic age. For one thing there was more analysis and less theory. Instead of the idealized concept of The Poet as we find him in Emerson's essays, one finds more attention given to the practical problems of the writer and his art. Abstraction gave way to practical reviewing in the critic's columns of *The Atlantic Monthly, The Galaxy, Scribner's, Harper's Magazine,* or *The Century.*

A critical essay was no longer a work of art or a lecture to be delivered with grace and careful revision, as was the case with Poe's *Poetic Principle;* instead it had to meet a vastly enlarged reading audience and an editor's deadline. Criticism became more of a business and less of an art. Technical matters displaced philosophy. In place of Emerson's "metre-making argument" one finds Lanier's involved and specialized *Science of English Verse*. Occasional discussions of the theory of fiction like George Parsons Lathrop's essay "The Novel and Its Future" (1874) or James's "The Art of Fiction" (1884) were the exception rather than the rule. More often the call was for special essays on individual authors, Hawthorne, George Eliot, Turgenev, Balzac, Flaubert, Zola. Stedman, it is true, devoted himself to books on the art of poetry, but they, too, were increasingly technical. Behind the multiplicity of reviews and articles, however, there was a recognizable substratum of theory, an effort to understand the meaning of realism and to give it certain aesthetic principles and comprehensible aims. In the subsequent pages we will attempt to gather the threads of this somewhat groping literary speculation and place it against the background of the period, as well as to see it in relation to the romantic theories of poetry and the organic conception of art which formed the basis of criticism in the prewar decades.

I.

The literary world in the 1870's dallied like the lover in Henry James's symbolic tale "Benvolio" (1875) between two mistresses, the lovely and fragile Scholastica, his first love, and the Countess, a worldy and fascinating widow. American criticism, confronted by an ever-widening gulf between ideals and social facts, hesitated like James's young poet, unable to make up its mind between the world of science and the world of dreams, between the ethics of Emerson and those of Boss Tweed, or between the ideals of the Enlightenment and the actuality of Zola's *L'Assommoir*. The older poetic masters of New England's golden day, Emerson, Longfellow, Whittier, and Lowell—remained as honored and revered household gods, while among the newer generation the muse of prose fiction gradually supplanted the muse of poetry.

Disturbing and challenging was the intellectual prospect in 1870: the beckoning voice of Darwinism, Herbert Spencer and the evolutionary spirit, Positivism, the novels of George Eliot and Turgenev, the ogre of French realism, the menace of scientific determinism, the twilight of religious orthodoxy. Yet, for the time the national mood was one of great hopes and high visions: "the genial romanticism of Victorian evolution" was to prevail.[3]

Among the critical spirits of the seventies, one distinguishes three different groups: the professional scholar-critics like T. S. Perry, T. W. Higginson, W. C. Wilkinson, G. P. Lathrop, E. P. Whipple, and M. C. Tyler; the young and active reviewers, notably James and Howells, who devoted themselves almost exclusively to the field of fiction; and the poet-critics, Whitman, Lanier, and E. C. Stedman.[4] The latter group became the spokesmen for what may be called the twilight of transcendental thought in in criticism. They sought to blend the earlier idealism with the idea of progress emanating from Spencer, Tyndall, and Comte and thus to find a reconciliation between science and literature.

In *Democratic Vistas* (1871) Whitman lent a new emphasis to the older, romantic concept of the poet as the representative voice of democracy. His faith somewhat shaken by the social and political chaos of the first Grant administration, a society "canker'd, crude, superstitious, and rotten," he nevertheless held firmly to his ideal of a brotherhood of self-reliant men led by the bard, or "literatus," who "while remaining fully poet, will absorb whatever science indicates."[5] In his poetic vision of the future harmony of America Whitman was followed by Lanier in the South for whom a tall stalk of corn became the symbol of the poet-soul, appointed to lead the vanguard of his time, teach chivalry, and reconcile "the heart-perplexing opposites" of the age.

3. V. L. Parrington, *The Beginnings of Critical Realism in America* (New York, 1930), p. 190.

4. The criticism of Lowell, of considerable extent in the 1870's and beyond, must be passed by in this chapter with only this very general observation: in his critical essays written in the seventies he centered his attention on the earlier English poets, perpetuating in general the transcendental ideals of Coleridge. As such, of course, he contributed to the prevailing romantic tone of literary theory during that period.

5. Walt Whitman, *Complete Prose Works* (Boston, 1898), p. 246, and elsewhere in *Democratic Vistas*.

Lanier, at the close of the decade, sought to combine the various sides of his complex mind—music, poetry, and scholarship—in his curiously learned lectures at Johns Hopkins University and the Peabody Institute on the science of English verse, Shakespeare, and the novel. The books of criticism which resulted from his ranging over German aesthetic theories, evolutionary science, and the modern novel are a strange melange of scholarship, moral fervor, and prophetic vision. They glow with a message of harmony and rhythm for a world of conflict and change. Lanier dreamed of a literary criticism in harmony with the evolutionary principles of Spencer, an upward law of social progress, or "etherealization," a physics of metrical systems, an exact science of acoustics for music and verse, a fundamental unity among all the arts, and (like Whitman) a democratic millennium in which man, wafted on the wings of beauty and goodness, would become self-governing.[6]

In this vision of a shimmering harmony of "the lens, the laboratory, and the millennial rocks" Whitman and Lanier were joined by a third poet-critic, E. C. Stedman, a New York stock broker turned poet (himself a schizophrenic symbol of these divided years).[7] Like them, Stedman envisaged a great future for poetry when science and art would join hands.[8] Whether any of

6. For the many statements of Lanier which make up his philosophy of criticism turn to *The Science of English Verse* (1879), *The English Novel* (1883), and *Shakespeare and His Forerunners*, 2 Vols. (1901). In *The Complete Writings of Sidney Lanier*, Centennial Edition, 10 Vols. (Baltimore, 1946), consult especially Vols. II, III, IV and the thorough introductions to these volumes. See also Gay Allen, "Lanier as a Literary Critic," *Philological Quarterly*, XVII (April, 1938) and Philip Graham, "Lanier and Science," *American Literature*, IV (Nov., 1932).

7. Hamlin Garland, who knew Stedman in the nineties, described him as "a poet driven to imperil his life in every way in the war of business—yet enjoying it." (*Roadside Meetings*, New York, 1930, p. 337.)

8. In his *Victorian Poets* (Boston, 1875) and *Poets of America* (Boston and New York, 1885) Stedman gave voice to many of the neo-romantic ideas in criticism and established himself as the most representative critic of the time. He applied to poetry the Spencerian principle of progress from the homogeneous to the heterogeneous; he envisaged a harmony of art and science; admired the classics and, like Arnold, preached the gospel of Hellenism in the marts of trade. According to G. E. De Mille, *Literary Criticism in America* (New York, 1931), p. 137, Stedman heralded the break, about 1880, from ethical to aesthetic criticism in America by championing the cult of beauty and idealizing Tennyson. Although he has been regarded as the spokesman of a declining genteel tradition, he nevertheless was among the first critics to apply scientific thought to poetry and, surprisingly, defended Whitman.

them foresaw the kind of poetry which would be written by T. S. Eliot and Ezra Pound is an interesting if futile speculation, but it is clear that for the next few decades their hopes for a poetic renaissance were unrealized. The novel, or the prose "romance" as Howells preferred to call it, emerged as the most vital literary form of the age, and in the hands of the younger generation of the seventies, Howells, James, Bret Harte, Eggleston, Mark Twain, and DeForest, its possibilities were explored both in theory and in practice. The novel quickly allied itself with the new psychology of Wundt, Helmholtz, and other German behaviorists, centered its attention on the analysis of manners and character, and discovered its most intriguing case study in the young American woman.

Howells, as editor of *The Atlantic Monthly,* the most influential periodical of the decade, was carving for himself a permanent niche in the realm of letters with his travel-sketches and character delineations, *Their Wedding Journey* (1871), *A Chance Acquaintance* (1873), *A Foregone Conclusion* (1875), and *The Lady of the Aroostook* (1879). Howells' formula for realism was to stay within the pattern of the love story, but to blur its conventional effects in the interests of psychological analysis of the feminine oversoul. The tone of these books was not realistic, but romantic, picturesque, charming, quaint, imaginative. "Ah! poor Real Life, which I love, can I make others share the delight I find in thy foolish and insipid face?" This idealization of the commonplace with its effort to look upon man, not in his heroic phases, but rather "in his habitual moods of vacancy and tiresomeness," was typical of the more forward-looking elements of the aesthetic temper of the 1870's. It grew in part from the "rare, precious quality of truthfulness" which George Eliot[9] found in Dutch paintings, from the heroic portraits of plain people by J. F.

9. George Eliot and Turgenev were the two European novelists who most widely established the standard for American critics of the 1870's in their quest for a philosophy of realism in fiction. George Eliot's psychological interest in character appealed to progressive critics and her strong didactic tone permitted conservatives to champion her as opposed to the greater frankness of the French novel. Her role in the struggle for realism was widely discussed in the periodicals by James, Howells, T. S. Perry, W. C. Wilkinson, G. W. Cooke, Lanier, and other critics of the period.

Millet, and from the enigmatic character studies of Turgenev.[10]

In his many reviews of the fiction of Henry James, Harte, Eggleston, Mark Twain, DeForest, and others, Howells sought to establish for reality a median position. Truth, accuracy, life-likeness, verity were qualities he sought, but he preferred Hawthorne's term "romance" to the newer word "novel" for prose fiction, and he looked beyond literalism to "the finer air of romance" and poetry. The novel represented a certain realistic tendency for which his imaginative temper was not, in the seventies, well suited. In 1879, reviewing James's *Hawthorne,* he demurred at the writer's synonymous use of the two terms: "The romance and the novel," Howells wrote, "are as distinct as the poem and the novel." It was not until 1884 that he was able to recognize "the prevalence of realism in the artistic atmosphere" and to associate it with the novel, a form quite apart from his early love —romance.[11]

Criticism in the seventies, groping for clear principles, was vacillating, provincial, self-conscious, timid, and boldly assertive. T. W. Higginson urged novelists to pursue that "daring Americanism of subject" which had brought such success to Cooper and Mrs. Stowe.[12] On the other hand, T. S. Perry disparaged a too exclusive nativism: "There is an American nature," he admitted, "but then there is human nature underlying it, and to that the novel must be true before anything else."[13] Did realism mean a "slice of life," an exact reproduction of characters and incidents

10. As in the case of George Eliot, it was Turgenev's middle course between excessive romanticism, on the one hand, and French naturalism, on the other, which helped American critics to define realism as a philosophy of compromise and mediation. In *French Poets and Novelists* (1878) Henry James found Turgenev's view of the human spectacle to be "more general, more impartial, more unreservedly intelligent than that of any novelist we know." G. P. Lathrop in *The Atlantic Monthly,* XXXIV (Sept., 1874), 321, wrote: "Of all the eminently realistic novelists, Turgenieff is, I imagine, the most vigorous, acute, and delicate."

11. See his reviews in *The Atlantic Monthly,* XLIV (Aug., 1879) and LXV (Feb., 1880). Also his review of Bellamy's *Miss Ludington's Sister* in *The Century Magazine,* XXVIII (Aug., 1884) where he says the author combined the elements of the romance and the novel by taking "some of the crudest and most sordid traits of our life, and has produced from them an effect of the most delicate and airy romance."

12. T. W. Higginson, "Americanism in Literature," *The Atlantic Monthly,* XXV (Jan., 1870), 63.

13. T. S. Perry, "American Novels," *The North American Review,* CXV (Oct., 1872), 366.

from contemporary society? But that, complained an *Atlantic* reader, would sink fiction "to the level of the police records." The true artist must differentiate his work from that of the photographer and make his personages "move on an ideal plane, parallel with yet above the real."[14] V. L. Parrington wrote: "To most Victorians realism meant Zola, sex, and the exploitation of the animal, and all the pruderies of the Age of Innocence rose up in protest against defiling letters with such themes."[15]

A writer in *Scribner's* declared flatly that "there should be a purpose in every work of art." Subtler minds put it more skillfully. J. H. Morse, for instance, agreed that all true work should play into the hands of honor and morality but added that all good art resents the imposition of a too formal didacticism. George Parsons Lathrop, discussing "The Novel and Its Future" in *The Atlantic Monthly* defined realism as a mediating philosophy between the familiar and the extraordinary, and between "the seen and the unseen of human nature."[16] T. S. Perry concurred: "The idealizing novelist will be the real novelist. All truth does not lie in facts."[17] These critics, like James, Howells, Lanier, and others, in different ways and with varying emphasis, were attempting to work out a balanced view of art, applied primarily to the novel, in which a grasp of actuality did not exclude the imagination and a scientific discipline of method did not prevent a healthy moral tone, or even (in the best sense) an idealized view of human nature.

Standing apart from all the reviews and critical books of the 1870's, however, are the two volumes of Henry James, *French Poets and Novelists* (1878) and *Hawthorne* (1879). Despite some obvious weaknesses and arbitrary judgments, these books have outlived the emotional literary controversies of the seventies and will continue to be read for their superior verbal grace and skillful literary portraiture. The strongly critical bent of James's mind, his serious conception of the critic's task, and his vast

14. *The Atlantic Monthly,* XLI (Jan., 1878), 132.

15. V. L. Parrington, *The Beginnings of Critical Realism in America,* p. 237.

16. George Parsons Lathrop, "The Novel and Its Future," *The Atlantic Monthly,* XXXIV (Sept., 1874), 321.

17. T. S. Perry, "American Novels," *loc. cit.,* p. 378.

curiosity about the technical side of artistry in fiction raised his work to a higher level than the more conventional didacticism and rule-of-thumb classification of much contemporary criticism. It was his advanced, impressionistic method which elicted puzzled or unfavorable reactions from the reviewers, even Howells complaining that James seldom allowed a clear positive or negative judgment to emerge from his multitude of observations and qualifications.[18] Few in 1878 agreed with Brander Matthews, who called *French Poets and Novelists* "by far the finest collection of purely literary criticism which has been published either in this country or in England" since Lowell's essays, with which it was favorably compared.[19] Although many of the reviews of James's *Hawthorne* were unfavorable enough to provoke some acid comments from him in private letters, a few discriminating reviewers recognized his critical objectivity and his detachment from the romantic worship of Hawthorne as a literary idol. W. C. Brownell in *The Nation* saw it as a new and audacious venture in descriptive and analytical criticism.[20] James was charged, however, with an excessively patronizing attitude toward the New England provincialism of Hawthorne.

James had arrived in 1880 at his ideal concept of a critic through his study of the methods of Arnold, Goethe, and especially the French school of Edmond Scherer and Sainte-Beuve. Of the latter he wrote: "I take him as the very genius of observation, discretion, and taste." No narrow lawgiver or rigid censor, Sainte-Beuve was instead "the student, the inquirer, the observer, the interpreter, the active, indefatigable commentator, whose constant aim was to arrive at justness of characterization."[21] Not all of James's early criticism conformed to this high standard or to that of Scherer whom James admired because he was undogmatic, unencumbered by theories, and had "truly devout patience" in

18. William Dean Howells, "Recent Literature," *The Atlantic Monthly*, XLII (July, 1878), 118-119.

19. Brander Matthews, *Library Table*, IV (March 30, 1878), 197. Cited in R. N. Foley, *Criticism in American Periodicals of the Works of Henry James from 1866 to 1916* (Washington, D. C., 1944), pp. 13-14.

20. W. C. Brownell, "James's Hawthorne," *The Nation*, XXX (Jan. 29, 1880), 80-1.

21. Henry James, "Sainte-Beuve," *The North American Review*, CXXX (Jan., 1880), 56, 68.

reserving judgment. His essay on Baudelaire, for instance, was a statement of Victorian propriety expressing its distaste for "the rags, bad smells, and unclean furniture" of the Gallic mind, not a just characterization of the author of *Les Fleurs du Mal*. Flaubert, too, was unsympathetically handled, but in the fine portraits of Turgenev and Balzac and in occasionally brilliant passages on Gautier, George Sand, and on Hawthorne's novels, James showed the critical mastery which was later to become his signature in *Partial Portraits, Notes on Novelists,* and the famous Prefaces.

The central conflict in James's mind during his residence in Paris in 1875-6 was to work out a compromise between his own inherited Anglo-Saxon moral idealism (tinged with a genteel distaste for the uglier facts of life) and his strong distrust of the French "lightness of soil in the moral region." He admired the intense artistic devotion to form of Daudet, Goncourt, and Zola, but was repelled by their "ferocious pessimism and handling of unclean things."[22] Balzac, he thought, could be ranked close to Shakespeare but for his one fault—"he had no natural sense of morality."[23] Turgenev alone among the Continental novelists satisfied James's "Puritan habit" without violating his aesthetic honesty and realism. The great Russian combined the method of a searching realist with an "ideal of delicacy" and, although inclined toward pessimism, his view of life was for James "more impartial, more unreservedly intelligent, than that of any novelist we know."[24]

In its sharp fluctuations of taste and a certain unevenness of tone, James's criticism shared much of the intellectual vacillation of the 1870's. The conflicting tendencies of a transitional age confronted him as they did his contemporaries: English wholesomeness as opposed to French naturalism; the "ideal of joy" in contrast to unrelenting facts of nature and science; ethical idealism as against artistic honesty and realism; art-for-art's sake versus decency and morality; content versus form in fiction. Yet James stood apart from the age in the subtlety of his expression and the depth of his intellectual concerns. If he was inconsistent, he

22. *The Letters of Henry James,* ed. Percy Lubbock (New York, 1920), I, 104.
23. Henry James, *French Poets and Novelists* (New York, 1878), p. 113.
24. *Ibid.*

showed great promise and flashes of genius unmatched by other American critics. If he wavered in judgment, it was in part because his wide knowledge of contemporary fiction enlarged the scope of his thinking, and his cosmopolitanism made it more difficult to encompass the intellectual disparities of the age. No one has characterized more succinctly the conflicts and cross-currents of the critical temper of these years of hesitation than Henry James when he described, in the language of gentle satire, "that admirable time in which nothing was so romantic as our intense vision of the real. No fool's paradise ever rustled to such a cradle song.... We knew we were too critical, and that made us sublimely indulgent. . . we dreamed over the multiplication table; we were nothing if not practical."[25]

II.

The critical controversy over realism, not unlike other literary trends, had its negative as well as its positive side. Negatively it took the form of an attack upon the past and upon those literary traits which the modern temper felt were the excesses of outworn romanticism, sentimentalism, and a pretentious display of the lofty, the noble, and the serious. Beginning in the late sixties, this assault was most vigorous among the humorists, Bret Harte, Mark Twain, Bill Nye, John Hay, Artemus Ward, John Phoenix, and others who combined tall-tale exaggeration with an amorphous body of literary and social criticism to produce a kind of concerted broadside against the declining romantic tradition. In their quite informal, but nevertheless effective, way these men helped clear the ground for more theoretical critics to articulate an aesthetics of realism. By means of slang, misspellings, dialect, colloquialism, parody, buffoonery, burlesque, and just plain ridicule the humorists slashed away at Scott, Coleridge, Ossianism, Cooper, "goody-goody-ism," flim-flam charlatanism, and all manner of what Mark Twain termed "sappy inanities." Twain burlesqued the noble savage, poked fun at Franklin's moral seriousness, parodied Coleridge, and in *Innocents Abroad* rebuked the culture-seekers. Harte parodied Cooper and Whittier, Nye wrote

25. "The Next Time," *Novels and Tales of Henry James* (New York, 1909), XV, 167.

a comic history of the United States, and other western realists, by deflating the polite tradition of the East, demonstrated in no uncertain terms the *un*importance of being earnest.

On the positive side, however, the years from 1880 to about 1887 witnessed the flowering out of the uncertainties and hesitations of the seventies in a burst of creative activity that one may justly name "The Triumph of Realism." These seven or eight years saw the publication of more superior fiction than any similar period in the century. Howells wrote *A Modern Instance, The Rise of Silas Lapham,* and *Indian Summer*—his best novels—in those years; Mark Twain produced his two masterpieces, *Life on the Mississippi* and *Huckleberry Finn;* James continued his prolific career of the 1870's with *Washington Square, A Portrait of a Lady* (usually regarded as the finest of his early novels), *The Bostonians, The Princess Casamassima,* and many of his best *nouvelles.* Henry Adams' *Democracy* and *Esther,* Hay's *The Breadwinners,* Cable's *The Grandissimes,* Woolson's *Anne,* E. W. Howe's *The Story of a Country Town* and much of the representative work of the local colorists in short fiction—all belong to the early eighties. It is scarcely an exaggeration to speak of this period as a kind of minor renaissance in American letters. Coming in the midst of the "tragic era" and The Gilded Age during which historians have said that the nation plunged recklessly toward outward expansion and inward defeat,[26] it seems necessary to attempt an explanation of this phenomenon. For if the historians are right, then literary realism like Crane's Maggie "blossomed in a mud puddle."

Many forces and a variety of factors, social, economic, political, intellectual and cultural, entered into the changing literary temper of the 1880's, nor is it possible here to take account of them all. Regional and sectional conflicts were softened by the repeal of the Reconstruction Act in 1878, the strikes and economic disturbances of the previous decade tapered off, the ferment and excited tone of the seventies sobered perceptibly, and the national temper grew more settled, more mellow, more practical. Somehow an adjustment came into sight between the older ideals and the newer

26. F. O. Matthiessen, *Henry James: The Major Phase* (New York, 1944), p. 186.

facts of society. In the warfare of ideas a temporary truce helped to bring about a stabilization of opposing intellectual pressures. The extent to which literary criticism contributed to this newer synthesis, it will be our purpose to indicate.

The eighties were the epoch of Howells and James. When young Hamlin Garland first went to Boston he found reviewers speaking of them "as if they were some sort of firm, or at least literary twins." There was truth as well as wit in George Moore's remark that Henry James came to Europe and studied Turgenev while Howells remained in America and studied Henry James. They corresponded frequently and discussed each other's work. They were critical, but mutually admiring. Unquestionably the two most provocative critical essays of the early eighties were Howells' "Henry James, Jr." in *The Century* (1882) and James's famous "The Art of Fiction" in *Longman's Magazine* (1884). James was the most active critic of the period writing the articles which were published in 1888 as *Partial Portraits*. Howells devoted himself largely to fiction until his contract with *Harper's* established him as the leader of the cause for realism after 1887. Walt Whitman's *Specimen Days* (1882), Lanier's *The English Novel* (1883), and Stedman's *Poets of America* (1885) were among the significant critical volumes of the eighties. Perhaps the most far-reaching influence upon the literary world in the early eighties was the marked shift of emphasis from cultured Boston and Cambridge to bustling New York. *The Atlantic Monthly* lost prestige while *The Critic,* established in 1881, became one of the liveliest critical journals; *Harper's Magazine* and *The Century* rose to leadership among the literary periodicals.

Howells set off a literary bombshell of international proportions when, out of strong personal friendship for James and a changing philosophy of art, he attempted to defeat the growing critical dissatisfaction with James's work. He spoke of his friend as the leader of the new school of novelists which was rapidly relegating Dickens, Thackeray, Trollope, and Reade to the category of an outmoded past. This school derives, Howells said, from Hawthorne, George Eliot, and the milder realism of Daudet rather than from Zola. It eschews moving accidents, passion, and

[129]

adventure, and prefers psychological analysis of character. It is James, he concluded, "who is shaping and directing American fiction."[27] A year or so later James returned the compliment (with reservations) in a letter to Howells in which he warmly praised Daudet, Goncourt, and Zola for their honesty and seriousness in contrast to "the floods of tepid soap and water which under the name of novels are being vomited forth in England." "I say this to you," James went on, "because I regard you as the great American naturalist. I don't think you go far enough, and you are haunted with romantic phantoms and a tendency to factitious glosses, but you are in the right path."[28]

Thus James sought to stiffen the realism of Howells, while Howells, by lingering over the romantic qualities of James's characters and emphasizing his debt to George Eliot rather than the extreme French school, was trying to soften the realism of James. Meanwhile English critics blustered and fulminated over Howells' cool relegation of Dickens and Thackeray to an outworn past and American reviewers continued to lump both James and Howells together as "scientific novelists" who excluded virtue, pathos, passion, and the deeper sympathies in their overemphasis on "morbid analysis," pessimism, realism, and photographic fidelity.

In 1883 Sidney Lanier's *The English Novel* was published posthumously from his earlier lectures. Lanier understood the deeply conflicting currents of doctrine which confronted the artist and thinker in an age of science and pragmatism. His predilection was for poetry and the past, but he was sufficiently modern to recognize the vitality of the novel as the art form of the future, and he selected George Eliot as the archetype in the realm of fiction. Rejecting Zola as morally corrupting, Lanier felt that he saw in George Eliot the reconciliation of science and art. "The great modern novelist is at once scientific and poetic," he said, "and here, it seems to me, in the novel, we have the meeting, the reconciliation, the kiss, of science and poetry."[29] Lanier likewise combined his theory of literary evolution with a faith in social

27. William Dean Howells, "Henry James, Jr.," *The Century*, XXV (Nov., 1882), 29.
28. *Letters of Henry James*, I, 104.
29. *Complete Writings of Sidney Lanier*, IV, 61.

progress. He cited Spencer and John Fiske to support the view that progress could best be measured by the development of the strong, self-reliant individual. In the stress he placed on character and ethical value which the novels of George Eliot exemplified, Lanier envisaged a future utopia "when the control of the masses will be more and more relegated to each unit thereof, when the law will be given from within the bosom of each individual—not from without."[30]

Without practical experience in fiction, possessed of the higher, poetic idealisms of the seventies, and with a passion amounting to religious zeal for a system of aesthetics which could encompass the polar extremities of scientific thought and moral idealism as they impinged on the intellectual American of 1880, Lanier made a gallant, if somewhat desperate effort at critical synthesis. He belonged to the neo-romantic afterglow rather than to the movement toward realism and collectivism of the later 1880's. The battle of the periodicals over the novel, meanwhile, took on renewed interest in a three-way argument touched off by Charles Dudley Warner's article in *The Atlantic* in April, 1883. Warner resurrected the cause of Sir Walter Scott and pleaded for a return to chivalry, romance, truth, virtue, justice, and happy endings. The purpose of the novel, he expostulated, was "to entertain." He argued that Scott and Cervantes represented not only romance and realism, but two universal attitudes toward life and concluded that Sir Walter had restored the balance between chivalry and realism which the followers of *Don Quixote* had destroyed. He attacked "modern fiction" for its morbidity, pessimism, psychological "analysis," and despondent tone.[31]

Mark Twain countered the traditionalism and romantic idealism of his friend Warner with a vitriolic blast in *Life on the Mississippi* at the "Sir Walter Disease" of the South in which he attributed the sentimentalism and unreality of that region to "the pernicious work" of Scott, his "jejune romanticism," fantastic heroes, and grotesque chivalry. He lamented the decline of

30. *Ibid.*, II, 275.
31. Charles Dudley Warner, "Modern Fiction," *The Atlantic Monthly*, LI (Apr., 1883), 464-74.

Cervantes' prestige and the "debilitating" effect of Scott's books on the South. Henry James entered the fray in his essay on Daudet in *The Century* where he begged to differ from Warner in his definition of the novel as entertainment. "I should say that the main object of the novel is to represent life," he wrote and hinted that Warner was defending the rosewater school of thought which would make the novel "as comfortable as one's stockings, or as pretty as a Christmas card."[32]

James's essay, together with "The Art of Fiction," "DeMaupassant," and other fine critical articles of this period, reappeared a few years later in *Partial Portraits* (1888). The volume, received with mixed feelings by the reviewers who were again irked by its apparent lack of clear opinions and logical structure, must now be regarded as a supreme example of James's mature impressionism and the best single body of criticism to appear in America between 1870 and 1900. George E. Woodberry, who reviewed the book for both *The Nation* and *The Atlantic Monthly,* grumbled about the author's lack of convictions[33] and lamented his refusal to make arbitrary judgments. "He does not favor, apparently, what is known as final criticism," Woodberry wrote, and his essays are "in the main an expression of the personal preferences of his own temperament, which may or may not be valid in the case of others."[34] Yet James had in this volume most nearly approached his own ideal of criticism, the qualities he admired in Scherer and Sainte-Beuve—vast appreciation of the subject, justness of characterization, tireless search for the motivating principle of a writer's work, in short a three-dimensional, literary portrait in words. As in *French Poets and Novelists,* James again displayed a verbal skill and intellectual flexibility which American critical writing had not shown since Poe, and he made of criticism not a bar of moral judgment but a fine art. In addition,

32. Henry James, "Alphonse Daudet," *The Century Magazine*, XXVI (Aug., 1883), 506.

33. G. E. Woodberry, "James's Partial Portraits," *The Nation*, XLVII (July 26, 1888), 75-6.

34. G. E. Woodberry, "Partial Portraits," *The Atlantic Monthly*, LXII (Oct., 1888), 566.

he succeeded in bringing together into a finely drawn synthesis many of the warring elements in the critical thought of the period. The masterly essay on DeMaupassant, for instance, illustrated the astonishing lengths to which the critic could go in allowing perfect freedom to the artist without wholly abandoning his inherited moral preferences. From the old struggle between Anglo-Saxon decency and French sensuality James emerges (almost) unscathed with his faith in freedom of subject for the novelist. "Let us then leave this magnificent art of the novelist to itself and to its perfect freedom. . . . Let us not be alarmed at this prodigy of M. de Maupassant who is at once so licentious and so impeccable."[35]

James's classic essay, "The Art of Fiction," has become a landmark in the history of American criticism. Its prominence is surely due, in part, to the fact that it is a work of art in itself written with dignity and seriousness of tone, yet not without a realistic touch which preserves it from the Arnoldian solemnity and orotund qualities of some literary declarations of the nineteenth century. In the development of American criticism, however, its importance lies in the effort to preserve something of the organic concept and the moral idealism of romantic critical theory without depriving the practising novelist of the freshness which comes from absolute artistic freedom and contemporaneity of subject. Only James's verbal skill and flexible impressionistic language could weave into something like a harmonious pattern the relative and absolute implications of such topics as freedom versus moral elevation, selection versus literalism, incident versus character, the "romance" as opposed to the "novel." At the start James is apologetic about attempts to deal with such a broad field as fiction in theoretical terms. He is somewhat weary of academic generalizations and dichotomies. Nevertheless he will risk sparring with such things because he feels that to become conscious of itself is the beginning of sophistication and the lifeblood of art. A good novel is organic, to be sure, but it is an *aesthetic* consistency rather than a cosmic one. The good novelist is the legislator of his given subject, not the legislator of the universe. The

35. Henry James, *Partial Portraits* (New York, 1888), p. 287.

"donnee" is his real concern. "A novel is a living thing," he writes, "all one and continuous, like any other organism and . . . in each of the parts there is something of the other parts."[36]

Paradox rests at the basis of the essay. On the one hand, the novel aims primarily to represent life, and "life" is defined as nothing less than "all feeling, all observation, all vision." On the other, "Art is essentially selection, but it is a selection whose main care is to be typical, to be inclusive."[37] A moral conscience and social responsibility are integral to the highest art, yet the artist must not be deprived of his freedom of subject or handling. Only those readers who could rest in an ultimate ambiguity and content themselves with a subtly phrased and highly refined-upon contradiction in theoretical criticism could fully understand James's essay. He insisted upon a finely shaded conscience, as much a matter of taste as of ethics, in which the moral tone of the work of art is in the end determined by the refinement and intelligence of the artist. "In proportion as that intelligence is fine will the novel, the picture, the statue, partake of the substance of beauty and truth."[38]

American criticism in the early 1880's, with James as its leading practitioner, thus took its stand midway between the extremes of Anglo-Saxon moral soundness and the French tradition of scientific realism. It aimed to preserve, if possible, the best elements of both. Idealism, with its puritan tinge, and realism, with its Gallic taint, were brought toward a point of harmonious mediation in the skillful language of *Partial Portraits* and also in some of the best work of Lanier, T. S. Perry, Burroughs, J. H. Morse, Brander Matthews, and other critics of the period. In this effort, criticism reflected the relative adjustment of forces in other areas of the national consciousness. In social thought the proponents of collectivism developed a more pragmatic and common-sense attitude toward reforms, but individualism, buttressed by the theory of the survival of the fit, still remained the essential American philosophy. The early eighties may be called The Triumph of Realism, but not of a realism which denied the earlier idealism and the higher sympathies. It was a realism which included

36. *Ibid.*, p. 392.　　　37. *Ibid.*, p. 398.　　　38. *Ibid.*, p. 406.

them, and it bore fruit in the best work of the leading American novelists of the age, when the bright Victorian skies had deepened in tone, but were not yet darkened by the mechanistic and deterministic tendencies of continental naturalism or native collectivist thought.

III.

The economic novel came of age in the late eighties and early nineties. The abortive activities of the Knights of Labor during the railroad riots of 1877, Greenback unrest, and Granger discontent were revived with renewed vigor in a wave of labor-capital disputes which turned the attention of literary America to social problems. When Howells, in 1886, began his monthly column, "The Editor's Study," for *Harper's Magazine* he immediately became the focal point of a new kind of realism—the realism of social criticism. Collectivist thinkers rallied round his standard, Utopians like Edward Bellamy, Richard T. Ely, and Lawrence Gronlund found sympathetic reception for their books, and young radicals like Garland and H. H. Boyesen looked to him as the guide, philosopher, and friend of the new dispensation. From 1887 until about 1894 literary America moved away from the moderate realism and objectivity of the early eighties and into the more intensified atmosphere of "The Years of Protest." Humanitarianism and collectivism challenged the twin gospels of wealth and economic individualism. The novel, used as a bar of social justice, suffered as an art form. The field of criticism became a sparring ground between the disciples of Howells and the exponents of romance. The question which hovered in the balance during these years was: should the novel subserve the interests of reform, or should the higher cause of Art alone determine its form and its content?

A survey of the writing of the most active critics during these years of social ferment leads to the conclusion that their efforts were, in the main, directed toward a compromise between extremes rather than an aggressive championship of opposing views. Howells' *Criticism and Fiction* (1891), Higginson's *The New World and the New Book* (1891), Boyesen's *Literary and Social Silhouettes* (1894), and Garland's *Crumbling Idols* (1894) emphasized a theory of art which would express the democratic ideals of the Declaration of Independence and the aspirations of new world equalitarianism. But none of these volumes espoused a sociological collectivism or a philosophy of determinism. On the other hand, conservative critics like H. W. Mabie in *My Study Fire* (1890), George E. Woodberry in *Studies in Letters and Life* (1890), and W. C. Brownell sought a compromise between romance and realism, a kind of humanistic ideal founded upon universal rather than nationalistic principles. Both schools shared the idea that the novelist was an artist and public teacher, rather than a reporter of facts. F. Marion Crawford's *The Novel: What It Is* (1893) defended popular fiction on the grounds of pure entertainment, while Henry James's *Essays in London* (1893) and *Picture and Text* (1893) continued his high standard of critical impressionism and analysis.

Howells' defense of the Haymarket "anarchists" and his strong indictment of their "civic murder" in 1887 marked the change in his thinking from romance and character delineation to social problems in fiction. Three years earlier, in an anonymous review of John Hay's *The Breadwinners,* he had cautiously stated his belief that strikes were the right of workmen provided that they did not use violence. He felt it was time the novelist considered the problems of workingmen in fiction, "as we saw them in fact during the great railroad strike."[39] Although in 1886 he made his famous declaration that "the smiling aspects of life" in America were the more representative and that the novelist should "seek the universal in the individual rather than the social interests,"[40] Howells came more and more to identify the aims of fiction with the economic unrest of the late 1880's. During his years of reviewing for *Harper's* when he defended liberal causes and somewhat tactlessly assaulted the great English novelists of the past, Howells became a martyr for the realistic side, and it is difficult to exaggerate the extremes of vituperation and adulation which were showered upon him from opposite camps. The anti-

39. William Dean Howells, "The Breadwinners," *The Century Magazine,* XXVIII (May, 1884), 153.

40. William Dean Howells, "The Editor's Study," *Harper's Magazine,* LXXIII (Sept., 1886), 641.

Howells crusade accused him of intemperateness, arrogance, narrowness, and prejudice. Aldrich wondered if his mind was "unbalanced," Scudder accused him of having "diseased" views of society and disowned him as a former *Atlantic* editor.[41] Even his friends, Henry James and Higginson, raised their eyebrows when *Criticism and Fiction* appeared in 1891 and wished he had not associated himself so exclusively with a single school of thought. James wrote to him: "I am surprised, sometimes, at the things you notice and seem to care about. One should move in a diviner air."[42] But others warmly defended him. Boyesen praised his "Frank and fearless attacks . . . upon the worn-out romantic ideals," and Higginson ranked him with Emerson as a liberator of American ideals of art.[43]

Criticism and Fiction occupies a curious place in the history of American criticism and in Howells' own intellectual development. Appearing at a time when its author was most absorbed in the problems of social injustice, the volume was not significant as a plea for critical realism in fiction. Its two main themes, suggested by the title, were (1) a belittling of criticism and the critical profession as a narrow, unrewarding activity, and (2) a disparagement of the tradition of the novel from Scott to Thackeray as too romantic and unqualified to interpret the realism of American life. It offended all but the most ardent disciples of Howellsian realism. As a book it lacks coherence and singleness of aim. Put together hastily and without much editing from many reviews in *Harper's* which had been written over a period of five years, the book loses force and point.[44] The strongest pronouncements of "The Editor's Study" defending the collectivist ideas of

41. H. E. Scudder, "Mr. Howells's Literary Creed," *The Atlantic Monthly*, LXVIII, (Oct., 1891), 569.

42. *The Letters of Henry James*, I, 136.

43. T. W. Higginson, *The New World and the New Book* (Boston, 1892), p. 15. For a thorough analysis of this controversy see Leonard Lutwack, "William Dean Howells and 'The Editor's Study,' " *American Literature*, XXIV (May, 1952), 195-207.

44. Everett Carter, "William Dean Howells' Theory of Critical Realism," *A Journal of English Literary History*, XVI (June, 1949), 151-66, asserts that the book must be rejected "as a hastily contrived product of the scissors and pastepot" and does not truly represent Howells' theory of critical realism as expressed in some of the earlier articles in The Editor's Study of *Harper's Magazine*. Yet the question remains: why did Howells tone down the social criticism of his earlier essays?

Bellamy, Gronlund, Ely, and Henry George were omitted. The "smiling aspects" passage which dated back to 1886 was repeated with slight alterations, although it was inconsistent with the more humanitarian and reformist tone of the conclusion. Yet, despite these weaknesses, *Criticism and Fiction* was widely influential on both sides of the Atlantic and has been frequently cited ever since as a manifesto of realism in American fiction. Certain passages in it carry the warm fervor of a dedicated spirit. Like Garland, Whitman, Higginson, and other literary patriots, Howells was striving to associate literature with the older democratic ideals which he felt ebbing away in the increased conflicts of industrialized urban society. He dreamed of a great future for America "when the mass of readers, now sunk in the joys of mere fable, shall be lifted to an interest in the meaning of things through the faithful portrayal of life in fiction." Echoing Emerson and Whitman in their belief in the high office of the artist as a leader and teacher of men, he spoke in elevated tones of the need for art once again to devote itself to the service of humanity. He cited Ruskin and Morris in his belief that "Art, indeed, is beginning to find out that if it does not make friends with Need it must perish."[45] In his attack on "romantic novels," Howells paradoxically used the tone of romantic criticism. Hence his anomalous position as the leading modernist in fiction urging a doctrine of art called "realism" which differed only in the contemporaneity of its subject matter from the democratic idealism and romantic elevation of the earlier nineteenth century.

The storm of protest over *Criticism and Fiction* may have led Howells to change his tone in later critical volumes from literary prophecy to reminiscence and appreciation. *My Literary Passions* (1894) and *Literary Friends and Acquaintances* (1899) were pleasantly non-controversial. But if one were to sum up the qualities of Howells as a critic, it must be said that for him criticism was always a secondary interest. He once confessed that he disliked that form of writing and resented its intrusions upon his writing career. "Essaying has been the enemy of the novelist

45. William Dean Howells, *Criticism and Fiction* (New York, 1891), pp. 184, 186-7. See also other passages in the concluding chapter.

that was in me," he wrote to Aldrich. "One cannot do both kinds without hurt to both."[46] His reputation as a social thinker must rest mainly upon his fiction, where his economic views of the late 1880's and 1890's were most clearly set forth. *The Minister's Charge* (1886), *Annie Kilburn* (1888), *A Hazard of New Fortunes* (1889), and *A Traveller from Altruria* (1894) developed his concept of the 'complicity' of society, his admiration for Tolstoi, his indictment of uncontrolled economic individualism, and his hopes for nationalizing railroads, telegraphs, and mines. In these novels and in his private letters the advanced nature of Howells' collectivist thinking was revealed, for in them he could project his ideas through character and situation and partially shield himself from the harsher commitment of direct prose. "I should hardly like to trust pen and ink with all the audacity of my social ideas," he said in a letter to James in 1888.[47] For all his effort to define the novel as a servant of social reform, the romantic side of Howells' nature restrained him from allowing his lovely and fragile ideal of Art to prostitute itself unconditionally to the social and economic pressures of "The Years of Protest."

In 1894 Hamlin Garland, the most ardent of Howells' young disciples, published *Crumbling Idols,* a critical manifesto of the new realism which carried even further the literary progressivism of *Criticism and Fiction.* It contained the same dedicated spirit, a tone of romantic nationalism, and a plea for change, evolution, relativism, and regionalism in art. In conservative circles it was coldly received. A critic in *The Atlantic Monthly* thought it dogmatic, naïve, and extravagant—"so many explosions of literary jingoism and anarchy."[48] Garland himself, many years later, recalled that it seemed "a young man's screech." In impassioned language he called for a renewed subjectivity in literature and pointed to the South and the West as the coming literary centers of the nation. The book invented a new term, "Veri-

46. *Life in Letters of William Dean Howells,* ed. by Mildred Howells (New York, 1928), II, 138. See also p. 144: "I hate criticism. . . . I never did a piece of it that satisfied me."
47. *Ibid.,* I, 417.
48. C. M. Thompson, "New Figures in Literature and Art: III. Hamlin Garland," *The Atlantic Monthly,* LXXVI (Dec., 1895), 840.

tism," which Garland found from reading Eugène Véron's *Esthetics* and Max Nordau's *Conventional Lies*.[49] "My conception is that realism (or veritism) is the truthful statement of an individual *impression* corrected by reference to the fact."[50] Impressionism in art and literature was to supplant both literalism and romanticism. The Veritist is true to life, but he is at heart an idealist, a prophet, and a visionary. "The realist or veritist is really an optimist, a dreamer. He sees life in terms of what it might be, as well as in terms of what it is; but he writes of what is, and, at his best, suggests what is to be, by contrast."[51]

"He aims to hasten the age of beauty and peace by delineating the ugliness and warfare of the present. . . . He sighs for a lovelier life."[52] Garland's book recognized the principles of Howells for what they were—a revived romanticism of attitude with contemporary life as the writer's subject matter.[53] The tone of revolt and challenge again recalled Whitman or Emerson. Although Garland was at the same time writing fiction for B. O. Flower's *The Arena* on the single-tax and the plight of the western farmer, *Crumbling Idols* scarcely touched the problem of social reform in art. Like Howells, his economic views and his literary criticism remained in separate compartments of his mind. He urged the writer to strive for a kind of aesthetic realism of atmosphere, local and authentic in coloring, and advised him above all to be "true to himself." Veritism, he wrote, "aims at embodying in art the common landscapes, common figures, and common hopes, and loves and ambitions of our common life. It loves normal people, unarranged landscapes, and colors that are not 'harmonized.' "[54]

49. Hamlin Garland, *Roadside Meetings*, p. 32.

50. Hamlin Garland, "The Productive Conditions of American Literature," *Forum*, XVII (Aug., 1894), 690.

51. Hamlin Garland, *Crumbling Idols* (New York, 1894), p. 52.

52. *Ibid.*

53. See, as one among many instances, Howells' comment on Boyesen's *The Mammon of Unrighteousness* (1891): "It is boldly realistic, and it is at the same time poetical, as realism alone can be. . . ." It depicts both "the beauty of the ideal" and "the ugliness of the material." ("The Editor's Study," *Harper's Magazine*, LXXXIII [July, 1891], 317.)

54. Hamlin Garland, "Mr Howells's Latest Novels," *The New England Magazine*, II, n.s. (May, 1890), 249.

In its impressionism, its subjectivity, and its shift from the word realism to veritism, *Crumbling Idols* echoed Howells' idealization of the commonplace and, at the same time, revealed more clearly that Howellsian realism contained a powerful strain of the romantic. Also, the book dramatized the distinction between the native realism of Howells and the greater objectivity and scientific discipline of Henry James and the French school.

What, then, was the relation of literary criticism to other aspects of national thought during these "Years of Protest?" Did it directly reflect the social and economic unrest of the 1887-1894 period? Or did it stand in an ivory tower of high-minded ethics and aesthetic taste? The main current of criticism seems to me to have followed a course somewhere between these alternative extremes. On the one hand, a candid observer must admit that criticism, even of the Howells-Garland-Boyesen school, fell well short of advising the novelist to become a disciple of French naturalism or an apologist for a socialistic order of society. Boyesen, one of the vigorous Howellsians, defined realism as follows in *Literary and Social Silhouettes* (1894):

I do not mean by realism, of course, merely the practice of that extreme wing of the school which believes only that to be true which is disagreeable and conscientiously omits all cheerful phenomena. . . . Broadly speaking, a realist is a writer who . . . deals by preference with the normal rather than the exceptional phases of life.[55]

Even Edward Bellamy, who came the closest in practice to applying the novel to the cause of social revolution, wrote of his intention in *Looking Backward*:

I had, at the outset, no idea of attempting a serious contribution to the movement of social reform. The idea was of a mere literary fantasy, a fairy tale of social felicity. There was no thought of contriving a house which practical men might live in, but merely of hanging in mid-air, far out of reach of the sordid and material world of the present, a cloud-palace for an ideal humanity.[56]

"A fairy tale of social felicity," "an age of beauty and peace," "the

55. H. H. Boyesen, "The Progressive Realism of American Fiction," *Literary and Social Silhouettes*, p. 71.

56. Edward Bellamy, "How I Came to Write *Looking Backward*," *The Nationalist*, I (May, 1889). Cited in A. E. Morgan, *Edward Bellamy* (New York, 1944), p. 224.

devotion of art to the service of humanity"—these phrases of Bellamy, Garland, and Howells hardly suggest that the realists in fiction were, as one conservative critic called them, "the morbid, the cynical, the naturalistic, and the decadent in our present day literature."[57] Likewise they do not indicate that Realism sought "an exact reproduction of real life," or, as Maurice Thompson hysterically charged, its proponents taught "that marriage is a failure, that home is a brothel, that courtship is lewd, that society is an aggregation of criminals."[58]

If, however, the extreme wing of the traditional-minded school of critics set up a "devil-theory" of the realists in their anxiety to protect literature from the hordes of atheism and immorality, on the other hand, the modernist critics equally erred in their attacks upon effete romanticism, escapism, and didacticism. There were, of course, among the adherents of "romance," critics like Marion Crawford who held a vested interest in historical romance. Crawford held that the novel was a "pocket theatre" whose main purpose was "to amuse and interest the reader," and maintained that it "must deal chiefly with love, for in that passion all men and women are most generally interested."[59] And there were such Don Quixotes of "romance" as Maurice Thompson tilting at the windmills of literary pessimism, realism, agnosticism, debauchery, Zolaism, illicit love, and Henry James and preaching the gospel of optimism, chivalry, wifehood, heroism, moral rectitude, and Scott.[60] But there were more balanced spokesmen of the romantic school like H. W. Mabie, John Burroughs, Richard Watson Gilder, and W. C. Brownell who pursued a saner ideal of art. Mabie, for example, held that romance and realism were two eternal types in fiction and that, while fashions change, each is "necessary to the complete expression of

57. Richard Burton, "The Healthful Tone for American Literature," *Forum*, XIX (April, 1895), 251.

58. Maurice Thompson, "The Turning of the Tide," *The Independent*, XLVIII (Jan., 1896), 238.

59. F. Marion Crawford, *The Novel: What It Is* (New York, 1893). See especially pp. 11, 43, 49, 57.

60. Maurice Thompson, *The Ethics of Literary Art* (Hartford, Conn., 1893). See pp. 30 ff., 60 ff. and elsewhere.

human nature and human life."[61] Gilder, as editor of *The Century,* has been singled out by hostile critics as the cynosure of stiff-necked Victorian gentility in criticism. Yet it was Gilder who privately supported Howells during his embattled years in "The Editor's Study" and who, with certain reservations as editor of a dignified monthly, recognized the "voice of conviction" in the work of the realistic school of fiction.[62] W. C. Brownell, another of the conservative group, became the foremost American Arnoldian and leader of the neohumanists in criticism.

American literary criticism during "The Years of Protest" from 1887 to 1894 stood aside from the social unrest and collectivistic tendency of the period. One cannot deny that a certain division of mind led Howells, Garland, Boyesen, and others of the modernists to hold up romantic and aesthetic standards of criticism while in their fiction and private letters they were espousing a strong program of social betterment. Furthermore, in their tendency to avoid "palpitating divans" and shrink from the franker realism and veracity of continental literature, most American critics may justly be accused of "Victorianism" in its less favorable sense. Even among the realists there was, as Henry James remarked, a tendency toward "romantic phantoms" and "factitious glosses." In this respect, criticism failed to guide the novel into channels where it could touch the note of tragedy and give expression to some of the deeper maladjustments of man in relation to the world about him. Although Howells and his fellow writers well understood such things, their volumes of criticism turned away from them to the safer and less controversial ground of aesthetics and higher ethics.

On the other hand, both schools of criticism during these years sought a standard of judgment which could transcend sociorealistic demands upon the writer and both refused to confine his aims to those of recording or remedying inequalities in the economic life of the nation. During a time of transition and re-

61. H. W. Mabie, "The Two Eternal Types of Fiction," *Forum,* XIX (March, 1895), 44.

62. H. W. Mabie, "Certain Tendencies in Current Literature," *New Princeton Review,* IV (July, 1887), 1-13. See also Leonard Lutwack, "William Dean Howells and 'The Editor's Study,'" *loc. cit.,* pp. 199-200.

orientation when the novel, and literature in general, was still a potent force in forming public opinion, Howells and his fellow critics seriously felt their responsibility as teachers and leaders of society. They sought to reestablish the older harmony between democratic aspirations and literary aims. If this was becoming increasingly difficult during the social tensions of the 1890's, it cannot be to their discredit that they still held to an earlier orthodox faith that man could, in some measure, determine his own fate—or at least that the solvent for social and economic hostilities in an age of waning religious and moral ideals must be discovered in some form of Christian idealism beyond the material advantage of any class or group. In their effort to find such a standard in the novel, both the pro-Howells and the anti-Howells critics were one.

The urge toward economic reform and social protest began to wane about 1894 with the subsiding of the Populist Revolt and the decline of labor strikes. Garland described his decision to give up reform fiction and turn to poetry and stories of the west.

I was not alone in this reaction from the ethic to the aesthetic. Clemens was passing through the same phase. Howells, though still exemplifying the socialistic concept in his novels as well as in his essays, was each month less direct about its expression. The reform impulse was steadily waning in power with us all.[63]

After *A Traveller from Altruria* (1894) Howells returned to his earlier studies of character and social manners in *The Landlord at Lion's Head* (1897) and *The Son of Royal Langbrith* (1903), while his literary criticism relaxed from the "strong reverberations" of The Editor's Study to the milder reminiscence of The Easy Chair. In 1896 he wrote to a friend: "I am rather quiescent in my social thinking just now."[64] As the pendulum of literary thought in America swung once more toward "the old, exiled romance," a younger generation of realists arose to champion the cause of fidelity, while the reading public devoured Stevenson, Kipling, Conan Doyle, Du Maurier's *Trilby,* Anthony Hope's

63. Hamlin Garland, *Roadside Meetings*, p. 187.
64. *Life in Letters of William Dean Howells*, II, 70.

The Prisoner of Zenda, and such historical romances as Siencie-wicz' *Quo Vadis?* and Hall Caine's *The Christian.*

IV.

The Yellow Nineties, the Mauve Decade, The Purple Cow Period, The Age of Carved Cherry Stones, The Genteel Tradition —in whatever colors or figures of speech one may paint the shifting hues of *fin de siècle* romanticism—it was a phase of The Age of Innocence which continues to capture the imagination of the historical-minded. It was an Age of Confidence, too, in which the bracing athleticism of the Message to Garcia, the moral righteousness of John L. Sullivan on the temperance platform, and the swashbuckling adventure fiction of Marion Crawford could thrill the popular mind, while intellectuals grew excited over Max Nordau's prophecy of the degeneration of civilization[65] and exerted their aesthetic emotions about Nietzsche, Ibsen, Wagner, Tolstoi, and art-for-art's sake. A mild poetic revival was set off by the publication in 1890 of Emily Dickinson's posthumous work. Crane, Garland, Madison Cawein, and Aldrich published slim volumes of minor verse with a note of sadness or decadence, and Ella Wheeler Wilcox addressed her poems of passion to palpitating spinsters. The 'dinkey magazines' flourished in the nineties, the Gibson Girl fluttered adolescent hearts, and funny fellows like Gelett Burgess, George Ade, and Mr. Dooley amused the reading public. The oldest generation of literary gods was gone— Holmes, Lowell, Whitman—and Howells, by the end of the decade, had outlived his reputation as a radical propagandist to become a figure of eminence and respect, reclining in *Harper's* Easy Chair. Henry James lurked dimly among the marquees in the London theatrical world, an increasingly suspect figure of the literary expatriate. Instead of the more vigorous Howells-and-

65. In 1895 the periodicals reverberated with pros and cons over the publication of Max Nordau's *Degeneration,* an anticipation of Henry Adams' theory of historical entropy, but with stronger sociological implications. Nordau listed among the degenerating influences of society: Nietzsche, Ibsen, Wagner, Maeterlink, Swinburne, symbolism, mysticism, pre-Raphaelitism, and most advanced art tendencies. Conservative American critics used his book as an argument against "the art of the Parnassians, the decadents and aesthetes, and certain types of realists." See Max Nordau, "Society's Protection Against the Degenerates," *Forum,* XIX (July, 1895), 543.

James era of the 1880's, there was now an interlude of high romance (*When Knighthood Was in Flower, Richard Carvel,* and *Monsieur Beaucaire*), domestic sentiment (*David Harum,* a combination of right thinking and bad grammar, B'gosh school), and uplifting piety (Charles Sheldon's *In His Steps*).

What were the currents of literary doctrine during these halcyon years? The old warfare of the periodicals continued without abatement. The adherents of romance, sensing a popular swing to their cause, redoubled their attacks upon Zolaism, morbidity, pessimism, and decadence in modern fiction. Aldrich, Mabie, C. D. Warner, Richard Burton, and others called for a new and healthful tone, a revived idealism and morality.[66] The Zolaistic movement was anathematized in verse by Aldrich as "a miasmatic breath blown from the slums." W. R. Thayer gleefully pronounced the doom of realism and stated: "Zola's influence is dead."[67] H. W. Mabie spoke of the "reappearance of the old-time story of romance and adventure"[68] and ranked James Lane Allen's *The Choir Invisible* (1897) just below *The Scarlet Letter.* Allen, a long-time foe of Henry James and the advanced school of realists, invented a new set of antitheses for criticism when he contrasted "the Masculine and Feminine Principles in art." Taking a mediating stand, he argued that the prevailing tone of literature in this "Age of Carved Cherry Stones" had been that of gentility, feminine delicacy, and refinement. He called for a restoration of the balance, a resurgence of "the Masculine Principle, possessing Virility, Strength, and Massiveness" and maintained that there was no necessary contradiction between the two principles.[69] The greatest weakness of the romantic reviewers, however, was the tendency to confuse the popular with the excellent. They erred on the side of provinciality and superficiality when they heralded *The Prisoner of Zenda* as a triumph

66. Richard Burton, "The Healthful Tone for American Literature," *Forum,* XIX (Apr., 1895), 250.

67. W. R. Thayer, "The New Story-Tellers and the Doom of Realism," *Forum,* XVIII (Dec., 1894), 470.

68. H. W. Mabie, "The Two Eternal Types in Fiction," *Forum,* XIX (March, 1895), 44.

69. James Lane Allen, "Two Principles in Recent American Fiction," *The Atlantic Monthly,* LXXX (Oct., 1897), 435-6.

of the adventure story over "the depressing introspections of the psychologists" and overpraised such books as Hall Caine's *The Christian,* Sheldon's *In His Steps,* Richard Harding Davis's *Soldiers of Fortune,* and Du Maurier's *Trilby.* At the same time they either ignored or mentioned with indifferent praise the novels of Howells, Crane's *Maggie* and *The Red Badge of Courage,* Norris's *McTeague,* Mary Wilkins' *Pembroke,* James's *The Turn of the Screw, The Spoils of Poynton,* and *What Maisie Knew.* Typical of the tone of popular right-wing criticism in the extreme genteel tradition is a review of *McTeague* by Nancy Huston Banks in *The Bookman* which began as follows:

The passing of morbid realism has never been quite so complete as the healthy-minded hoped it would be, when it was swept out of sight five or six years ago by the sudden onrush of works of ideality and romance, which arose like a fresh, sweet wind to clear the literary atmosphere. In this resistless new movement toward light and peace, these black books were cast aside and forgotten, and there was fair hope for a time that the celebration of the painful and the unclean had passed from fiction forever.[70]

Poor Howells and James, poor Norris and Stephen Crane!

The realists were by no means silent, however. H. H. Boyesen replied to the anti-Zola crusade by blaming the romantic fiction of Rider Haggard, Stevenson, Conan Doyle, and S. R. Crocket for the recrudescence of the "feudal ideal" among young people and upheld the superior moral wholesomeness of Zola and Daudet "who give an exact and vivid reflection of an ugly reality" and hence become "unintentional" moralists.[71] The realists in criticism were unquestionably the better prophets. Howells supported Crane and Garland, reviewed sympathetically the books of Boyesen and Miss Wilkins, and defended Henry James, Mark Twain, and Frank Norris. Yet even Howells, in his anxiety to discover the qualities of realism in new books, tended to puff out of all just proportion such authors as Brand Whitlock, and it should be noted that even while admiring *McTeague* as the last word in

70. Nancy Huston Banks, "Two Recent Revivals in Realism," *The Bookman,* IX (Mar.-Aug., 1899), 356.

71. H. H. Boyesen, "The Great Realists and the Empty Story-Tellers," *Forum,* XVIII (Feb., 1895), 728.

realistic fiction, he qualified his remarks by a nostalgic sigh at the passing of the old-fashioned ideal of a novel "as something which may be read by all ages and sexes," and urged that Norris had not told the whole truth because he left beauty out. "Life is squalid and cruel and vile and hateful," Howells wrote, "but it is noble and tender and pure and lovely, too."[72]

In 1893 Garland wrote the first sympathetic review of Stephen Crane's obscure and anonymous *Maggie,* describing it as "a story which deals with vice and poverty and crime . . . not out of salaciousness, but because of a distinct art impulse to utter in truthful phrase a certain rebellious cry. It is the voice of the slums."[73] Crane himself said of it: "I had no other purpose in writing *Maggie* than to show people to people as they seem to me."[74] He wrote to Lily Brandon in 1896 that his creed of art was identical with that of Howells and Garland: "that art is man's substitute for nature and we are most successful in art when we approach nearest to nature and truth. . . ."[75] Traditional critics, however, found the work of this enigmatic young genius too outspoken and "vulgar." A reviewer in *The Bookman,* for instance, thought *The Red Badge of Courage* powerful, but morbid, distorted in emotion, and "much in need of being assisted into sunlight and a natural, normal growth."[76]

Mary Wilkins' *Pembroke* (1894), fully as depressing in tone as *Maggie,* was treated with greater understanding by respectable critics because it did not deal with improper relationships. H. E. Scudder straddled the issue: "a genuine artistic achievement, in spite of the crumbling materials out of which it is built."[77] But *The Critic* was greatly impressed with Miss Wilkins' stark portrayal of the flint-like hardness of the latter-day Puritan and

72. William Dean Howells, "A Case in Point," *Literature* (March 24, 1899).

73. See Garland's *Roadside Meetings,* 198.

74. Quoted in H. F. West, *A Stephen Crane Collection* (Hanover, N. H., 1948), x-xi. Cf. Crane's hint of a humanitarian purpose in *Maggie* (*The Bookman,* I [May, 1895], 229.) See also Crane's statement: "I try to give the readers a slice out of life." (Quoted in M. Schoberlin, *Sullivan County Sketches* [Syracuse, N. Y., 1949], p. 20.)

75. Schoberlin, *op cit.,* p. 19.

76. Nancy Huston Banks, "The Novels of Two Journalists," *The Bookman,* II (Nov., 1895), 219-20.

77. H. E. Scudder, "Marcella and Pembroke," *The Atlantic Monthly,* LXXIV (Aug., 1894), 274.

spoke of the "tremendous power" and "concentrated intensity" of the book.[78] *The Landlord at Lion's Head* (1897) won back for Howells much of his lost critical support; the characterization of a Harvard "jay," Jeff Durgin, was regarded as an achievement equal to Silas Lapham or Bartley Hubbard, "a concrete prediction of a type which threatens"—the selfish, skeptical social climber without a conscience. Henry James, however, continued to be "praised with faint damns." His "terrible story" *The Turn of the Screw* was characteristically reviewed in *Current Literature:* "We quite fail to understand Mr. James's strange appetite for the horrible. . . . Lovers of children will own him a grudge for libelling their favorites."[79]

In the guerilla-fights of the nineties between critics of the realistic and romantic schools, during which neither side paid much attention to the intellectual validity of their arguments and often groped blindly amid the smoke of their own verbal cannonading, an occasional voice of reason and sanity could be heard above the din. One of these was that of Frank Norris whose *The Responsibilities of the Novelist* (1903) calmly shifted the basis of the discussion to new ground. Norris was temperamentally a romantic who possessed an abiding faith in the serious purpose of literature. He ranked the novel even above the Pulpit and the Press (his capitals) as the vehicle for instructing and enlightening the public. Like Whitman, Howells, and Garland, Norris was a literary populist who associated the aims of literature with the democratic idea: "The People have a right to the Truth, as they have a right to life, liberty, and the pursuit of happiness," he felt, and this high duty fell upon the shoulders of the novelist. All good novels have a purpose—to express the truth about contemporary life, not to amuse the public with historical romance or cloak-

78. Anon., "Pembroke," *The Critic*, XXII (July 21, 1894), 35.

79. Anon., "Library Table: Glimpses of New Books," *Current Literature*, XXV (March, 1899), 213. Although this was the predominant tone of the American commentary on James during the 1890's, it was not the only one. A notable exception was Cornelia Atwood Pratt's article, "The Evolution of Henry James," *The Critic*, XXXIV (Apr., 1899), 338-42, which gave superlative praise to James's brilliant short fiction and his novels: ". . . as feats of execution, as plastic performances, there is simply nothing in our language with which to compare them. They are final. They stand alone."

and-dagger adventure. But, above all, Norris refused to be confused by the realism vs. romance debate. He pointed out that a true distinction between the two is that romance "is the kind of fiction that takes cognizance of variations from the type of normal life," while realism "confines itself to the type of normal life." Thus Zola, who deals with the sordid, is not, as he has been called, a realist, but is, on the contrary, "the very head of the Romanticists." And Howells, who is a realist, is "as respectable as a church and as proper as a deacon."[80] Thus Norris, with one stroke, cut the ground from under those guardians of propriety who had quite falsely associated the Howellsian school of fiction with the sordid aspects of French naturalism and confronted them with the startling fact that Zola was indeed in their own camp! Norris sought in his own fiction a "Romance of contemporary life" ("As much romance on Michigan Avenue as there is realism in King Arthur's court") and he disavowed the "harsh, loveless, colorless, blunt tool called realism."[81] And he recognized that the two schools were not mutually opposed, but instead were "constant qualities of every age" and would always represent different ways of looking at life.[82]

Henry James similarly disdained the battle of the inkpots between the genteel and the worldly critics, and he continued to refine upon his masterly technique of literary portraiture. If his criticism of the nineties lacked entirely the nationalistic note of Howells, Garland, or Norris, it possessed instead a finesse and discrimination unequalled among his American contemporaries. His *Essays in London* (1893) and *Notes on Novelists* (1914) contain the same fine perceptions as did his earlier books. They continue to be considered the finest criticism of the *fin de siècle* period. His basic theory of art had not changed. He still glimpsed a realism which could blend with higher ideals,—"the very ideal of the real, the real most finely mixed with life, which is in the last analysis the ideal."[83] He still admired Zola's large

80. Frank Norris, "A Plea for Romantic Fiction," *The Responsibilities of the Novelist* (New York, 1903), p. 215.

81. *Ibid.*, p. 214.

82. "The True Reward of the Novelist," *ibid.*, p. 20.

83. Henry James, *Notes on Novelists* (New York, 1914), p. 396.

canvas and condemned his lack of "the finer discriminations," but he did not attempt to tag him with any "ism." He continued to believe it possible to preserve "the English instinct of reticence" without sacrificing the candor of continental writers, but he came more and more to admire Flaubert's technical mastery and to minimize his objectionable subjects. *Madame Bovary,* James now felt, "confers on its sufficiently vulgar elements of exhibition a final unsurpassable form."[84] His ideal of criticism was an artistic one—to achieve an indefatigable suppleness. His stated definition of the critic's function belongs with the classic utterances of that art:

To lend himself, to project himself, and steep himself, to feel and feel till he understands, and to understand so well that he can say, to have perception at the pitch of passion and expression as embracing as the air. . . . Just in proportion as he reacts and reciprocates and penetrates, is the critic a valuable instrument.[85]

With his flexible mind and dexterous pen, James represented a high standard of the literary critic. He took his position aside from the norm of criticism in the nineties; he moved in a realm quite apart from moral judgment and condemnation (yet still not beyond the pale) and he brought American critical writing to a point of refinement where none, in his day, could emulate him. His method had evolved into an elaborate kind of psychological portraiture which undertook to enmesh his subject subtly and delicately "in a multitude of fine perceptions." He circled about the subject, weaving around it "a new closeness of texture" so that the result was neither censure nor approbation, but understanding.[86] And yet he never quite lost sight of the basic critical distinction of the age: he sought to blend the views of the realists with those of the romanticists in a new and admirable synthesis which was superior to both. Among the wealth of brilliant critical observations in the collected prefaces to the New York edition

84. *Ibid.,* p. 80.

85. Henry James, *Essays in London* (1893), p. 265.

86. The phrases are quoted from Morris Roberts, *Henry James' Criticism* (Cambridge, Mass. 1929), p. 66. My discussion of James's criticism throughout has been indebted to Roberts's admirable study.

of his works is this, from *The American,* where he says the final word on the artist as realist or romanticist:

he commits himself in both directions; not quite at the same time or to the same effect, of course, but by some need of performing his whole possible revolution, by the law of some rich passion in him for extremes. . . . His current remains therefore extraordinarily rich and mixed, washing us successively with the warm wave of the near and familiar and the tonic shock, as may be, of the far and strange.[87]

V.

From *Democratic Vistas* (1871) to the publication after the turn of the century of Henry James's famous critical Prefaces American criticism sought, largely in terms of the novel, to define the function of the artist within the framework of a society faced with the increased social and intellectual pressures of an industrial democracy. The essential problem which confronted artist and critic alike was how to retain a residue of moral and aesthetic idealism while at the same time remaining true to the reality of American life with its accelerated tendency toward materialism, determinism, and ethical indifference. The widening gulf between literary ideals and social facts seemed, at times, almost unbridgeable, yet in the best work of such men as Whitman, Lanier, James, Howells, Garland, Norris, Perry, and a few others there may be seen a steady effort to express some kind of synthesis and to work out a harmony among opposing forces. During the thirty years we have been considering the pendulum swung back and forth between the ideals of romance and those of realism, and whatever values emerged from the controversies of the critics lay in the antithetical and, at the same time, reinforcing counterpoint between the two.

Literary and intellectual historians have often regarded the essence of realism in fiction and criticism during those years in terms of a progressive "rise" of scientific modes of thought and journalistic methods of expression out of the ashes of a worn-out romantic faith. Yet such an evolutionary interpretation of the period somewhat falsely assumes a steady march of the realistic

87. Henry James, *The Art of the Novel,* ed. Richard Blackmur (New York, 1934), p. 31.

emphasis, and the gradual emergence of a new and vigorous reality in art and critical theory over the old, unfit romance. But, as we have attempted to show, it was the interrelationship between the two ideals that was most significant for American criticism in the late Victorian age. Furthermore, one searches in vain throughout the entire thirty-year period for a coherent rationale of naturalism, or even a conscious critical realism for the novel. It seems best, then, to regard the Victorian ideal of criticism as a synthesis of the claims of romantic and realistic principles. Viewed unsympathetically, this "romantic vision of the real," as Henry James called it, was a Victorian compromise. Yet a more generous estimate would see in it the quest for a new orthodoxy and a fresh vision of reality, a steady effort to work out an adjustment between critical extremes during a period of intellectual upheaval and social change. The aesthetic philosophy called realism was the literary aspect of a broader intellectual struggle between a teleological and a scientific reading of the universe. The result of that philosophical controversy was the pragmatic compromise of William James whereby the older absolutes were preserved and held in balance with utilitarian and relativistic modes of thought. James's will-to-believe and pragmatism were a philosophical mediation, a Victorian compromise in the same sense that his brother's critical position mediated between the two basic critical doctrines of the time.

The earlier realism, seen in its historical setting of Victorian America when literature was still a powerful channel of communication and a guiding force, represents for the historian of ideas one of the most interesting 'units' in American literary history. The sharp critical battles, the literary experiments, the flourishing monthlies with their serialized fiction and eagerly read review columns, the patronage by Howells of young disciples, the large personal correspondence among leading literary men and women —all these helped to give the American "realism" the authentic air of a "movement."

From the social and political desperations of The Gilded Age and Reconstruction decades, American criticism for the most part stood somewhat aloof. It neither espoused a subservience of literature to the business ethics of Jay Gould nor did it strongly champion a collectivist protest against political and economic deviation. Instead, it grounded its hopes on a return to the earlier democratic faith that the individual consciousness contained the will and the strength to bring about necessary reforms in society. In short, the Victorian orthodoxy, as expressed in critical theory, was conservative in temper, Christian in spirit, and humanitarian in outlook. Except for occasional expressions of protest by Howells and Garland, it turned away from militant and outward means of reform. On the other hand, it is unjust to hold that the Genteel Tradition in criticism urged an escapist program or a priestly withdrawal into the academy or the drawing room. Rather it maintained the old-fashioned belief that the frictions of an increasingly industrialized and stratified society might be assuaged by a literature which, without sacrificing the authenticity which a realistic and analytic method could bring, still upheld a broad standard of ethical and aesthetic decorum.

Three main schools of critical thought manifested themselves in the closing decades of the century. First, and most aggressive in their opinions, were those critics who followed Whitman and Emerson in their close association of literature with the democratic idea. Howells was the champion of this group and many of the leading critics of the period shared, in some measure, his views— Higginson, Garland, Norris, Lanier, Stedman, and Boyesen. In varying ways these men gave expression to the idea of scientific progress in the arts, the faith in a successful union of scientific and artistic methods in fiction, and the concept stemming from Taine that nationalistic and environmental factors weighed strongly in evaluating literary accomplishment. Second, in contrast to these literary democrats and believers in progress, were the neo-humanist critics who sought a universal standard of reference in the great tradition of world literature. Thomas S. Perry, Brander Matthews, W. C. Brownell, Woodberry, Gilder, and Mabie all possessed a scholarly awareness of the literature of the European past which they brought to bear in their search for broad, human values independent of race, place, and time. Sometimes, it must be admitted, this group confused tradition with a narrower concept of Victorian gentility and prudishness, but their ideal of criticism, at its best, was based upon that of Arnold and Goethe. Third, in a class almost by itself, was the criticism of Henry James influenced by Sainte-Beuve and Edmond Scherer—impressionistic, objectively analytical, and concerned with matters of technique in the novel—endeavoring to understand a work of art in terms of the background, development, and motivating "center" of the author's mind. If we allow for its one weakness, a narrowness and limitation of scope, and if we judge it purely as an art in itself rather than as a branch of cultural history, American criticism in this period reached its highest level of achievement in the work of James.

In his theory of the novel James managed to preserve the elements of the organic concept of art, but in a delimited and technical sense as applied to the work itself. He also preserved a residue of the moral idealism and transcendentalism of the mid-century. The two sides of his mind, its traditionalism and its modernism, are everywhere apparent in his critical and his creative work. He was at once in protest against romantic attitudes and an inheritor of them. The fact that he chose the novel as the object of his literary devotion contributed even more to his suspicion of the accepted critical terminology of his day, since many of the words were coined during the transcendental movement and carried implications which could not easily be applied to the fiction of the post-war decades. "Beauty," "truth," "organicism," "romance," "ideal"—these were a part of the Coleridgean inheritance. They were so much a part of the critic's vocabulary as to leave him almost wordless without them. James and Howells and their contemporaries used them inevitably, but in James's case with a growing sense of their inapplicability to the novel of realism. Had he devoted his critical powers to the literature of the past—to epic poetry or the drama—he might have found the romantic inheritance more suited to his material. But the vitality of the French novel, the pressures of competing for an audience of his own, and the necessities of evolving an original technique in fiction—such matters affected his critical thought and led him more and more to substitute impressionism for literary standards.

James's work stands almost alone in the criticism of the genteel decades, if we measure that body of work against world standards of critical writing. Nevertheless, if it is possible to evaluate so varied an accomplishment as a whole, American criticism between 1870 and 1900 performed with a high degree of skill the inevitable task of a generation—to harmonize the old and the new. The problem was more difficult than it was for the earlier generation partly because of the multiplicity of materials for the critic to comprehend and account for, and because of the accelerated pace of social change. In those picturesque years of outward expansion and awkward growth, nothing seemed more permanent than change itself. Scientific and material progress threatened to absorb most of the vitality of a generation. The literary critic was often bewildered and uncertain whether to look backward to a passing stage of intellectual accomplishment or forward toward a receding ideal which mocked him from the future; whether to look East to the strongholds of tradition and Europe or West to the unexplored innocence of the national psyche. But the effort, if not always the accomplishment, of aesthetic and critical theory was to harmonize the extremes in a new vision of reality and to achieve a moment of stability between adverse and conflicting pressures. Realism, sympathetically viewed, was this synthesis. Unsympathetically seen, it was a Victorian compromise in criticism.

In the last analysis our attitude toward the criticism of the genteel decades will rest upon our interpretation of this Victorian synthesis or, more specifically, on our willingness to accept or reject the unfavorable estimation placed upon the period as a whole by the liberal generation of the twenties. Its weaknesses have been fully explored. It was a Gilded Age, a genteel age, imbued too much with the cheerful optimism of Spencerian evolution and the smiling aspects. Accordingly criticism and fiction failed to express a tragic sense of life. Even James and Howells felt that Hardy, Tolstoi, Dostoevsky, and Turgenev were too gloomily depressed for American conditions and did not sufficiently hold to the "ideal of joy." A certain prudish gentility likewise helped to prevent the fiction of realism from handling the deeper passions, perversities, sex themes, and tragic realities of existence. Still, in the best sense, realism was a steady effort to work out an adjustment between critical extremes. In practice it produced a great quantity of spirited and intelligent commentary. Toward the social and economic deviations of The Gilded Age, it was at once a reflection and a protest. In theory the best of the realists rejected both literalism as a method and determinism as a philosophy. Still, they sought to mirror contemporary society faithfully. The literary counterpart of pragmatism, realism was a mediating force, and in the vigor and activity of the sharp debates it provoked, it provides the historian of criticism with a highly rewarding perspective for a study of American critical thought and practice. The Genteel Tradition and The Age of Innocence, as those phrases have been used, belong to the old-fashioned irrevocable past, but the intellectual aspirations and literary aims of that period are not without import for a later, even more bewildered generation.

John H. Raleigh

REVOLT AND REVALUATION
IN CRITICISM
1900-1930

IF THE YEARS from 1870 to 1900 were marked by the spirit of compromise and attempted synthesis, those from 1900 to 1930 were decidedly not. There is continuity between the two periods in that the nineteenth century battle for "realism," which was essentially a struggle for freedom of expression, was carried on into the twentieth century, becoming a total demand for total freedom. But, as the distance of Dreiser from James and Howells would indicate, the early years of the twentieth century were ushering in a new era, confused, extremist, great in both creativity and destructivity, an age which has proved to be both the terror and the delight of man and may well be the despair of the historian. For the twentieth century has confused or bemused its most acute observers. Fascinated and horrified by the onrushing character of his age Henry Adams wrote to Elisabeth Cameron in 1915:

Seventy-Seven all told, and I've outlived most things at that. As far as I can see, I've outlived the world too, and have nothing to go on looking for. I've outlived at least three quite distinct worlds since 1838, but this last one exploded ten years ahead of my calculated time, and caught me unexpectedly. . . .[1]

1. *Letters of Henry Adams, 1892-1918*, ed. Worthington Chauncy Ford (Boston and New York, 1938), p. 630.

With more equanimity but with the same sense of essential chaos George Santayana wrote in 1931:

For my part, though a lover of antiquity, I should certainly congratulate myself on living among the moderns, if the moderns were only modern enough, and dared to face nature with an unprejudiced mind and a clean purpose. Never before was the mental landscape so vast. What if the prospect, when the spirit explores it, seems rather a quagmire, as it were the Marshes of Glynn, rich only in much reeds and rank grasses. Has not the spirit always loved the wilderness?[2]

It is, first, appropriate and symbolic that Henry Adams should have been obsessed by "explosions" and that he should have been preoccupied in his later years with physics and with drawing analogies between human history and so-called laws of physics. As the epistemological implications of biology haunted the late nineteenth-century imagination, those drawn from physics lurk behind the consciousness of the twentieth. For the final significance of science for the layman, aside from his appreciation of the material benefits that it accrues and the intellectual daring and brilliance behind it, is that it points up the precariousness of the human condition, and science from Galileo to Einstein has been in effect a prolonged assault on human pride.

Darwin had dealt what appeared to be the final blow, proof of basic animality. But for worshippers of progress this passage of the species from simple to complex organism was cause only for delight. And, as Butler and Shaw demonstrated, a satisfying religion could be made out of evolutionism itself. Furthermore the solid earth had not yet melted, and Darwin's animal still inhabited a world of absolutes—Space, Time, and Causality. While this organic machine could be depressing in itself, yet it had a kind of solidity that was comforting. Much of the Sophoclean sweep and scope and the note of inevitability that pervades some Victorian literature, as in the novels of George Eliot, derives from the transferring of these supposed attributes of the physical world to an assumed moral universe.

But hardly had Darwinism been heard, interpreted, and assimilated, when physics, primarily, and other sciences, announced

2. George Santayana, *The Genteel Tradition at Bay* (New York, 1931), p. 17.

that time, space and causality were all illusions, the very universe itself a brief dream in the cosmic reaches of time. If nineteenth century biology had forced man to look back to the primeval slime, twentieth century physics has forced him to look back behind that to stellar explosions and an expanding and dying universe. And this concept in its turn has been both depressing and exhilarating, as the case may be: on the one hand, the bizarre melancholy of Adams, or the romantic despair of Bertrand Russell's "The Free Man's Worship":

That Man is the product of causes which had no prehension of the end they were achieving; that his origin, his growth, his hopes, his fears, his loves, his beliefs, are but the outcome of accidental collocations of atoms . . . that all the labors of the ages, all the devotion, all the inspiration, all the noonday brightness of human genius, are destined to extinction in the vast death of the solar system. . . .[3]

On the other hand, this world of merging opposites and disappearing boundaries whose only consistency lay in its indeterminacy, has had its apotheosizers as well. (James Huneker was one.)

Despairing or hopeful, these non-scientists who have meditated upon the implications of twentieth century physics are still bound together by a common uncertainty: they do not really *know* what physics says. Every educated reader of the time could read and, within limits, understand Darwin; no one, outside the initiate, can genuinely understand modern physics. And it is science that has become perhaps the great symbol of the specialization of knowledge which has removed intellectual affairs in the twentieth century from the check of experience or even ordinary logic. Thus whatever science has said by way of content, its technique can only serve to furnish the layman with the sense of uneasiness that ignorance breeds.

But if the twentieth century brought with it disintegration and indeterminacy, other factors, as if in compensation, were moving towards an unprecedented synthesis and integration. It was and is the chief anomaly of the twentieth century that, amid the cries of despair over the fragmentation and compartmentalization of

3. *Selected Papers of Bertrand Russell* (Modern Library, n.d.), p. 3.

knowledge and even of mind itself, never has an age so vigorously pursued—between wars—organization and integration, and offered so many creeds that promised to make all men alike forever. And in the closing years of the nineteenth century and in the early years of the twentieth a major intellectual shift toward collectivist thought occurred; from dualism to monism, from absolutism to relativism, from individualism to institutionalism. As D. F. Bowers has pointed out, Dewey's instrumentalism is perhaps less indebted to the Jeffersonian tradition than it is to Darwin and Hegel (Dewey's intellectual heroes in his formative years), with the Darwinian concepts of man as an animal among others and an evolutionary monism, and the Hegelian insistence upon history as process and upon institutionalism.[4] Thus too the Progressivist ferment that animated the national life during the opening years of the century was a curious and paradoxical amalgam of laissez-faire and collectivist doctrine.

Caught between these differing yet complementary forces, literature and criticism have generally expressed a minority position, decrying both the fragmentation of knowledge and self and the collectivization of society. It is the assumption of most serious literature of the last few decades that somehow civilization itself has gotten off its proper track or that it is advancing on a wrong line. Hence the preoccupation of criticism, especially in the twenties, with a "usable past" or with tradition, as if somehow culture could push civilization back to where it had gone astray and start it off once more aright.

It is doubtful then if any body of literature has ever been so vehemently critical and so against the status quo as has the literature, American or European, of the twentieth century. But neither has this literature, in its turn, been immune from the apocalyptic tendencies of its age, and it is doubtful too if any other age has been offered so many and so differing diagnoses and panaceas by its writers. Literary criticism has thus tended to veer from one extreme position to the other.

But dismay and decay are not the only characteristics of the

4. D. F. Bowers, "Hegel, Darwin, and the American Tradition," *Foreign Influences in American Life,* ed. D. F. Bowers (Princeton, 1944).

era. It is commonly said that Western civilization in the last four decades has been chiefly distinguished by a "lack of values." But this description is true only when we add the adjective "common" to the noun "values," for it could be argued just as plausibly that the age suffered from a plethora of values. As the old creeds and beliefs and assumptions sank to extinction, an army of ideas sprang up to take their place. And if the age had undergone the ultimate despair, it had at moments, as in pre-World War I America, millennial insights and expectations as well. If depression was deep and muted at times, hopes have run high and eloquent at others.

As if to reflect the contradictory tendencies of the age and its alternations between heat and cold, literary criticism took three distinct, although overlapping, directions in the period from 1900 to 1930. First, the initial quiet decade developed into an efflorescent period of creativity and of political and cultural idealism during the years preceding America's entry into World War I; underneath this was gathering a strong and multifarious critical movement that was concerned with evaluating, negatively, American culture and that was to receive its fullest expression in the twenties; finally, and taking still another direction in the twenties, the early criticism of Eliot and Pound, with its internationalist outlook and its emphasis on analysis of literary technique, began to be heard.

I.

The century began quietly enough. Van Wyck Brooks in *The Confident Years,* quoting Ambrose Bierce, characterizes the years 1900-1910 as the "weak and fluffy" decade:

It was ironical in retrospect that the decade of Roosevelt and the "strenuous life" should have been, as Bierce said, weak and fluffy, but so it seemed to be in the literary world, especially if, like Bierce himself, one thought of literature as virtually identical with fiction. Under a sky whose fixed stars were Mark Twain, Howells, and Henry James, no new talents had appeared of comparable size. . . .[5]

For Dreiser had scarcely begun, Mrs. Wharton had not yet arrived, Norris, Crane, Harland, Boyeson and Frederic were dead,

5. Van Wyck Brooks, *The Confident Years* (New York, 1952), p. 322.

Fuller was writing less and less, Bierce had ceased to write, Garland had not realized his early promise, and Hearn had disappeared.

And literary criticism itself was notable for its lack of centrality and cohesion, and, with the exception of Huneker, for its withdrawn character, the most eminent practitioners being solitaries such as Santayana or John Jay Chapman or W. C. Brownell. "Is a man to have an opinion [in America]?" asked Chapman in 1910; "Then he must make it himself."[6] Santayana described the late nineteenth century intellectual life at Harvard, where young America was introduced to the things of the mind, as:

It was an idyllic, haphazard, humoristic existence, without fine imagination, without any familiar infusion of scholarship, without articulate religion: a flutter of intelligence in the void, flying into trivial play, in order to drop back, as soon as college days were over, into the drudgery of affairs.[7]

Brownell devoted a large part of his long career to urging upon Americans, as had his master Arnold, the centrality and the high critical intelligence of French culture. His own age he regarded an an epoch of "exaggeration and fantasticality."[8] And for all his intelligence and wit, and his commitment to the future in his avowed political liberalism, Brownell was yet the voice of Victorianism, however enlightened, and could not speak to the younger minds of his time nor appreciate its literature. The nascent generation, generally and unjustly making Howells the villain, thought that most of its elders were flaccid and timid. Speaking of the cultural atmosphere of the time when he was at Columbia, Randolph Bourne said:

Every one . . . bemoaned the lack of critics, but the elder critics seemed to have lost all sense of hospitality and to have become tired and a little spitefully disconsolate, while the newer ones were too intent on their crusade against puritanism and philistinism to have time for a constructive pointing of the way.[9]

6. John Jay Chapman, *Learning* (New York, 1910), p. 15.
7. George Santayana, *Character and Opinion in the United States* (New York, 1920), p. 51.
8. W. C. Brownell, *Standards* (New York, 1917), p. 121.
9. Randolph Bourne, *The History of a Literary Radical* (New York, 1920), p. 22.

The latter part of Bourne's statement would seem to indicate that things were beginning to happen, as indeed they were. For all the potentials of the great creative and critical outburst that was to occur after 1912 lie implicit in the early years of the century, and some have their roots back in the nineties themselves. In poetry, as Howard Mumford Jones points out in *The Bright Medusa,* much of the characteristic attitude and substance of later poetry was anticipated in the work of Santayana, Moody, Stickney, and Lodge. Like later poets, this now neglected group was at odds with the industrial order, was pessimistic over the demise of Christianity, and was searching, unsuccessfully, for an adequate myth.[10] In the novel, the furor over Dreiser's *Sister Carrie,* while it delayed publication of the book itself, indicated that the fight for "realism" that had animated the late nineteenth century was to be extended to a fight for "naturalism." And in fact the notorious American prudery, while genuine, is liable to be overestimated. As Van Wyck Brooks says:

. . . The romantic prudery of the time was more marked in America than in France or England, though not as much as Americans sometimes thought. For Zola's English publisher had been imprisoned for two years, as Flaubert was prosecuted, like Beaudelaire, for pornographic writing. There was no consistency in American prudery and it was not to be forgotten that Havelock Ellis' *Studies in the Psychology of Sex* was published in America when it was prohibited in England.[11]

In criticism itself the work of Huneker, however superficial and journalistic, was not only lively and new, it led directly to Mencken and it pointed generally to the major interests of later generations. In the nineteenth century criticism tended to be either nationalistic, as in the case of Emerson and Whitman and even chauvinistic as in the case of their lesser followers, or Anglophile and ethical. The asumption generally of the latter group was that literature was English in substance and didactic in intent. There was a further assumption, so deep-set as to be virtually unquestioned, that art was literature and nothing else. Huneker attacked each of these shibboleths. To a literary world

10. Howard Mumford Jones, *The Bright Medusa* (Urbana, 1952), p. 47 ff.
11. Brooks, *The Confident Years,* p. 303.

[165]

that was concerned generally with Tennyson or Browning or Meredith, Huneker brought Ibsen, Strindberg, Becque, Hauptmann, Sudermann, Gorky, Maeterlinck, and D'Annunzio. If he took up English writers, it was someone like Shaw, the anti-Victorian iconoclast. His method was avowedly anti-moralistic and impressionistic. Thus he cried up Conrad because the novelist was not a propagandist but was a "disinterested artist." At the end of *Promenades of an Impressionist* he proclaimed: "The foregoing memoranda are frankly in the key of impressionism. They are a record of some personal preferences, not attempts at critical revaluation."[12] And he boasted: ". . . I have promenaded my dearest prejudices, my absurd illusions."[13] By the same token he urged the young twentieth century to cease celebrating the accomplishments of its parent, the nineteenth, and to work with the present.

The artist who turns his face only to the past—his work will never be anything but an echo. To depict the faces and things and pen the manners of the present is the task of great painters and novelists. Actualists alone count in the future.[14]

The disappearance of absolutes and the dissolution of age-old boundaries that so disturbed the orthodox were gloried in by Huneker:

Old frontiers have disappeared in science and art and literature. We have Maeterlinck, a poet writing of bees, Poincaré, a mathematician opening our eyes to the mystic gulfs of space; solid matter resolved into mist, and the law of gravitation questioned.[15]

Finally Huneker considered all artistic expression his province and recounted his enthusiasm over music (although he did not like Schönberg or the general direction of contemporary music) and painting as well. In short, Huneker's function and historical importance was to celebrate the exciting new world, in literature and in the other arts, that was opening up, not only in England but more especially in Europe generally, and to be impressionis-

12. James Huneker, *Promenades of an Impressionist* (New York, 1910), p. 389.
13. *Ibid.*, p. 390.
14. *Ibid.*, pp. 228-9.
15. James Huneker, *Unicorns* (New York, 1917), p. 20.

tic rather than rigorous in method, and to be bohemian (". . . art and alcohol are inseparably wedded"[16]) rather than moral in spirit and attitude. In certain ways Huneker was uncannily prophetic, and in 1917 he said: "The fiction of Henry James is for the future."[17]

If Huneker is important for nothing else, he is historically significant for his link with Mencken, who regarded Huneker as his John the Baptist, and in 1929 Mencken paid his tribute. All the critics of the twentieth century, said Mencken, were eternally in Huneker's debt, for he had cleared the way. Huneker had related art to "living ideas, to all the great movements of human forces, to life itself."[18] "He emancipated criticism in America from its old bondage to sentimentality and stupidity, and with it he emancipated all the arts themselves."[19] There is doubtless an excess of enthusiasm here, but Huneker *was* a trail-blazer and an innovator and thus constitutes an appropriate introduction to an era of criticism that was finally to pride itself on its revolutionary character.

While Huneker was performing his largely solitary labors in the early years of the century, there was gathering quietly all the potentials for the critical debate that was to animate the teens and twenties. More's first book, on Benjamin Franklin, appeared in 1900; Mencken's *George Bernard Shaw* in 1905; Babbitt's *Literature and the American College* and Brooks's *Wine of the Puritans* in 1908; Herbert Croly's *The Promise of American Life* in 1909; Pound's *The Spirit of Romance* and Spingarn's *The New Criticism* in 1910; Bourne's *Youth and Life* and the Marxist publication *Masses* in 1911; the magazine *Poetry* in 1912; and John Macy's *The Spirit of American Literature* in 1913, the year in which Bourne himself graduated from Columbia. Here are the embryonic conditions for almost everything that was to happen: the Humanist critique (More and Babbitt); the Nietszchean assault (Mencken); the "usable past" (Brooks); the rebellion of the young (Bourne); the poet as critic and the flight

16. James Huneker, *Variations* (New York, 1921), p. 137.
17. Huneker, *Unicorns*, p. 53.
18. *Essays by James Huneker*, ed. H. L. Mencken (New York, 1929), p. xxi.
19. *Ibid.*, p. xxiii.

to Europe (Pound); the "pure" critic (Spingarn); the Marxist analysis (the *Masses*); the Poetic Renaissance (*Poetry*); and the liberalist revaluation of American history (Croly and Macy). And Freud and Fraser were in the air. The central history of American criticism from 1900 to 1930 is largely the history of the development of these conflicting forces, and the significance of that period lies in the final meaning of the conflict.

From 1912—with the advent of the so-called Poetic Renaissance—to 1917, everyone agreed that something was happening. It was a time of high spirits and aspiring idealism, qualities which were not to survive the moral debacle of the twenties. Edmund Wilson ascribed the feeling of liberation that writers felt at the time to three factors: first, the shadow of Big Business seemed to be passing away; second, Woodrow Wilson, for all his faults, seemed to be like some of the earlier presidents, in that he was a writer and a thinker, and he had thrust America onto the world stage; and third, "a livid spark seemed to flash from the American labor movement in the direction of the Russian revolution."[20] But even more important was the feeling that the arts themselves were juvenescent. There was, first, an enormous amount of professional talent expended in the promotion and production of all forms of art. Howard Mumford Jones, who was living in Chicago during this period, records some of the activity in Chicago:

As one who knew Chicago life . . . I can say that at the Chicago Art Museum I saw for the first time the Armory Show of 1913, including the "Nude Descending a Staircase"; that . . . I first heard Stravinsky's *Le Sacre du Printemps;* that the only time I ever witnessed Wagner's *Ring* was in a series of magnificent productions by the Chicago Opera Company . . . that my first Greek play was Maurice Brown's *The Trojan Women* . . . that the first book I ever had published was a translation of Heine's *North Sea Poems,* brought out by the Open Court Publishing Company of Chicago, which supported the *Monist,* a journal of international thought. . . .[21]

A consequent spirit of joyousness and expectation seemed to animate the young of that youthful day. *Poetry* in its first memora-

20. Edmund Wilson, *Classics and Commercials* (New York, 1950), p. 106.
21. *Op. cit.,* p. 7.

ble issue, for October, 1912, printed Pound's poem on Whistler, wherein, in spite of the assault upon America, hope is the note:

> You and Abe Lincoln from that mass of dolts
> Show us there's chance at least of winning through . . .

And the editors of this journal, which was to publish the best of the new poetry, announced as their hopeful intention: "We believe that there is a public for poetry, that it will grow."[22] Capturing the spirit of the times even better perhaps was Margaret Anderson's introduction to her *Little Review*: "Life is a glorious performance: quite apart from its setting, in spite of the kind of 'part' one gets, everybody is given at least his chance to act . . . And close to Life . . . is this eager, panting Art who shows us the wonder of the way as we rush along."[23]

It was a time too of expectant experimentation in all fields, and the *New Republic* launched its career in 1914 in precisely this vein: "The *New Republic* is frankly an experiment. It is an attempt to find a national audience for a journal of interpretation and opinion."[24] In the other arts, revolutions were in the making. According to Meyer Schapiro: "About 1913 painters, writers, musicians, and architects felt themselves to be at an epochal turning-point corresponding to an equally decisive transition in philosophical thought and social life."[25]

In painting proper the great symbol was the Armory Show of 1913 which introduced the modern French masters to the American public, and is called by Schapiro, "The great event, the turning point in American art . . ."[26]

Literary criticism itself received a tremendous impetus from two non-literary sources, politics and youthful iconoclasm. Partly as the result of the reinterpretation of American history that scholars like Smith and Beard and Veblen and others were instituting, partly because of the continuing assault upon the bourgeoisie, which the nineteenth century had inaugurated,

22. *Poetry,* I (October, 1912), p. 27.
23. *Little Review,* I (March, 1914), p. 1.
24. *New Republic,* I (November 7, 1914), p. 3.
25. Meyer Schapiro, "Rebellion in Art," *America in Crisis,* ed. Daniel Aaron (New York, 1952), pp. 205-6.
26. *Ibid.,* p. 203.

partly because of Progressivist agitation, the rising generation was inveterately radical. Van Wyck Brooks points out that when Max Eastman arrived in Greenwich Village in 1907, he found that the atmosphere was socialist rather than esthetic.

For many of the rising generation, moreover, literature was not so much an art as a "kind of social dynamics," as Floyd Dell was to call it, something that had once been used to build up taboos and was now being used to break them down again.[27]

Some of the dreams of the young literary left were perfervid. In his autobiography Joseph Freeman tells how before the first World War young radicals had visions of a socialist utopia and a magical union of art and politics. Their hero was Floyd Dell: "The flavor of 1912 was caught by Floyd Dell when he called it the Lyric Year. A new spirit had come to America, and not in politics alone."[28]

Allied to the political impulse was a "youth" movement which was smashing the old taboos and declaring for a new world of youth and freedom: Mencken, Shaw and Wells being the prophets. Edmund Wilson was perhaps typical of this new generation in his choice of literary heroes: "I had been stimulated at boarding-school and college by the examples of Shaw and Mencken and, to a lesser extent, by that of James Huneker."[29] And this movement toward freedom, led principally, it would seem now, by Mencken, was finally successful. In spite of the fact that Sinclair Lewis in his Nobel Prize speech of 1930 could declare that American culture was still under the thralldom of Howells, there can be no doubt that what Howells stood for or was supposed to have stood for—enervating gentility—had long since disappeared. According to Wilson: ". . . when I came on the scene [circa 1919], the battle had mostly been won: I was myself a beneficiary of the work that had been done by Mencken and others."[30] The War itself, before the ensuing disillusion and cynicism, gave an even greater impetus to youthful aspirations and provided an international flavor. In the preface to *Letters*

27. Brooks, *The Confident Years*, p. 373.
28. Joseph Freeman, *An American Testament* (New York, 1936), p. 37.
29. Wilson, *Classics and Commercials*, p. 114.
30. *Ibid.*

and Leadership (1918) Brooks took note of Pierre de Lanux's *Young France and New America* which had proposed a union of all the young people of the West, to usher in the New World. It was not to be, said Brooks, for America still did not know itself; it has only a "fierce rudimentary mass-mind."[31] But even the early Brooks, for all his melancholy trenchancy, shared, it would seem, in the early hopes, and he invariably tacked on a happy ending to his pervasive critiques, as in *Letters and Leadership*. And in his influential *America's Coming-of-Age* he urged the intellectuals to the great task: "To quicken and exhilarate the life of one's own people ..."[32] Even Mencken professed to see a few pin-points of light in the primordial darkness:

... the most important change that has come over American literature in my time is this: that American satire, which once aimed all its shafts at the relatively civilized minority, now aims most at the imbecile majority.[33]

In the area of purely literary criticism the great symbol was Spingarn's famous lecture "The New Criticism" which—although it seems to have had no palpable effect—was welcomed with enthusiasm because of its iconoclasm. In Spingarn's throwing out of all the "rules" of the game, such as history, genres, style, and periods, in his interest in the creative process itself, in his cosmopolitan championing of Croce, and in his slaying of the moral dragon, he embodied the deep-set antagonism of the younger writers to the logic-chopping, the dry academicism, the narrow Anglophilism, and the "moral printer" attitudes that had constituted one of the main strains in American criticism. Mencken himself grudgingly congratulated *this* college professor, and he bestowed on Spingarn his supreme accolade—acknowledgment of belligerency: "Against the whole corps [of critics], moral and esthetic, psychological and algebraic, stands Major J. E. Spingarn, U. S. A."[34]

But the most genuinely symbolic figure for the ante-bellum

31. Van Wyck Brooks, *Letters and Leadership* (New York, 1918), p. XVI.
32. Van Wyck Brooks, *America's Coming-Of-Age* (New York, 1915), p. 171.
33. H. L. Mencken, *Prejudices: Fourth Series* (New York, 1924), p. 138.
34. H. L. Mencken, "Criticism of Criticism of Criticism," *Criticism in America*, ed. Joel E. Spingarn (New York, 1924), p. 177.

era is perhaps Randolph Bourne, who was, in fact, regarded as the leader of freedom-loving youth in their attack on their tyrannical and timid elders. "This Older Generation," an essay included in Bourne's *History of a Literary Radical,* indicts the elders for clinging to the repressive verities of Protestant religion and New England morality, for denying the existence of social problems, for selfishness, and for timidity, especially as concerns death and sex. At one time Bourne thought that he and the younger men were winning completely the battle for freedom, and he spoke hopefully of "the widening and deepening of the American imagination. We are adrift in a far wider sea than our own forefathers. We are far more adventurous in personal relations, far more aware of the bewildering variousness of human nature."[35]

But Bourne died young and he died a social outcast (because of his opposition to the entry of America into the War). And in his demise he is perhaps an even more eloquent, if melancholy, symbol of our period as a whole, for the high hopes that crystallized in 1912 proved extravagant, and the real history of the period from 1900 to 1930 is written in the vast and elaborate negative criticisms of American civilization of Mencken, More, Brooks and others, and in the flight to Europe of Eliot, Pound, and others. The short-lived *Seven Arts,* with which Bourne was connected, is perhaps the most accurate bellwether of all. It began in November of 1916, proclaiming:

It is our faith and the faith of many, that we are living in the first days of a renascent period, a time which means for America the coming of that national self-consciousness which is the beginning of greatness.[36]

But the opposition of the editors to the War lost them their subsidy, and in October, 1917, on the verge of bankruptcy, they pleaded, in vain as it turned out, for support. There had been a "current," a desire of American youth for art and freedom: "Across this current, like a sudden dam, came the war. It carried with it a menace to what we believed to be the promise of Ameri-

35. *Op. cit.,* p. 188.
36. *The Seven Arts,* I (November, 1916), p. 52.

can life."[37]   And indeed the "promise of American life" turned
into the frenzy of the 1920's, and the youthful dreams of 1912
turned finally to dust.

II.

But almost from the beginning of the century and underneath
the optimism and the hopes that marked the years from 1912 to
1917 there was gathering steadily a large and important body of
criticism, directed as much at American life itself as at literature.[38]

37. *The Seven Arts,* II (October, 1917), p. v.

38. The time-honored way in which to deal with the period under consideration
from Bernard Smith's *Forces in American Criticism* (1939) to William Van O'Connor's
An Age of Criticism (1952) is by classifying in rough chronology, the various schools
of criticism: Impressionism, Liberalism, Humanism, Freudianism, etc.   Charles I.
Glicksburg, for example, in the lengthy introduction to his anthology *American Literary
Criticism* (New York, 1951) summarizes the period as follows:

During the first fifty years American criticism has passed through many meta-
morphoses; it has been prolific, undeniably alive.   Impressionism, humanism, pure
aestheticism or "expressionism," modeled on Croce's philosophy of art, creative
criticism, liberalism, and radicalism and their reflection in *belles lettres,* the attempt to make literature fundamentally a criticism of life, the sturdy growth of
interest in our native literary tradition, its origins, history, folklore, and development,
the reinterpretation of the shaping influence of the frontier, the popular vogue of
psychoanalysis and the amazing effect it had on both writers and criticism, the
sudden emergence of naturalism and a new experimental literature . . . (p. 14).

Glicksburg attempts to give every devil his due and his account is accordingly innocuous.
With other historians a bias generally intrudes.   Smith is a Marxist, while O'Connor is
inclined to think what he calls "analytical criticism," the prevailing mode of the last
decades, as a supreme consummation.   Norman Foerster's *American Criticism* (1928)
is in many respects still the best book on the subject because of its solid, detailed,
independent analysis, but it is chiefly concerned with nineteenth century figures, Poe,
Emerson, Lowell and Whitman, and deals in summary fashion with the twentieth
century from a New Humanist point of view.

There are, of course, other ways in which the critical conflicts of the time have
been viewed.   William A. Drake in the introduction to his anthology *American Criticism* (New York, 1926), pp. vii-xii, not attempting synthesis, said: "We stand today
in the center of a vast disintegration" (p. vii).   More intrepid analysts have tried to
clarify and codify the "vast disintegration."   Foerster's introduction to his *American
Critical Essays* (London, 1930) professed to see four sets of "bewildering" conflicts;
modernist skeptics vs. ancients; romantics vs. realists; humanists vs. naturalists; and
scholars vs. critics.   Underlying these conflicts, he claimed, were two antithetical ways
of approaching literature: the "foregrounders," including inpressionists and expressionists;
and the "backgrounders," including the nationalists and the humanists.   James C.
Bowman in his *Contemporary American Criticism* (New York, 1926, pp. vii-ix) discerned four groups of conflicts: nationalism vs. internationalism; formalists vs. expressionists; moralists vs. Mencken-ites; and esthetes vs. "message-hunters."   Lewisohn in
the introduction to *A Modern Book of Criticism* (New York, n.d., pp. i-iv) saw the
age as in conflict between traditional authoritarianism and nascent freedom of expression.   Percy Boynton in *The Challenge of Modern Criticism* (Chicago, 1931) saw

This movement was to gather force and cogency and culminate in the Battle of the Books of the twenties. Writing retrospectively in 1924, Joel Spingarn remarked: "In the last twelve or fifteen years, side by side with the so-called 'poetic Renaissance,' there had developed what is probably the first fundamental discussion of the nature of criticism in American literature."[39]

This discussion was "fundamental" in two ways: it attempted to formulate first principles for literary criticism and it attempted to assay the fundamental assumptions of American culture. While the critical and the cultural concerns overlapped—Mencken, for example, blamed the moralistic bias of Anglo-American criticism on Anglo-American culture—and were reciprocal—Spingarn's theories were as much beholden to cosmopolitanism as to the more abstract principles of Croce—they can nevertheless be discussed separately.

In the debate over literary criticism proper the most notable characteristic is the number of conflicting theories

---

the period as the coming-of-age of American culture: "Long ago, Matthew Arnold . . . pointed out that a time of true creative activity must be preceded by a time of criticism." (p. 13).

Two contemporary assessments of interest, because of the eminence of their authors as critics, are those of Edmund Wilson and T. S. Eliot. Wilson thought there were five groups, ostensibly exchanging ideas but in actuality mutually exclusive: Mencken and Nathan; T. S. Eliot; the Neo-Romantics, like Millay or Fitzgerald; the Social-Revolutionaries, like Gold or Dos Passos; and the Psychological-Sociologists, like Brooks or Krutch. (*The Shores of Light,* New York, 1952, p. 367 ff.) Eliot's opinion of the American critical scene in the twentieth century is negative, to put it mildly. "We generally agree in conversation that the amount of good literary criticism in English is negligible." ("Criticism In England," *Athenaeum* 4650, June 13, 1919, p. 452.) Reviewing Foerster's *Reinterpretation* in 1929 Eliot gave a sketch of American literary criticism. In the late nineteenth century, while President Eliot and Kittredge dominated Harvard, literary studies in America tended to the Teutonic. Now there was a tendency to fly in the other direction and give contemporary literature an exaggerated importance. Latterly there had been three generations of American critics. Babbitt and More constituted the first generation and their strength lay in their de-provincialization of American criticism, replacing the fireside criticism of Lowell with the harder standards of Taine and Renan. The next generation, of which Mencken and Brooks were good examples were "merely querulous." But the third generation, "Mumford, Munson, and Allen Tate," among others, were disciples of the first; and in the universities Foerster was its representative. ("American Critics," *Times Literary Supplement* 1406, January 10, 1929, p. 24.) Thus (making Allen Tate a Humanist!) Eliot made Humanism the only substantial critical movement in America, and, later on, he broke with Humanism. Significantly, the only American critic about whom Eliot was enthusiastic was Poe, the eternal pariah.

39. Spingarn, ed., *Criticism in America,* p. 2.

that were advanced. In the twenties there began to appear the first collections of those critical symposia which have since become a minor national industry, and, unless the editor himself possessed or professed a certain bias, the collections were remarkable for the number of contradictory critical ideologies they advanced. Spingarn's own anthology, *Criticism In America* (1924), is one of the best examples, for it included pieces by Woodberry, Brownell, Brooks, Babbitt, Mencken (represented twice), Eliot (represented twice), Sherman, Ernest Boyd, and Spingarn himself. Temporally considered these critics represent almost three generations of American criticism, Woodberry and Brownell having been born in the 1850's, Spingarn himself in 1875, and Brooks, Eliot and Boyd in the late 1880's. And much of what happened to literary criticism during the early years of the twentieth century is indicated by the distance between the sober restraint of Woodberry and the flamboyance of Mencken, between the pragmatism of Brownell and the theoretical fireworks of Spingarn, and between the moralism of Babbitt and the estheticism of Eliot.

Both Woodberry and Brownell were avowedly conservatives, and Woodberry, fearing that the historical approach to literature was to be discarded, pleaded in his "Two Phases of Criticism: Historical and Esthetic" for a balance between the two concerns: the historical for "interpretation" and the esthetic for "judgment." Brownell, attempting to keep the famous Victorian balance between the moral and the esthetic, while at the same time being concerned with the problem of "objectivity," urged likewise an amalgam of the philosophic or historic interest along with an evaluative and esthetic one.

But after these two older critics came the deluge: Babbitt's Humanism, Spingarn's Expressionism, Mencken's Impressionism, Sherman's Nationalism or "Puritanism," Brooks's Liberalism and the "Usable Past," and Eliot's concern with analytics and European traditionalism. (Boyd's essay is essentially an attack on Sherman.) While none of these theories in themselves won the day or could be said to have expressed majority opinion, collectively they signify two things: first, a rejection of the immediate past, namely the imagined heritage from the nineteenth century; and second, the advent of an age that was to agree on nothing and get down to first principles in everything. In both of these aspects this collection signalized an increased catholicity of critical principles and critical judgments. The literary journals of the nineteenth century were perhaps most inclined to argue over the merits of particular authors, but those of the twentieth have been inclined rather to argue over critical assumptions and principles themselves.

And indeed the arguments were so fundamental that they brought literary criticism into a direct and dramatic juxtaposition to life, more direct and dramatic, perhaps, than ever before in American history, with the possible exceptions of the cases of Emerson and Whitman. For the problems that were argued were ultimately cultural in the largest sense of that word. As Van Wyck Brooks said of his own work and that of his friend Bourne:

If our literary criticism is always impelled sooner or later to become social criticism, it is certainly because the future of our literature and art depends upon the wholesale reconstruction of a social life all the elements of which are as if united against the growth and freedom of the spirit. . . .[40]

To this should be subjoined Ludwig Lewisohn's observations on the fundamental character of the Great Debate: "This debate concerning critical methods was, in other words, a debate between philosophies, cosmogonies, religions, races. It was a conflict over the future of American civilization."[41]

On the surface the Great Debate was an immediate protest against specific flaws, and as such was marked by vigor and acrimony. The acrimony was deplored by some; it was gloried in by others, such as Mencken[42]; but the wisest observation on this *furor criticus* was Lewisohn's:

. . . the rise of the critical spirit with a given civilization is a symptom of health and maturity. Such it has undoubtedly been in contemporary

40. Brooks's introduction to *The History of a Literary Radical,* p. xxii.
41. Ludwig Lewisohn, *Expression in America* (New York, 1932), p. 423.
42. H. L. Mencken, *Prejudices: Third Series* (New York, 1922), p. 178.

America. For the critical spirit had hitherto been no force in American life.[43]

In the first place, the Battle of the Books, like its older archetype and like all serious discussions, was in some sense an attack on pride. "American optimism" was the name given to it by most of the critics, while Babbitt and More, as classicists, gave it its classical name. Babbitt, for example, approvingly quoted an eighteenth century Frenchman: "If I am to judge by myself, man is a stupid animal."[44] And: "Now the true leader is a man of character, and the ultimate root of character is humility."[45] Thus the real intellectual temper of the age was that of Kipling's "Recessional" and the implicit injunction was that you could not climb to heaven by building a tower of gold. Moreover, the humility, in many cases, extended to the self. As young Edmund Wilson reminded his fellow critics: "At best, we have produced no literary critics of the full European stature: the much abused Paul Elmer More remains our only professional critic whose learning is really great and whose efforts are ambitious."[46] And he concluded: "We have the illusion of stronger [than the preceding generation] vitality and of greater intellectual freedom, but we are polyglot, parvenu, hysterical and often illiterate."[47]

In the second place, men of such diverse opinions, as More, Mencken, Brooks, and Pound all could and did agree on one thing: a far-reaching indictment of American culture, and the indictment is strikingly similar wherever one looks in the period. It had all been said before, in one way or another, by Poe, Hawthorne, Melville, Henry James, and Whitman, but never had it been said so vociferously and so completely by so many contemporaneous writers, as was the case in the years from 1912 on. Brooks's *America's Coming-of-Age* is perhaps the classic statement—America is divided into "Highbrow" and "Low-

43. *Op. cit.*, pp. 416-17.

44. Irving Babbitt, *Rousseau and Romanticism* (Boston and New York, 1920), pp. 366-7.

45. Irving Babbitt, *Democracy and Leadership* (Boston and New York, 1924), p. 35.

46. Edmund Wilson, "The All-Star Literary Vaudeville," *American Criticism: 1926*, ed. William A. Drake (New York, 1926), p. 347.

47. *Ibid.*, p. 357.

brow," both hopelessly unbalanced; it is too much committed to materialism; a sound and balanced individual cannot develop in the midst of such contradictions; American literature has always been missing something: it is either too gross or too ethereal: it tends to banal moralizing; America's best writers have always been out of touch with this lopsided culture; in American culture the "lowbrow" is apotheosized; America is a great mass of unfocused energy waiting for the organizing culture to galvanize it into proper action. Behind and below the entire unhappy scene is a narrow Puritanism which, although it has changed its form, has never relaxed its grip on the American mind. The reaction to Brooks's early work is perhaps best summed up in Edmund Wilson's imaginary dialogue between Brooks himself and Scott Fitzgerald, where Fitzgerald says to the older man: "The other day, one of the youngest of our number, reading your essay, *The Literary Life,* broke down in a wild fit of weeping and cursed God for having made him an American."[48] The essential indictment was repeated endlessly and elaborated monumentally by various critics—some followers of Brooks, others opposed to him—throughout this period. Harold Stearns's symposium *Civilization in the United States* is but the largest and most systematic working out of this thesis. As Mencken said in an essay entitled "On Being An American": "Apparently there are those who begin to find it disagreeable—nay, impossible. Their anguish fills the Liberal weeklies, and every ship that puts out from New York carries a groaning cargo of them . . ."[49]

America is hypocritical, anti-intellectual, Puritanical, materialistic, timid, mass-minded, machine-dominated, conformist, atomized, restless, cultureless and joyless, although it systematically cultivates a synthetic optimism—so it goes in some fashion or another with practically all the critics of the period, the only notable exception being Stuart Sherman, with his unsure and changing conceptions of Puritanism. Even a Marxist and a Humanist could, with a few frictions, see eye to eye on this nega-

48. Wilson, *The Shores of Light,* p. 159.
49. H. L. Mencken, *Prejudices: Third Series* (New York, 1922), p. 9.

tive assessment. To a man, all the critics agreed that America needed a central culture and that it needed a class of men to administer that culture, in short some kind of intellectual aristocracy. Brooks, Mencken, Babbitt, More, Sherman, Lewisohn, and Eliot, despite all their differences, would all assent to this notion. It is, for example, one of the explicit themes of Waldo Frank's *The Re-Discovery of America* in which it is said: "With tragic need, America needs groups. Groups to capture our chaos as consciousness captures the sense."[50]

It is when we come to the specific individual panaceas that the period begins to seem as chaotic as these men thought America was, and the traditional grouping of esthetes, impressionists, Humanists, Liberals, Marxists, and Freudians does not help much to banish chaos. Perhaps Stuart Sherman, who began as a Humanist, verged into a narrow and militant nationalist of the third-generation-Protestant-Anglo-Saxon stripe, and finally finished his career as a rather liberal book reviewer, should be considered a symbolic figure for the period. In practice this meant that Sherman disliked Dreiser for one set of reasons in his early stage, disliked him for other reasons in his middle stage, and then *liked* him for still other reasons in his last stage. And so it went: Babbitt and More urging their brand of Humanism; Lewis Mumford calling for a coming to terms with mass machinery; Mencken for an intellectual aristocracy and light from Europe; Floyd Dell for Marxism; Santayana for detachment; Lewisohn for self-expression; Pound and Eliot, by example anyway, for flight to Europe; Sherman for a return to his conception of Puritanism. Moreover, the cross-references are equally bewildering. Dreiser is a culture-hero for Mencken, a culture-villain for Babbitt, and a talented culture-"hyphenate" for Randolph Bourne. Everybody took up the subject of Whitman; almost everybody, including More, thought that Whitman was good but not great, and all disagreed as to what was lacking. As the central thesis of all these critics was that America lacked

50. Waldo Frank, *The Re-Discovery of America* (New York, 1929), p. 279.

a central culture and a critical tradition, their own practice seems to bear them out. A Marxist, Calverton, had this bilious observation to make:

. . . a series of shallow rationalizations, a puffery of the inessential, a confused scribbling about morality, a blathery defense of slap-stick emotionalism, a projection of a *new* approach that antedates Goethe, onslaughts on the business man's psychology, sedate apologies for traditions, archaeological remnants of deceased social epochs, denunciations of psychological and historical esthetes, vain retreats to Horace and Aristotle, all subsidized by a wealth of allusion and imagery but a paucity of insight and analysis.[51]

In a less doctrinaire spirit Edmund Wilson has made the same point:

What we lack, then, in the United States, is not writers or even literary parties, but simply serious literary criticism . . . Each of these groups does produce, to be sure, a certain amount of criticism to justify or explain what it is doing, but it may, I believe, be said in general that they do not communicate with one another; their opinions do not really circulate.[52]

To get a less confused picture of the period it is necessary to take a larger view and a more abstract perspective, and this is to see that however the *content* of the various arguments varied, the form, like the aim, was invariably the same.

First the parallel to Matthew Arnold, whose example and precepts were very much in the minds of these critics as frequent reference and quotations show, is instructive. Like him, they were trying to "create a situation" and to carry out Lowell's famous prescription that before America could get a literature it needed a criticism. Like Arnold also, they were basically and essentially ethnological, given to brandishing cultures at one another. They thought too that literature was a criticism of life. Even Arnold's methods—the use of irony and raillery and the penchant for colorful "catch" words and phrases—were habitually employed. Moreover, to broaden the analogy, the desire of these critics to ransack the past for norms with which to correct

51. V. F. Calverton, *The Newer Spirit* (New York, 1925), p. 152.
52. *The Shores of Light*, p. 369.

the present and guide the future, was but a continuation of a habit of thought which was endemic in the nineteenth century and of which Arnold was only one exemplar. Santayana has labeled this future-past obsession one of the veritable hall-marks of nineteenth century thought:

Everywhere in the nineteenth century we find a double preoccupation with the past and with the future, a longing to know what all experience might have been hitherto, and on the other hand to hasten to some wholly different experience, to be contrived immediately with a beating heart and flying banners. The imagination of the age was intent on history; its conscience was intent on reform.[53]

And this, said Paul Elmer More, was only what the great tradition of critics in some way or another had always done, and in an essay on Arnold he named this tradition—Cicero, Erasmus, Boileau, Shaftsbury, Sainte-Beuve, and Arnold—and described its characteristics:

They are the exemplars—not complete individually, I need not say—of what may be called the critical spirit: discriminators between the false and the true, the deformed and the normal; preachers of harmony and proportion and order, prophets of the religion of taste. If they deal much with the criticism of literature, this is because in literature more manifestly than anywhere else life displays its infinitely varied motives and results; and this practice is always to render literature itself more consciously a criticism of life.[54]

It was in this general spirit that American critics addressed themselves to the problem of American culture. But of "harmony," "proportion," "decorum," in the Great Debate, there is little, if any, and to return to Arnold once more, the difference between Arnold and the American critics is equally instructive. In Arnold's most famous historical drama, Hebraism vs. Hellenism, there is not a good-evil antithesis but rather two complementary sets of virtues, either of which becomes evil only when it is overemphasized, and a negative cultural situation results only when one of the twins is excluded. In short, Arnold's drama

53. George Santayana, *Winds of Doctrine* (New York, 1913), pp. 7-8.
54. Paul Elmer More, *Shelburne Essays (Seventh Series)* (New York, 1910), p. 218.

of Western history was over-simplified, if you will, but it was balanced and did not run to extremes.

The spirit, however, that informed the historical dramas of the American critics of the twenties was radical and extremist. Its classic expression is given, strangely enough, in an autobiographical revelation of a religious nature by one of its leading figures, namely Paul Elmer More. In *Shelburne Essays* (Sixth Series), in an essay on St. Augustine, More introduces the subject by recounting his own religious experience. He had been brought up a Calvinist, had lost his faith and tried to find a substitute for faith in increase of knowledge, but this was vanity:

And then, just as the vanity of this pursuit began to grow too insistent, came the unexpected index pointing to the new way—no slender oracle, but the ponderous and right German utterance of Baur's *Manichaisches Religionssystem*. It would be impossible to convey to others, I cannot quite recall myself, the excitement amounting almost to a physical perturbation caused by the first glimpse into the mysteries of independent faith. It was not, I need scarcely say, that I failed even to see the extravagant and materialistic tendencies of the Manichaean superstition; but its highly elaborate form, not without elements of real sublimity, acted as a powerful stimulus to the imagination. Here, symbolized by the cosmic conflict of light and darkness, was found as in a great epic poem the eternal problem of good and evil, of the thirst for happiness and the reality of suffering, which I knew to lie at the bottom of religious thought and emotion. How shall monotheism account for this discord of the world?[55]

More goes on to point out that, because of St. Augustine, who never seemed to be able to purge his own soul of his early Manichaeanism, a strong infusion of Manichaeanism, which at one point in the early Christian era theatened to win the day, was infused into and has remained in Christianity itself. And More's own attitude, although he consistently attacked any form of absolutism, had a tendency toward Manichaeanism, or what he called, in other contexts, "dualism": the world and human experience are made up of conflicting opposites, which it is impossible to synthesize.

55. Paul Elmer More, *Shelburne Essays (Sixth Series)* (New York, 1909), pp. 65-66.

What differentiates most of the American critics from Arnold is precisely this tendency toward what might be called a cultural Manichaeanism, which not only dramatized history, as a set of running antitheses, but often constructed a melodrama, a set of conflicts between absolute blacks and whites, good and evil. Babbitt's historical drama, for example, went something like this: there were certain Oriental virtues and certain Occidental vices, perpetually clashing in a kind of universal melodrama. In the Occident itself Babbitt inclined to Coleridge's view that Plato and Aristotle, between them, held the intellect of the Western world in fee. In any event certain parts of Plato and all of Aristotle constituted the good and for centuries have fought the evil, which reappears again and again, in various guises, but preeminently in Rousseauism. Within modern times then it is the inheritors of Aristotle battling with the Rousseauites. Coming to America, in its relation to Europe, we find certain American vices battling certain European virtues. American history itself is made up of a series of radical antitheses: Washington (good) vs. Jefferson (evil); Edwards (good) vs. Franklin (evil); the "saving remnant" vs. the mob. So that you could begin with Buddha and draw a line down through Aristotle, through Washington, through Edwards, through the "saving remnant" and finally arrive at Irving Babbitt. Now there were, of course, other factors operating in Babbitt's drama of history, such as the famous and ubiquitous three-fold distinction between the naturalistic, the humanistic and the religious. But the basic tenor was in the direction of this cultural Manichaeanism.

And it is this cultural Manichaeanism that unites most of the critics of the period. Each turned to the past, saw this past as a cultural warfare between good and evil, sought out what was thought to be good, and said, in effect, to his fellow critics, "History is on my side," and to his countrymen, "Follow me to the Promised Land which, as History proves, lies in the direction in which I am pointing."

The Manichaean drama varied enormously, of course, in individual cases. It could be cosmic and religious in scope and nature as with More, or it could be nationalistic and secular, as in the case of Van Wyck Brooks, or, as we know, all history is always on the side of the Marxists. It was mass repression vs. individual self-expression for Lewisohn, the machine vs. the humane for Mumford; the promise of America vs. the fulfillment for Brooks; the aristocratic principle vs. the mob for Mencken; the bourgeoisie vs. the proletariat for the Marxists. Practically all of these historical dramas predicted a dualism between the glowing vision of what America had promised to be and the dank reality of its actual accomplishment. Their mutual method was to belabor one another with great blocks of history and culture in a civil war that raged throughout the twenties and reached its climax in the battle between the Humanists and their opponents in 1929 and 1930.

In retrospect the supreme irony, in view of his own penchant in the religious sphere for Manichaeanism, is that More, who was thought to be the "absolutist" of American criticism, was actually a good deal less absolutist and a great deal more flexible in specific judgments than many of his "liberal" opponents. In what is, so far as I know, his largest and most inclusive statement about history, "The Quest of A Century," he subsumed all man's experience, from ancient Hindus to modern Americans, under a drama, the terms of which are rest, which is relatively good, and change and motion, which are necessary but relatively evil. But the real evil is the irreconcilability of the two terms:

It is possible, I believe, to view the ceaseless intellectual fluctuations of mankind backward and forward as the varying fortunes of the contest between those two hostile members of our being,—between the deeply-lying principle that impels us to seek rest and the principle that drags us back into the region of change and motion and forever forbids us to acquiesce in what is found.[56]

He then goes on to show that the Hindus tried to achieve the impossible, a complete commitment to rest, by explaining away change as an illusion; that the Greeks, temporarily, achieved a

56. Paul Elmer More, *Shelburne Essays* (*Third Series*) (New York, 1906), p. 245.

balance between the two principles; that the nominalist-realist controversy of the Schoolmen was essentially a debate over this same dilemma; and that modernism and the belief in progress constitutes as complete a commitment to change as was the Hindus' commitment to rest. And, finally, he observes: "The meaning of all this is quite plain: there is no reach of the human intellect which can bridge the gap between motion and rest."[57] Religion tries to veil this gap, metaphysics to explain it away, but the only way to live with it is to find a middle way. And More, in other fields, was always and actively against extreme positions of any kind. As he said in "The Demon of the Absolute": "This Demon of the Absolute is nothing else but rationalism, what Francis Bacon called the *intellectus sibi permissus* or, if you wish it in plain English, reason run amuck."[58] And again, "For there are no absolutes in nature; they are phantoms created by reason itself . . ."[59] More goes on to show, with some justice, that other critics were generally more absolutistic than was he. Mencken's drama of himself battling the college professors was, according to More, sheer extravagance: "On one side is set up a monster of pedantry and over against him is ranged the genius who champions complete irresponsibility of temperament."[60] Again More attacks Spingarn for this same touch of fanaticism: ". . . we have scholars like Mr. Spingarn, who, with the involved sort of pedantry common today, teach a ready public that art is only expression and criticism only impression."[61] And there was, in most of these critics, a tendency towards absolutism or what I have called cultural Manichaeanism, and I suspect that when the final history of the period is written Paul Elmer More will go down as more of a "liberal" and many of the others as more "authoritarian" than once they were thought to be.

But it is not surprising that the Manichaeanism that seems to lurk, conscious or unconscious, in the human mind, should have

57. *Ibid.*, p. 263.
58. Paul Elmer More, "The Demon of the Absolute," in Charles I. Glicksburg, *American Literary Criticism* (New York, 1951), p. 258.
59. *Ibid.*
60 *Ibid.*, p. 261.
61. *Ibid.*, p. 262.

erupted in literary criticism, as it did in the nineteenth century and even more vehemently in the twentieth. A hundred years before so stout a rationalist as James Mill had said to his son that he was surprised that, what with the decline of formal Christianity, this had not already happened; as Mill says in the *Autobiography*:

The Sabaean or Manichean theory of a Good and an Evil principle, struggling against each other for the government of the universe, he would not have. . . . condemned: and I have heard him express surprise, that no one revived it in our times. He would have regarded it as a mere hypothesis; but he would have ascribed to it no depraving influence.[62]

Not all the notable critics of the day, however, were engaged in constructing historical dramas. In fact it was precisely the objection of Spingarn, Pound, and Eliot that these cultural speculations were not, properly speaking, criticism at all. And for Eliot the unconscious attempt to make literature a substitute for religion was a lamentable *mélange des genres*.

III

Spingarn, it is true, took up the problem of history, but he solved it by denying its validity. It should not concern the critic: "We have done with the history and criticism of poetic themes,"[63] and he went on to attack such historical critics as Taine. In this respect he has some affinities to certain practitioners of what we now call "The New Criticism." Yet Spingarn's "New Criticism" failed to capture distinguished supporters and to build up a school as the other "New Criticism" so notably has done. And Spingarn failed because he lacked what the "New Criticism" indubitably possesses, that is, a method of analyzing specific works of literature. On the other hand, Pound and Eliot succeeded in influencing other critics because they provided specific examples of practical criticism and because they were concerned with the methodology of criticism, all this enhanced by their authority as poets. In fact it is im-

62. John Stuart Mill, *Autobiography* (Oxford World Classics, 1924), p. 33.
63. Joel E. Spingarn, *Creative Criticism* (New York, 1917), p. 33.

possible to assess the significance of Pound and Eliot in criticism without assessing their aims and influence as creative writers.

For they were engaged most deeply in their early careers in effecting a revolution in poetry, and it is not presumptuous to say that they have been the Coleridge and Wordsworth of their time. Against a background of war, revolution, and a passionate upsurge of ideology, they have striven for and been successful, like the Romantics a century before, in bringing poetry back to the vernacular and in claiming for poetry the right to use "unpoetic" subjects—"dolts," operating tables, and young men carbuncular. As eighteenth century rhythms and diction had seemed stilted and conventional in the early nineteenth century, so late Victorian poetry, which was essentially a continuation of Romantic modes, seemed stultifying to the twentieth. Fully conscious himself of this historical role, Eliot said in *The Use of Poetry and The Use of Criticism*:

I myself can remember a time when some question of "poetic diction" was in the air; when Ezra Pound issued his statement that "poetry ought to be as well written as prose"; and when he and I and our colleagues were mentioned by a writer in *The Morning Post* as "literary bolsheviks" . . . But I think that we believed that we were affirming forgotten standards, rather than setting up new idols. Wordsworth, when he said that his purpose was "to imitate, and as far as possible, to adopt, the very language of men," was only saying in other words what Dryden had said, and fighting the battle that Dryden had fought. . . .[64]

And Dryden is celebrated for connecting the poetry of his time, which had fallen under the spell of the Donne or Milton tradition, to speech and to prose: ". . . if verse should not stray too far from the customs of speech, so also it should not abandon too much the uses of prose."[65] Milton had left the language like "the club of Hercules, which no lesser strength could wield."[66] But it was Dryden "who formed a language possible for mediocrity, and yet possible for later great writers to do

64. T. S. Eliot, *The Use of Poetry and the Use of Criticism* (Cambridge, 1933), p. 62.

65. T. S. Eliot, *John Dryden* (New York, 1932), p. 15.

66. *Ibid.*, p. 22.

great things with."[67] Thus the history of English poetry is a ceaseless dialectic between poetic convention and speech (and/or prose), and Pound and Eliot, among others, were attempting to perform the ever-recurring task of reminding verse of its verbal origins. It would be a mistake, of course, to multiply resemblances between Eliot and Pound and Wordsworth and Coleridge. As, in a sense, the Romantics had reacted away from "wit" and the "metaphysical conceit," the moderns have reacted back to it, in attempting to recapture verbal patterns that the Romantics and Victorians had abandoned. And while both the Romantics and the moderns have been in a sense under the spell of and have been influenced by French culture, in the one case it was a liberal political ideology, in the other it has been a scrupulously non-political esthetic.

In any event a change in diction, as Eliot said, is not a mere juggling of words, but is proof and example of wider changes in society as a whole: "Any radical change of poetic form is likely to be the symptom of some very much deeper change in society and in the individual."[68] It follows, naturally, that poetry and criticism go hand in hand: "I can only affirm that there is a significant relation between the best poetry and the best criticism of the same period."[69] And the great critics were the poet-critics, who united the two attitudes in their own persons. It is in this role that Pound and Eliot may be regarded as a counter-attack in criticism in the name of the poet himself. Most of the important critics of the time were not creative writers, and Norman Foerster in 1930 remarked: ". . . a divorce has occurred between criticism and the most vital creation."[70] But Pound and Eliot had long since set out to restore the union.

Moreover the times were propitious for a new approach. Conscious again of his historical role here Eliot said: "So our criticism, from age to age, will reflect the things that the age demands; and the criticism of no one man and no one age can be expected to embrace the whole nature of poetry or exhaust

67. *Ibid.*
68. Eliot, *The Use of Poetry*, p. 67.
69. *Ibid.*, p. 20.
70. Norman Foerster, ed. *American Critical Essays* (London, 1930), p. vii.

all of its uses."[71] Nor is it accidental that, at just this time, the logical positivists were descending on language to prove that the whole philosophical problem was essentially verbal and that psychoanalysis, the confessional for modern man, should be essentially verbal in approach. So in literary criticism Eliot and Pound, in their early days, converged on words and spoke from the point of view of the writer and not the Arnoldian critic of society. In fact Arnold himself was regarded as the enemy by Eliot: " . . . he [Arnold] was always getting off [specific literary criticism] into something else and this is to be regretted . . . he wasted his strength."[72] But Pound and Eliot were the veritable incarnation of the attitude of the young writer, who, finally, cares about nothing but the technique of writing. Malcolm Cowley in *Exile's Return* tells of receiving a letter from young Kenneth Burke, in which Burke voices the credo: ". . . to lie or cheat as a last resort, but never write any sloppy prose."[73]

Out of this same creative but anti-speculative attitude came Pound's various dictums: "I do not like writing about art. . . ."[74] Or: "I think we need a convenient anthology rather than a descriptive criticism."[75] Coupled to this was an historical attitude that said simultaneously all history is our province and that much of history is a mistake: "De Gourmont prepared our era; behind him there stretches a limitless darkness. . . ."[76] History, according to Pound, generally consists of times when the "Word" is pure and times when it is impure. As a writer you seek out the pure periods, not to find a Manichaean struggle, but rather to study verbal techniques for your own edification as a writer. In any event "All ages are contemporaneous."[77] And thus, in a sense, historical considerations do not count.

Eliot likewise urged a scrupulous regard for technique and an ahistorical attitude. In the "Perfect Critic" he said that all criticism in English since Arnold was either vague impression-

71. Eliot, *The Use of Poetry*, p. 134.
72. T. S. Eliot, *The Sacred Wood* (London, 1932), p. XIII.
73. Malcolm Cowley, *Exile's Return* (New York, 1934), p. 28.
74. Ezra Pound, *Pavannes and Divisions* (New York, 1918), p. 101.
75. *Ibid.*, p. 109.
76. Ezra Pound, *Instigations* (New York, 1920), p. 169.
77. Ezra Pound, *The Spirit of Romance* (London, 1920), p. vi.

ism or empty verbalizing. Criticism suffered from two complementary defects: it was always getting away from literature itself and when it did talk of literature it was vague and verbose.
It was not that one should not have opinions on morals, politics,
and religion, but these should be kept separate from literary
criticism. And in "The Function of a Literary Review," he
pronounced:

A literary review should maintain the application, in literature, of
principles which should have their consequences also in politics and
in private conduct; and it should maintain them without tolerating
any confusion of the purposes of politics or ethics.[78]

Out of this attitude came the famous definition of poetry as a
"superior form of amusement," the real intent of which is not
to say that poetry is un-serious but rather that is it "autotelic."

If the critic as critic should stay out of politics and morals,
he should also stick close to the text: "Analysis and comparison
methodically, with sensitiveness, intelligence, curiosity, intensity
of passion, and infinite knowledge: all these are necessary to the
great critic."[79] And "The critic is interested in technique—
technique in the widest sense . . . And to the poet only the
criticism of poets is useful."[80] At one time anyway Eliot said
that he did not believe that anybody except a creative writer
had anything worthwhile to say about writing, a proscription
which would have ruled out, by definition, most of the other
American critics of the time, and he would always say, in any
event, that the highest form of criticism is the criticism that
the creative writer himself performs on his own work.

His early attitudes on history, although more complex than
those of Pound and although all who have been influenced by
them—and the number seems legion—have over-simplified them,
have given currency to that same sense of timelessness that
Pound urges on the man of letters. The most famous pronouncement, of course, comes from that seminal essay "Tradition and
the Individual Talent": "The existing monuments form an ideal

78. T. S. Eliot, "Function of a Literary Review," *Criterion,* I (July 23, 1922), p. 421.
79. T. S. Eliot, "Criticism in England," *Athenaeum* 4650 (June 13, 1919), p. 457.
80. T. S. Eliot, "A Brief Treastise on the Criticism of Poetry," *The Chapbook* II
(March, 1920), p. 3.

order among themselves, which is modified by the introduction of the new (the really new) work of art among them."[81]

This intriguing and, it has always seemed to me, equivocal, statement, which is subsequently qualified in various ways, can be taken to mean many things, but in so far as Eliot has influenced the New Criticism, it has been taken in the same sense as his other famous pronouncement on history: ". . . to see the best work of our time and the best work of twenty-five hundred years ago with the same eyes."[82] As we know, Eliot has since moved on to perform once again the labors of Matthew Arnold, but in his early career he combined with Pound to produce a powerful climate of opinion which said in effect that the Battle of the Books of the twenties was not literary criticism at all and that the only function of criticism is to talk about literature and then to concentrate particularly on techniques and means. As the young Eliot said of the Elizabethans: ". . . we cannot grasp them, understand them without some understanding of the pathology of rhetoric. Rhetoric, a particular form of rhetoric was endemic, it pervaded the whole organism."[83] Thus to know the Elizabethan's verbal techniques is to know the Elizabethans.

Not the least of Eliot's appeal lay in the fact that his prose style seemed to exemplify his critical principles. Sober (if sometimes pompous), precise (if over fastidious), clear (if deceptively so), concerned with expressing clearly new ideas, it seemed to be a veritable embodiment of the new classicism that Eliot, following Hulme, was ushering in. While Eliot's ideas were directed at the fuzziness or vagueness of prevailing criticism, his style implicitly condemned verbosity or rhetorical flights.

Reenforcing all these counter-revolutions in criticism by Eliot and Pound was the fact that each had become an expatriate. By this act each indicated that he considered the Battle of the Books, which was essentially a search for a "usable" past in American terms, as a non-important scramble in a sub-culture or, at least, an unformed culture. Against America and the present, they asserted Europe and the past.

81. Eliot, *The Sacred Wood*, p. 50.
82. *Ibid.*, p. XVI.   83. *Ibid.*, p. 30.

The influence of Pound and Eliot, while not immediately discernible in the twenties, and although certainly its chief effect was to be felt later (after its original proponents were interested in different things), was nevertheless unmistakable. Edmund Wilson said in the twenties that criticism of the future was equally divided between the Manichaean and the "artistic" impulse: "It may be said that Mencken and Eliot between them rule the students of the Eastern universities."[84] In a sense this situation prophetically adumbrates the present contretemps in the academic world between historical studies and criticism.

IV

It remains to be asked—what happened to American criticism during the period? What was added that could be passed on to future generations? First, there was a shift in subject matter. The great Victorian authors, who had dominated critical thinking for decades, were pushed back, at the least, into the middle distance and, at the most, out of sight. The reputations of George Eliot and Dickens, for example, were at their nadir in the early years of the twentieth century. At the same time three new groups of interests emerged: American literature in its entirety; the generation of Wells, Shaw and Dreiser; and, later on, the generation of Joyce, Proust and Eliot.

Studies of American literature received impetus from various sources and directions. The most important perhaps was the liberalist revaluation, first sketched by Macy and later given epic sweep and documentation by Parrington. This great resettling was to have the effect of deflating the New Englanders and of making American literature seem to be cisatlantic and continental and linked to an ideology, the Jeffersonian, which lay at the very origin of American history. Parrington made his mistakes—they have been pointed out *ad infinitum* by subsequent critics and scholars—but his history still stands as the first and only literary history produced by an American about America that can bear comparison to the work of Brandes or

84. Wilson, *The Shores of Light,* p. 364.

Croce. It is not too much to say that practically all histories of American literature since the *Main Currents* are attempts to correct, not eradicate, Parrington's basic insight and metaphor, the most notable instances being Matthiessen's *The American Renaissance* and Kazin's *On Native Grounds.* The great conservative or the purely esthetic interpretations of American culture, which have so often been called for, have not yet appeared.

Parrington was an academician and was thus symptomatic of the institutionalizing of American literary studies that occurred in the twenties. It is true that serious scholarly histories, such as that of Moses Coit Tyler, and serious responsible criticism, such as Brownell's *American Prose Masters,* had been written earlier. The academically trained Stuart P. Sherman, in rebellion against the medievalism of Kittredge's Harvard, had long urged the serious study of American literature. And the *Cambridge History of American Literature* appeared in 1917-1921. Yet in 1928 Norman Foerster, in the introduction to *The Reinterpretation of American Literature,* could still call the state of American scholarship "deplorable." Not only were many of the relevant facts unknown, but there were no lucid generalizations to illumine the facts that were known.[85] But *The Reinterpretation* itself, called by Howard Mumford Jones "the key to much that has been written since"[86] was, in a way, a turning point, and its objective, organized scholarship devoted to American literature, has since been realized.

A third factor operating in the efflorescence of American literary studies was the rediscovery of complex and hitherto obscure literary figures such as Emily Dickinson, Melville, and Poe. At the same time the precarious reputation of Henry James began to assume the portentous face that it was to show to later generations. Even the fervently patriotic Stuart P. Sherman claimed that he "adored" this expatriate. And it was becoming apparent that American culture had produced not only *simplistes*—"Who reads an American book?" Sydney Smith had

85. *The Reinterpretation of American Literature,* ed. Norman Foerster, (New York, 1928), p. ix.

86. Howard Mumford Jones, *The Theory of American Literature* (Ithaca, 1948), p. 168.

asked—but perverse, tormented, ambiguous, complex writers, from whom, as in the case of Poe, wise corrupt old Europe herself was learning things she had not known or remembering things she had forgotten. At the same time the newer American writers were accepted, after some initial skirmishing, as serious and talented and worthy of critical analysis. Dreiser, especially, Sherwood Anderson, Sinclair Lewis, among others, all received their due. The poets were almost immediately recognized as important and were immortalized by having their work denominated a "Renaissance."

Simultaneously two new generations of European writers were engaging the attentions of American critics, and William A. Drake's *American Criticism, 1926* included essays on Arthur Symons, Anatole France, and Proust. The first generation, of which France and Shaw are good examples, was welcomed for its iconoclasm. But once the old taboos had been smashed, when Mencken's work had been done, the balance shifted to an esthetic emphasis and the next group of great European writers, such as Proust or Joyce, provided massive materials for esthetic analysis. The table of contents of Edmund Wilson's *Axel's Castle* (1931) sounds like a veritable roll-call of the literary movement and the European writers who were to engage the talents of American critics for years to come, down to and including the present day. The subject matter of *Axel's Castle* was "Symbolism" and the authors discussed were Yeats, Valery, Eliot, Proust, Joyce, Stein, de l'Isle-Adam, and Rimbaud. The amount of critical exegesis that has been performed on this movement and on these writers since 1931 staggers the imagination.

But not only the subject matter of criticism underwent a significant change during the period. Attitudes and assumptions altered radically as well. First, there was a new sense of spaciousness and amplitude, which came out in a variety of ways. Taboo subjects, such as sex, were brought out into the open. Old values were called into question and new ones were advanced. The subject matter and interests of criticism were enormously enlarged in various ways; there was first a horizontal extension, particularly into psychology, sociology, philosophical esthetics, and the other arts, and a further extension culturally by the taking into account of foreign critical theory. The table of contents of E. P. Burgum's *The New Criticism,* published in 1930, is instructive, for it included estheticians, both English and Italian, art critics, English and French, a music critic, a Spanish literary critic, a German historian, along with such standard inclusions as Spingarn, I. A. Richards, and Eliot. And in the introduction Burgum asserts that "new theories of aesthetics"[87] are being advanced, that "critics are seeking to bring to their knowledge of literature the aid of modern philosophy and psychology,"[88] and that modern research shows that "all the arts have a common esthetic element."[89]

Added to this theoretical expansion, there was a turning away from English literature as Huneker had signified, to the other literatures of Europe. Pound, in his usual fashion, made the strongest claim for European cosmopolitanism:

He [the true artist] writes not the popular language of any country, but an international tongue common to the excessively cultivated, and to those more or less familiar with French literature of the first three-fourths of the nineteenth century.[90]

Babbitt, More, Mencken, Lewisohn, Eliot and others all urged a cosmopolitan taste in literature. Lewisohn reminded his fellow critics in the battle that what they were going through was a struggle which literary men had had to go through in practically all the Western countries, and in the introduction to his anthology, *A Modern Book of Criticism,* which included essays by French, German, Irish, and American critics, he told the younger critics that they were not alone and that, first:

. . . their battle was fought and won in France thirty years ago; secondly, that in Germany, where the heritage of Goethe's supreme vision made the battle needless, a complete philosophical basis for the new criticism has been provided; thirdly, and most obviously, that the

87. E. P. Burgum, *The New Criticism* (New York, 1930), p. v.
88. *Ibid.,* pp. v-vi.
89. *Ibid.,* p. vi.
90. Pound, *Instigations,* p. 18.

chief creative minds of contemporary England and Ireland are fighting with them.[91]

If there was an extension in width in American criticism at this time, there was also an extension in depth, backward into time, and the massive door that the nineteenth century had opened on the fathomless abysses to the rear was now swung wide open. More's sweep was majestical—Oriental thought, Greek thought, western philosophical and theological speculations, all this backed by a solid factual knowledge of western history in general. His own sense of history was almost monstrous, a compound of horror and glory, and he said: "We are living in the past, we who foolishly cry out that the past is dead."[92] And further: "Great music is a psychical storm, agitating to fathomless depths the mystery of the past within us."[93] And again: ". . . genius itself is nothing other than the reverberation of this enormous past on the sounding board of some human intelligence."[94]

The Marxist critics, such as Calverton, helped to establish, even for non-Marxists, this sense of the enormity of the past and of the urgency with which one must travel back up the stream to ultimate sources. Moreover, the Marxist analysis of history had some of the appeal of the literary epic—sweep, drama, and inexorability. In the twenties, and even before, there began to appear the gigantic Marxist generalizations. In a short essay the writer would guide the reader, in wide dialectical sweeps, through the history of the Western world. This helped to establish a climate of opinion.

One of the major significances of this turning back to the sources was the resurgence of an interest that had always enchanted Western man, that is, Oriental thought and art. In this sphere one could bring together such mutual antagonisms as Pound and More. More's and Babbitt's interest was ethical and philosophical, while Pound's was largely esthetic; the common

91. Ludwig Lewisohn, ed. *A Modern Book of Criticism* (Modern Library, n.d.), p. iv. The introduction was written in 1919.
92. More, *Shelburne Essays* (Second Series), p. 65.
93. *Ibid.*, p. 64.
94. *Ibid.*, p. 65.

bond was a feeling that Western man and Western thought must arrive at a rapproachment with the East. Nor was it an academic interest, and Babbitt, for example, posed issues that today grow hourly more thunderous, when in 1924 he denounced the nations of the West both for their mutual slaughter and for inflicting "their imperialism and racial swagger on about nine hundred millions of Asiatics. . . ."[95]

But even more urgent and explicit was the desire to come to terms with Europe and the European heritage. At first glance it would appear, simply, that the literary center of gravity during the period had shifted from the eastern seaboard to the midwest. Whitman had predicted the shift in 1871, but history, as usual, was to move slower than its prophets' estimates. For it was not until the end of the nineteenth century that the switch from Boston to New York as center was finally accomplished. Even after that, writers, no matter what their origin, tended to gravitate to the east. But the essential talent in both imaginative and critical writing in the first decades of the twentieth century seemed to have come out of the Middle West, and Chicago was its Florence. This displacement however of the literary center of gravity was not simply another move in the great glacial shift of American culture towards the west, but was complicated by the fact that the atmosphere of literary Chicago was itself cosmopolitan. And it would be more proper to say that the literary milieu of Chicago in the early twentieth century was, as it has always been in the east, a complex of conflicting and complementary forces looking both before and after, to the Pacific and the future and to Europe and the past. As Sinclair Lewis pointed out, the original settlers of the Mid West in the nineteenth century fought soil and weather like a "Saxon peasant" in the year 1000, but the third generation was internationalist: "They and their families have in sixty years covered three centuries of cultural history, from Wesleyanism to Freudianism, from witchcraft to hysteria."[96] But this "jump from potatoes

95. *Democracy and Leadership*, p. 154.

96. Sinclair Lewis, *The Man From Main Street*, ed. Harry E. Maule and Melville Cane (New York, 1953), p. 176.

straight to Proust,"[97] said Lewis, was "characteristically" American. And thus Hemingway learned to write of his midwestern boyhood on the left bank of the Seine, and thus the age-old conflict between East and West that underlies American culture was not dispelled in the early twentieth century but shifted its standing-ground from the Atlantic seaboard to the heartland. If anything the problem was exacerbated during the period as a whole.

For it was as if the physiognomy of American criticism which hitherto had been, at its best, forward looking and prophetic, had now, at its best, become backward looking and critical. And the confusion of the period and the lopsidedness of the arguments demonstrate that American culture had still not solved its paradoxical relationship to Europe. It can be argued that there is no such problem, but I should be inclined still to agree with Santayana's celebrated formulation: "The country was new, but the race was tried, chastened and full of solemn memories. It was old wine in new bottles."[98] In a sense one might say that the Great Debate arose out of a mass feeling of guilt among the intellectuals that their culture had not fully realized its promises, as Eliot and Pound had said more explicitly.

For centuries the dream of a sanctuary in the West has haunted the European imagination, of which America is still a part. Practically all the European peoples, borne down on as they are by their mutual legions, with the great glacier which is Russia always at their backs, have instinctively and primordially placed their mythical resting place, their happy valley, in a region beyond the sea to the West. And America, the end product of the vast migratory movements that have agitated the peoples of Europe since the sixteenth century, was the literal incarnation of that dream. It has always been America's writers and intellectuals, those most haunted by the old dreams of the old world, who have lamented the tarnishing of the myth. This they still do, for the question is still open.

97. *Ibid.*, p. 177.
98. Santayana, *Winds of Doctrine*, p. 186.

C. Hugh Holman

THE DEFENSE OF ART:
CRITICISM SINCE
1930

A S FOR LITERARY CRITICISM," says Allen Tate, speaking of contemporary states of knowledge, "we here encounter a stench and murk not unlike that of a battlefield three days after the fighting is over and the armies have departed."[1] The fact that none of us can make a record of criticism during the last twenty-five years except as a combatant or as an injured bystander indicates the magnitude of the certain but now undetectable errors that a historian of criticism since 1930 is doomed to make.

In the first place, the historian is without the services of perhaps the justest, probably the most effective, and certainly the most authoritative critic of criticism—*time*; and he finds himself viewing, studying, and sometimes reverencing chaff that the winnowing of the years will utterly remove from later historical notice. We stand too near the stream of criticism in the thirties and forties to distinguish with certainty its main currents and its eddies. And this astigmatic view is still further distorted by the partisan passion with which the critical issues first swam into the historian's ken. When so fine a writer as Ernest Hemingway declares in 1932, "But regardless of how they [the New Humanists] started I hope to see the finish of a few, and speculate how worms will try that long preserved sterility; with their

1. Allen Tate, *The Forlorn Demon* (Chicago, 1953), p. 98.

[199]

quaint pamphlets gone to bust and into foot-notes all their lust,"[2] we know that he is almost ludicrously wrong; for the finish not merely of a few New Humanists, but of the entire movement had already been practically accomplished. Yet one who was thus passionately in the New Humanist struggle—whether for it or against it—will have difficulty relegating the movement to its quite minor role.

In the second place, the history of criticism, when it is accurately written, is more nearly a record of individual critical experiences with art than a chronicle of critical movements. Allen Tate seems unimpeachable when he declares, "It has seemed to me that the best criticism at all times has its best function in the ordering of original insights and in passing them on, through provisional frames of reference, to other persons secondhand."[3] The seminal critics in a given period, although they found its schools, in their individuality and insight transcend the schools they found. As Malcolm Cowley has pointed out, "Where Mr. Ransom and Mr. Tate, for example, are miles apart in many of their judgments, young Mr. X. who has listened to both of them and read both of them, seems to be a conglomeration or coagulation of Ransom and Tate. Young Mr. X represents the school—not Ransom, or Tate or Blackmur."[4] Here again we need the perspective of temporal distance in order to see which of the trees in our local forest outtop the rest.

However, criticism is an always unique fusion of the *Zeitgeist* and the critical personality, and no matter how individual he may be the complex of thought and event within which a critic works determines many aspects of his criticism, a point which Frederick A. Pottle has made convincingly.[5] So it is largely in terms of the various movements that have grown out of the peculiar demands of our age that I shall attempt to sketch the course of criticism in the past quarter of a century, noting the movements without

2. Ernest Hemingway, *Death in the Afternoon* (New York, 1952), p. 139.
3. Tate, *The Forlorn Demon*, p. 162.
4. Symposium on "The New Criticism," Act II, *American Scholar*, XX (1951), 220.
5. In "The Case of Shelley," *PMLA*, LXVII (1952), 589-608; "The New Critics and the Historical Method," *Yale Review* (1953), XLIII, 14-23; *The Idiom of Poetry* (Ithaca, N. Y., 1941), where he says, "In poetry each age has a *unique* problem," p. 31.

attempting a serious evaluation of them. I suspect that Philip Wheelwright is correct when he calls the "three elements of contemporary criticism—the anthropological, the psychological, and the semantic,"[6] but certainly the sociological and the historical need to be added if we are attempting a record rather than an evaluation. By such a method as I shall follow, however, movements which represented only immediately significant responses to the pressures of their age and which produced no critics of sufficient strength to give them enduring vitality come in for a disproportionately large share of the record; and by forcing the various critics into movements the distinctive qualities of individual critics are lost. For example, one feels fairly certain that a hundred years from now these "movements" will be forgotten and a few sharply defined critical personalities will seem to have held undisputed critical sway in the second quarter of the twentieth century. Furthermore, to attempt anything other than the loosest kind of chronology seems impractical for such a period. I shall attempt to discuss the significant "movements," or "group responses," taking them in general movement by movement.

The MLA Committee on Research Activities has declared that "The essential nature of literary criticism turns on value judgments. In all of its forms, literary criticism has evaluation or judgment as its purpose. It is this characteristic which distinguishes criticism from other forms of literary scholarship."[7] Wayne Shumaker has called the ultimate critical goal "the *full, evaluated apprehension of the critical subject matter*."[8] Each age creates the proposition or propositions which lie behind its value judgments, literary and otherwise. In a sense the broad types of criticism, what Allen Tate calls the "provisional frames of reference," are expressions of the propositions the age makes or accepts. When a proposition in an era is held with vigor and

6. Philip Wheelwright, "Mimesis and Katharsis: an Archetypal Consideration," *English Institute Essays, 1951* (New York, 1952), p. 5.

7. "The Aims, Methods, and Materials of Research in the Modern Languages and Literatures," *PMLA*, LXVII (1952), 29.

8. Wayne Shumaker, *Elements of Critical Theory* (Berkeley, Calif., 1952), p. 13.

reasonable unanimity, the criticism of that era presents a corresponding unity, and the proposition needs little defense, for it is not often attacked. But when an era contains conflicts between propositions that seem to struggle on fairly even grounds, the underlying judgments of literary critics become infected with the same "dissociation of sensibility"; and criticism, like literature, loses its unity and becomes a subject for endless dispute.

The contemporary period has been called an Age of Anxiety, of the Great Depression, of the *Beat* (as opposed to *Lost*) Generation, of Modern Man's Obsolescence, but not often, if at all, an age of hope or certainty or unity. It is because these epithets describe modern America with reasonable accuracy that the period has also been one of criticism, for an age becomes critical because there are elements in it that call forth criticism. It is the presence of passionately fought critical wars and not the presence of great critics that makes a critical period. Ours is a critical age because of the skepticisms with which art is viewed in our time—skepticisms that are the propositions of our era. The critic, when he is more than a mere reviewer or a historian, is the defender and justifier of art, either implicitly or explicitly, and current American criticism differs most from that of the past in the intensity and thoroughness with which it examines, by a variety of methods, the fundamental values of art—values which other, and perhaps happier, ages assumed without inquiry or analysis.

Of course, the basic attacks on the ultimate validity of literature which our age has made are not new. In some form or other they have been present and burgeoning throughout the century, but the stock market crash of November, 1929, with its attendant hunger, fear, breadlines, bonus marches, and Hoovervilles, produced an atmosphere of crisis within which technological man's implicit distrust of the arts sprouted, like bacteria in a heated culture, into explicit attacks upon the place and seriousness of artistic endeavor. It was the age of that unconscious parody of science-fiction, Rex Tugwell's "technocracy," when millions of people toyed seriously with the idea of evaluating man by an erg-meter to measure his expended energy. Little wonder that Allen Tate felt that "The poet finds himself balanced upon the moment when a world is about to fall."[9] "The realist and aesthetic critics found their claims diminishing under harsh dispute," Morton D. Zabel notes, adding that "the awakened sense of social responsibility in reformers took aesthetic and liberal doctrines as its chief object of attack."[10] In *Exile's Return*[11] Malcolm Cowley has given us a moving record of what it was like to have lived a life dedicated to art as religion and then suddenly to be thrown into the suffering of an economic collapse.

In such an atmosphere the old, steady, but almost imperceptible retreat of literature before the persistent attacks of scientific materialism, pragmatism and logical positivism, the new psychologies, and the economic interpretations of history became no longer an ordered and dignified withdrawal but a panic-stricken rout. Seemingly confronted on every hand by the demand that literature justify itself in other terms than its own, by a widespread questioning of its fundamental validity, the writer and the critic alike seemed naked and afraid. In 1931 in *The Literary Mind: Its Place in an Age of Science*, a book which Alfred Kazin has called "a literary man's contemptuous valedictory to literary men,"[12] Max Eastman wrote:

Poetry is compelled by its very nature to yield up to science the task of interpreting experience, of finding out what we call truth, of giving men reliable guidance in the conduct of their lives. . . . A "literary truth," may therefore be defined—provisionally at least—as a truth which is either uncertain or comparatively unimportant.[13]

The writer was challenged on every side and frequently from within his own conscience to justify his place in the community of men and to show his relevance to a world of economic and

9. As quoted in Alfred Kazin, *On Native Grounds* (New York, 1942), pp. 403-404.

10. Morton D. Zabel, *Literary Opinion in America*, Revised edition (New York, 1951), p. 33.

11. Malcolm Cowley, *Exile's Return* (New York, 1934; Revised edition, New York, 1951).

12. Kazin, *On Native Grounds*, p. 404.

13. Max Eastman, *The Literary Mind: Its Place in an Age of Science* (New York, 1931), pp. 239, 244.

social suffering. Only among the academic scholars and historians, and by no means always there, was the examination of literature free from this soul-searching self-scrutiny and this violent attack from without.

These pressures in a sense pushed literature into an uninhabitable corner, and the patterns of criticism in our day have been shaped by the kinds of defensive actions the critics have fought in behalf of letters. The wide disagreement among the defenders as to what the value of literature is resulted in their often forgetting their common enemies in their arguments over how to attack him and in their exerting much of the effort that might more fruitfully have gone into the study of literature in an internecine struggle over how it should be defended. The period has been, therefore, one of embittered war, of intemperate overstatement, of half-truths, and of strange bed-fellows. Of the criticism of the whole period it can be said, as Allen Tate remarked about his book *Reason in Madness*, that its "convention . . . is attack."[14]

I

EXTRINSIC CRITICISM: MARXIST

Critics who would defend the value of literature fall into two major groups: those who tend to make a synthetic approach, finding the chief value of literature in its extrinsic relation to society and civilization, and those who tend to make an analytic approach, expecting thereby to demonstrate the intrinsic value of literature. Certainly few critics—and one is tempted to add, no good ones—use one approach exclusively. Yet it is upon this division that sides were taken in the bitter critical wars of the thirties.

The most obvious and immediate effect that the depression had on literature was a great increase in the emphasis on literature as a social tool. Certainly the sociological interpretation of literature was not new. Critics and writers in America had struck the social note with vigor for more than a half century. The very pattern of political liberalism, with its doctrines of

14. Allen Tate, *Reason in Madness* (New York, 1941), p. x.

perfectibility and progress, had implicitly asked for a socially significant literature for more than a century. The development of the theory of realism and its later scientific mutation, naturalism, seemed almost to presuppose the social involvement of the writer and the critic. And there had always been a leftist element among American writers and critics. Yet criticism of a radically sociological nature did not exist in quantity until the impact of the depression made itself widely felt in the American literary world. Such a sociological approach, as René Wellek and Austin Warren have indicated, is "particularly cultivated by those who profess a specific social philosophy."[15] In a broad sense, the doctrines of Karl Marx provided such a social philosophy for many who were not formal Marxists or Communists as well as for the growing numbers of those who were.

"Marxist criticism," as William Van O'Connor has noted, "in the twenties had few practitioners and was uninfluential."[16] *The Masses,* under Max Eastman and Floyd Dell, had been far from socially doctrinaire. When Michael Gold began to edit *New Masses* in 1928, a criticism that was explicitly Marxist began to appear. But probably a more influential force was the impressive assertion of the social conscience as a critical litmus paper in Vernon L. Parrington's *Main Currents in American Thought* (1927, 1930). It was the suffering that the depression brought painfully home to the artist, however, that gave the greatest impetus to the sociological interpretation of literature. V. F. Calverton declared in 1930: "The growth of this social attitude in art is in response to a great human need, paramount in these times of severe strain."[17] Edmund Wilson has described the period this way:

. . . at the end of the twenties, a kind of demoralization set in, and this was followed by a shrinkage of those values, and for the writer the conditions became different again. There was suddenly very little

15. René Wellek and Austin Warren, *Theory of Literature* (New York, 1949), p. 89.

16. William Van O'Connor, *An Age of Criticism 1900-1950* (Chicago, 1952), p. 116.

17. V. F. Calverton, *The New Ground of Criticism* (Seattle, 1930), p. 38.

money around, and the literary delirium seemed clearing . . . and the stock market lay gasping its last. The new "classes" of intellectuals—it was a feature of the post-Boom period that they tended to think of themselves as "intellectuals" rather than as "writers"—were in general sober and poor, and they applied the analysis of Marxism to the scene of wreckage they faced. This at least offered a discipline for the mind, gave a coherent picture of history and promised not only employment but the triumph of the constructive intellect.[18]

Alfred Kreymborg caught the feeling that turned many writers to a social interest in his sonnet "American Jeremiad":

> . . . .
> What shall a lover sing when half the land
> Is driving cold and lives on dank despair?
> As long as inhumanity's in the hand
> That runs the race and whips the poor apart,
> Lovers must all embrace a bloody air
> And strangle men who starve the human heart.[19]

In 1931 in *Axel's Castle*, one of the landmarks in historical criticism in this period, Edmund Wilson said:

. . . the time is at hand when these writers, who have largely dominated the literary world of the decade 1920-1930 . . . will no longer serve us as guides. Axel's world of the private imagination in isolation from the life of society seems to have been exploited and explored as far as for the present is possible . . . in America the comfortable enjoyment of what was supposed to be American prosperity . . . has given way to a sudden disquiet. . . . The question begins to press us again as to whether it is possible to make a practical success of human society, and whether, if we continue to fail, a few masterpieces, however profound or noble, will be able to make life worth living even for the few people in a position to enjoy them.[20]

As early as 1923, V. F. Calverton had founded *The Modern Quarterly*, a magazine that continued as an effective leftist voice

18. Edmund Wilson, "Thoughts on Being Bibliographed," *Classics and Commercials* (New York, 1950), pp. 107-108.

19. *Proletarian Literature in the United States*, edited by Granville Hicks and others (New York, 1935), p. 171.

20. Edmund Wilson, *Axel's Castle* (New York, 1931), pp. 292-293.

until 1940 and that achieved *Monthly* status between 1933 and 1938. In 1925, in *The Newer Spirit*, he had demanded a "sociological interpretation of literature," declaring, "Although revolutions in esthetics are due to revolutions in ideas, every revolution in ideas is a consequence of a revolution in the social structure that the prevailing material conditions have produced."[21] Among the numerous books which his wide interests produced, Calverton's most important work is *The Liberation of American Literature* (1932), a Marxist attempt to interpret American literature in terms of the nature of the social forces in America. It was, perhaps, because Calverton remained an independent radical, outside the Communist Party, that Joseph Freeman declared, "For a long time, Michael Gold and I were the only literary critics in the United States attempting to evaluate art and literature by revolutionary standards."[22] In any event, *New Masses,* which was the organ of formal Marxist criticism, from its founding in 1926 to its merger with *Mainstream* as *Masses and Mainstream* in 1948, assembled as its contributors a preponderance of those in America who viewed literature through the frame of dialectical materialism. The chief in importance among them was Granville Hicks, whose *The Great Tradition* (1933), a Marxist history of American literature since the Civil War, is one of the critical landmarks of the Marxist thirties.[23] Speaking before the College Conference on English, Central Atlantic States, in 1934, Hicks defined the somewhat naive simplicity of the Marxist method as he and most of his *New Masses* associates employed it:

. . . we can understand an author best if we examine his relation to the social movements of his time and to the class alignments out of which they grow. . . . What we have to ask, it seems to me, is whether a work of literature contributes to a world-attitude that is compatible with the aims and tasks of the proletariat and whether it tends to

21. V. F. Calverton, *The Newer Spirit* (New York, 1925), p. 51.

22. Joseph Freeman, "Ivory Towers—White and Red," *New Masses* (Sept. 11, 1934), 21.

23. Other landmarks are Calverton's *Liberation of American Literature, Proletarian Literature in the United States,* and Bernard Smith's *Forces in American Criticism* (1939).

build up a system of responses that will permit the proletarian to play his individual part in the coming struggle.[24]

Among those who followed Hicks's simple and clear path, unobstructed by serious aesthetic issues, were "Michael Gold" (Irving Granich), Joseph Freeman, and Joshua Kunitz. To this group of revolutionaries there was added the emotion, intelligence, and sensibility of the recently returned "expatriates," who moved from Paris cafes to political conferences and exchanged Dada gestures for political action. The chief of these was Malcolm Cowley, who as literary editor of *The New Republic,* was keenly conscious of social meanings in the broad pattern of dialectical materialism but who never subscribed to any "formula" method for the criticism of art. In this period, too, the growing sense of social involvement which the last chapter of *Axel's Castle* demonstrated, led Edmund Wilson to be a critic of the same general type, although it seems always to have been Taine rather than Marx who has supplied the broad framework of Wilson's thought. Strictly academic figures, such as Newton Arvin, also found inspiration and method in Marxist thought, and his *Whitman* (1938) stands as a fine example of the scholarly use of the dialectical method.

In 1935, Hicks and others edited an anthology *Proletarian Literature in the United States*, with a thoughtful introduction by Joseph Freeman, whose autobiography, *An American Testament*, published the next year, is a sensitive record of a radical critic. *Proletarian Literature* assembled the best of the radical writings of the early thirties. It reads almost like a manifesto for a bright new future, but in reality it is the swan song of a movement; for it was true of this group, as Wellek and Warren point out about Marxist critics in general, "They tell us not only what were and are the social relations and implications of an author's work but what they should have been or ought to be. They are not only students of literature and society but prophets of the future, monitors, propagandists."[25] The recogni-

24. Granville Hicks, "Literature and Revolution," in *American Literary Criticism 1900-1950*, edited by Charles I. Glicksberg (New York, 1951), pp. 418, 422.
25. Wellek and Warren, *Theory of Literature,* p. 90.

tion of this quality in the mid-thirties, when the institution of the People's Front was increasing the "either-or" nature of Marx-ist criticism, spelled the virtual end of the movement, in a literary sense, although it has continued in the political and social sphere to the present.

However, forces were at work which were to rescue much of the strength of the Marxist position from the naive critical methods by which it had been expressed. In 1934 the John Reed Club of New York founded the *Partisan Review*, a journal which was to avoid the pitfalls of party-line criticism, and which after its reorganization in 1937 became under William Phillips and Philip Rahv a magazine of distinguished and distinguishing in-dependent liberal and radical art and criticism, a position which it holds with honor today. In 1936 the novelist James T. Farrell, alarmed at the too-simple yardstick employed in most Marxist criticism, in *A Note on Literary Criticism* sounded a call to his fellow Marxists to repent their errors, forget their simple judg-ments, remember that literature cannot be equated with politics, and begin evaluating it in aesthetic terms. Edmund Wilson, after the trip to Russia reported in *Travels in Two Democracies* (1936), became impatient with the doctrinaire nature of Marxist art and in *The Triple Thinkers* (1938) refuted the Marxist aestheticians in an essay, "Marxism and Literature."

The crucial date for many of the Marxists and near Marxist critics was 1939, the year of the signing of the Russo-German Pact and the beginning of the Second World War. Granville Hicks, the best of the "party-line" critics, left both the Party and its literary position, and many others followed his course. In that same year Bernard Smith published *Forces in American Criticism*, which stretched American literary thought and theory on the Procrustean rack of class consciousness and demanded a scientifically Marxist critical system. Upon this note of unwar-ranted optimism the "Red Decade" in American criticism ended.

Although almost dead as a critical movement by 1940, Marx-ism is still a force in American literary theory, both in the impact it has made on our liberal critics and writers and in the continuing work of men like James T. Farrell. His *The League of Frightened Philistines* (1945) vigorously defended naturalism against the charge of "irresponsibility," and *Literature and Morality* (1947), in addition to studies of Tolstoi and Dostoievsky, demanded a social morality for the artist. Edwin Berry Burgum, who had belonged to the *New Masses* group, in 1947 assembled some of his critical essays in *The Novel and the World's Dilemma*. Stanley Edgar Hyman, in *The Armed Vision* (1948), made studies of the leading critics and formulated an "ideal" critic, who is a Marxist (among many other things) with all the elements of aesthetic knowledge, sensibility, and learning, the absence of which in most Marxist critics has often been derided.

The Marxist movement in American criticism has been vigorous, ingenious, and religiously consistent; but it has produced little that is significant either in artistic theory or in practice. Yet, though strangely empty of achievement, the movement, for all its sound and fury, has enriched criticism and still enriches it. For the passionate sense of involvement in life, the response to human needs, the intense preoccupation with literature as a life force—all these elements have helped to keep criticism in our time away from one of its most enticing refuges, the ivory tower.

II

EXTRINSIC CRITICISM: NON-MARXIST

The Marxist and near-Marxist movement in American criticism did not exhaust what Solomon Fishman has called, "The special fascination that social questions have for American critics."[26] Throughout the thirties and the forties a variety of critics and historians sought to find and make negotiable for the present a non-Marxist "usable past." Although comparatively few of them looked with admiration upon the work itself, most of them shared the motives which led Van Wyck Brooks to undertake his five-volume appraisal of the American literary past—a desire to find and express "the use of tradition, which

26. Solomon Fishman, *The Disinherited of Art: Writer and Background* (Berkeley, Calif., 1953), p. vi.

establishes a consensus about the dead and which causes them to live again, to fructify the present, to fertilize existing minds, and to stablize our values."[27] In 1936 *The Flowering of New England*, the first volume of Brooks's *Makers and Finders: A History of the Writer in America, 1800-1915*, appeared.[28] It was true of the five volumes as F. O. Matthiessen observed about the first: "His method for the most part is biographical and descriptive; he devotes the major part of his effort to establishing the ambient atmosphere in which the writers did their work."[29] Broadly similar aims probably were behind Henry Seidel Canby's *Classic Americans* (1931), *Thoreau* (1939), and *Walt Whitman, An American* (1943). Although less uncritically genial, Constance M. Rourke explored the resources of American folk traditions and made them an illuminating point of entry into critical and cultural history. Her *American Humor* (1931) illustrated her method and rendered her death in 1941, before the completion of her proposed three-volume *History of American Culture*, a serious loss to American criticism. Van Wyck Brooks in 1942 compiled from the body of manuscript materials she left a representative statement of her positions in *The Roots of American Culture*. Howard Mumford Jones has examined the American past for the ideational content it has for the present in several loosely organized groups of essays and brief books, the most important of which is his critical record of American literary history, *The Theory of American Literature* (1948). Floyd Stovall, in *American Idealism* (1943), studied the American literary past in terms of a liberal idealism. All these writers, in varying ways, have felt the need which F. O. Matthiessen saw in Brooks "to provide American readers with an image of the nobility and assurance of our past. He seems to feel that what we need most now is restored confidence."[30]

27. Van Wyck Brooks, *The Writer in America* (New York, 1953), p. 62.

28. In the order of their subject matter chronology, the volumes of *Makers and Finders* are: *The World of Washington Irving* (New York, 1944), *The Flowering of New England* (New York, 1936), *The Times of Melville and Whitman* (New York, 1947), *New England: Indian Summer* (New York, 1940), and *The Confident Years: 1885-1915* (New York, 1952).

29. F. O. Matthiessen, *The Responsibilities of the Critic* (New York, 1952), p. 201.

30. *Ibid.*, p. 238.

Matthiessen himself is magnificently representative of another and a more seriously critical aspect of the search for a "usable past." Primarily a literary and cultural historian, he brought to his task a keen critical judgment, a sharply analytical method, and a liberal political awareness that gave edge to his studies of earlier cultures. In almost everything he wrote is to be discerned his attempt, as Henry Nash Smith expresses it, "to effect a synthesis of a theory of art (the organic principle), a theory of tragedy, and a thoroughgoing democratic theory. . . . The quest for such an integration governed his scholarship, his teaching, and his political activity."[31] In *American Renaissance* (1941) his method, the seriousness of his purpose, and the complex ambiguities of his mixture of orthodox Christian theology and political liberalism are most apparent.

Closely allied to this essentially historical approach and colored by the passion of a pointedly political orientation is Alfred Kazin's extended record of American prose in this century, *On Native Grounds* (1942). However, Kazin lacks Matthiessen's tolerance and his knowledge, and painfully impresses upon us his wish to make political affiliation a substitute for critical judgment, particularly in his unwillingness to recognize the contributions of the New Critics and of the Marxists to our letters and literary theory. Maxwell Geismar in his continuing multivolumed study of the American novel since the Civil War, three volumes of which have now appeared—*Writers in Crisis*: *The American Novel, 1925-1940* (1942), *The Last of the Provincials*: *The American Novel, 1915-1925* (1947), and *Ancestors and Rebels*: *The American Novel, 1900-1915* (1953)—has made a group of what he calls "individual studies of the novelists who reflect and also help to form our changing cultural scene."[32] The primary orientation is sociological and politically liberal.

At the time of the outbreak of the Second World War, one group of critics issued a hortatory call for "responsibility" on the part of the writer and reader. Certainly the most vocal and

31. *F. O. Matthiessen (1902-1950) A Collective Portrait*, edited by Paul M. Sweezy and Leo Huberman (New York, 1950), p. 59.
32. Maxwell Geismar, *The Last of the Provincials* (Boston, 1947), p. vii.

probably the most influential of these critics was Bernard De-
Voto, who as editor of the *Saturday Review of Literature*, did
battle against most of the critical schools. In *Minority Report*
(1940) he disavowed all critical systems, and in *The Literary
Fallacy* (1944) he attacked the idea that "literature is the measure
of life, and . . . that life is subordinate to literature."[33] Believing
that no other nation or age had had itself so misrepresented by
its writers, he sounded repeatedly the call to truth and responsibility. Although, in *The World of Fiction* (1950) he deals
almost exclusively with the psychology of fiction, it is to discredit
fiction as a truly significant portion of reality and to declare that
it is "a reader's reprieve and absolution that novelists, whatever
else they may be besides, are also children talking to children
. . . in the dark."[34] Archibald MacLeish in 1940 joined the attack on the current literary and scholarly scene with "The Ir-
responsibles," a call to sociological involvement for the writer.
This sometimes nationalistic and always liberal demand that
writers, scholars, and critics place social and political objectives
above all else has been common in much of our newspaper criticism and in *The Saturday Review*. It is a measure of the tendency of the extrinsic critic to surrender the critical function to
the hortatory office, whether Marxist, liberal, or nationalistic.

Yet, despite the tendency of the search for a usable past to
find in that past what it seeks, despite the fact that many of its
practitioners have, as Matthiessen has pointed out, never "mastered a method, and . . . write with the eloquence of innocence,"[35]
the sociological approach has brought new and vital viewpoints
to contemporary criticism and, in the work of men like Edmund
Wilson, Harry Levin, and Lionel Trilling, has kept invigorat-
ingly before the critical reader an awareness that literature has
a relevance to life, a relevance within which at least one of its
principal virtues may be found. Edmund Wilson, in an essay
on "The Historical Interpretation of Literature," says:

33. Bernard DeVoto, *The Literary Fallacy* (Boston, 1944), p. 43.
34. Bernard DeVoto, *The World of Fiction* (Boston, 1950), p. 22. The elipsis is
DeVoto's.
35. Matthiessen, *The Responsibilities of the Critic,* p. 245.

It is possible to discriminate in a variety of ways the elements that in any given department go to make a successful work of literature. Different schools have at different times demanded different things of literature. . . . In my view, all our intellectual activity, in whatever field it takes place, is an attempt to give a meaning to our experience. . . . The mathematician Euclid, working in a convention of abstractions, shows us relations between the distances of our unwieldy and cluttered-up environment upon which we are able to count. A drama of Sophocles also indicates relations between the various human impulses, which appear so confused and dangerous, and it brings out a certain justice of Fate . . . upon which we can also depend. The kinship . . . of the purposes of science and art appears very clearly . . .[36]

Perhaps the clearest statement of the complexity of the extrinsic view of literature is Harry Levin's:

. . . the relations between literature and society are reciprocal. Literature is not only the effect of social causes; it is also the cause of social effects. . . . The fallacy . . . is to equate art with society, to assume a one-to-one correspondence between a book and its subject-matter, to accept the literature of an age as a complete and exact replica of the age itself.[37]

Levin stresses "conventions," literary *genres* as shaping devices, and forms as "institutions," and attempts to create an institutional method. This process asserts an extrinsic frame within which the work of art is to be judged, but does not impose upon it any particular social or political view.

Lionel Trilling is as keenly aware of the complexities of the relationship between literature and society as Harry Levin, and he brings to his criticism the added forces of a strongly liberal political bias and a pervasive knowledge of and respect for the psychology of Sigmund Freud. His collection of essays on literature and society, *The Liberal Imagination* (1950), stands with the best work of Edmund Wilson, as a reminder that some of the most incisive thinking and writing about literature during the last quarter of a century has had a broadly sociological

36. Edmund Wilson, "The Historical Interpretation of Literature," *American Literary Criticism*, pp. 494-496.

37. Harry Levin, "Literature as an Institution," in *Literary Opinion in America*, edited by Morton Dauwen Zabel, Revised edition (New York, 1951), pp. 660-661.

orientation. He rejects the simplifications of the more naive sociological critics and urges upon his reader an awareness of the rich complexity of literature, but he asserts too that

In the United States at this time liberalism is not only the dominant but even the sole intellectual tradition. . . . These are not political essays, they are essays in literary criticism. But they assume the inevitable intimate, if not always obvious, connection between literature and politics. . . .

The job of criticism would seem to be, then, to recall liberalism to its first essential imagination of variousness and possibility, which implies the awareness of complexity and difficulty. To the carrying out of the job of criticizing the liberal imagination, literature has a unique relevance, not merely because so much of modern literature has explicitly directed itself upon politics, but more importantly because literature is the human activity that takes the fullest and most precise account of variousness, possibility, complexity, and difficulty.[38]

In the essays in the collection, Trilling argues that the relation between creative literature and ideas is of "insistent importance for the modern critic." He praises the novel as doing "the unremitting work of involving the reader himself in the moral life." He attacks the New Critics for their refusal to value the historical changes in the meaning of works. Yet there is a willingness in Trilling to use the tools evolved by various critical schools freely and gracefully and to deal with art as form as well as substance.

One of the most valuable of the extrinsic approaches is that of Frederick A. Pottle, whose *The Idiom of Poetry* enunciates his "Doctrine of Critical Relativism," which is proving to be a useful mediating position between the analytical and the historical critics. Pottle divides the intrinsic and extrinsic into the subjective and historical, thereby doing them a little disservice but with interesting results; for the division enables him to define criticism thus:

It should begin with an honest and unflinching statement of the critic's own successes in reading. It will not pretend to raptures where there were none. It will be particularly pleased when it finds that some door which was shut for the preceding generation is ajar or

38. Lionel Trilling, *The Liberal Imagination* (New York, 1950), pp. ix, xi-xii, xv.

swinging open. That is one half of criticism, the subjective or personal. But the true critic will know that poetry—or, let us say, a poem—is an immortal thing. His criticism is only a bit of its ever-expanding life. The whole poem is his criticism plus all the other criticism it has evoked. To his own evaluation the critic will add a selection from what critics of the past have said about it, by no means limiting himself to judgments that coincide with his own. That is the other half of criticism, the historical.[39]

Through all the shades of political, sociological, and historical coloration and with varying degrees of tolerance and indignation, the socially and historically oriented criticism of literature on non-Marxist terms has continued to be practiced with distinction during this time when the polar extremes of Marxist and analytical criticism have sometimes seemed to represent the whole of the significant critical activity.

III
PSYCHOLOGICAL CRITICISM

Among the most powerful forces in producing the complex of attitudes toward man and art that forced the twentieth century artist and critic into his various defensive postures were the "new" psychology and anthropology, with their inquiries into the substrata of human thought and feeling. Yet it has been from this same material that much contemporary writing has drawn both its subject matter and its manner, and much criticism has found a method for the effective examination of art, an explanation of its origins, and a reason for its existence. Hardly a school or a significant critic in the last quarter of a century has been free of the impact of various modern psychologies; almost every critical school has a psychological premise underlying at least a portion of its method; and many of the justifications of art have had psychological implications, whether expressed as the need of the individual, the catharsis of the author, or the record of the group mind. Furthermore, in the loosely defined conflict between extrinsic and intrinsic values for literature, psychology has often proved to be the happy middle ground

39. Pottle, *The Idiom of Poetry*, p. 41.

where the seeming opposites can be fused. Thus, for example, the Marxist critic, the liberal non-Marxist, the literary biographer, and the analytical critic may find in the theories of Sigmund Freud a confused but mistily common ground on which they may meet, and the sociologically oriented critic may share with the analytically minded one a common concern over that psychologically fathered but nondescript child, the myth.

Few writers and almost no critics have employed psychological theories as more than "keys" to open the doors to new understandings; and, although it has often been forgotten, it is important to remember Frederick J. Hoffman's caveat:

> The role of the critic is to examine quite objectively the ideologies of his time, with a view toward noting their applicability to or difference from aesthetics. If he is to be respected, he must also recognize quite candidly and intelligently the important modal differences between intellectual or scientific and emotional or aesthetic points of view.[40]

The use of psychology in criticism usually results in the study of the artist, the study of the creative process, or the study of the individual work in terms of the psychological truths and suppositions that it contains or that help to explain it.[41] For each of these processes the germinal spirit has been Sigmund Freud, although modifications by Carl Jung and others, and a frame of reference supplied by anthropology have acted to qualify both the rigor and the positivism of Freud's position. A portion of the confusion that has existed in the application of Freudian ideas to literary criticism is inherent in certain of Freud's own statements. For example, Freud's interest in the neurotic basis for art has nurtured the psychoanalytical approach to literary biography; his interest in the unconscious springs of human action has supplied a standard for judging the "truthfulness" of the artists's picture of the world; his exploration of the unconscious has helped to formulate a variety of literary manners. This con-

40. Frederick J. Hoffman, *Freudianism and the Literary Mind* (Baton Rouge, 1945), p. 94.
41. See the succinct summary of these alternatives in Wellek and Warren, *Theory of Literature*, p. 75.

flicting set of attitudes is clearly expressed in one of Freud's best known brief pronouncements on art:

The artist is originally a man who turns from reality; with his special gifts he moulds his phantasies into a new kind of reality, because he cannot come to terms with the demand for the renunciation of instinctual satisfaction as it is first made, and who then in phantasy-life allows full play to his erotic and ambitious wishes. But he finds a way of return from this world of phantasy back to reality, and men concede them a justification as valuable reflections of actual life. Thus by a certain path he actually becomes the hero, king, creator, favourite he desired to be, without pursuing the circuitous path of creating real alterations in the outer world. But this he can only attain because other men feel the same dissatisfactions as he with the renunciation demanded by reality and because this dissatisfaction, resulting from the displacement of the pleasure-principle by the reality-principle, is itself a part of reality.[42]

To this view of the artist as a creator of a kind of reality, Carl Jung's theory of the "collective unconscious," with its memory of our racial past, even of some levels of our pre-human past, added an importance that tended to convert Freud's neurotic into a shaman, a myth-maker speaking out of his unconscious a primordial truth.

This tendency to see art as the product of neurosis or as the expression of the "collective unconscious" results also in a tendency to view art as a vehicle for the psychoanalysis of its neurotic producer or as a reflection in terms of structure, image, and implicit meaning of a truth about a reality drawn in perceptual terms from the racial memory. The same dichotomy also produces the tendencies to employ psychology as a means of evaluating the subject matter of art or as a means of exploring the inner structure and meaning of art. Certainly none of these polarities are total, but they point directions in the application of psychological principles to critical practice.

The most obvious impact that Freud's ideas had upon the popular mind was in the demand for sex-freedom, the reaction

42. *The Collected Papers of Sigmund Freud* (London, 1924), IV, 19, as quoted in Hoffman, *Freudianism and the Literary Mind*, p. 95.

against repression, the rejection of the evil "puritan." Behind much fiction and polemical writing in our generation this attitude may be seen, and in the twenties and sometimes today as well it spills over into criticism. In 1926 Thomas Beer had found it an effective device for dissecting *The Mauve Decade*, and in 1930 Floyd Dell declared, "Religion aside, we may say that Art offers us a socially accepted alternative to the neuroses and psychoses which are the socially unacceptable ways of finding relief from lingering infantile anxieties."[43] But the best known and most influential critical work employing this interpretation of Freud's ideas was Ludwig Lewisohn's *Expression in America* (1932), which established the sexual life or inhibitions of the writer, either known or implied, as a standard for literary excellence.

Closely allied to this very simple application of Freud's ideas was the psychoanalytical approach to literary biography, an approach which was sometimes almost indistinguishable from the Lewisohn method. The twenties had seen Van Wyck Brooks's studies of Mark Twain and Henry James, Raymond Weaver's and Lewis Mumford's of Melville, and Joseph Wood Krutch's of Poe. All of these works suffered from an attempt to use art as a substitute for the psychiatrist's couch, and to discover the incident, fact, or abnormality out of which the accomplishments and the failures of their subject had arisen. While no one would deny the value of the tools that Freudian psychology gave the biographer, literary and otherwise, and while art certainly comments significantly upon the state of mind and feeling of its producer, the fact remains that the handling of psychoanalytical problems by these writers and critics of the twenties was generally naive and unrewarding. A similar naivete is to be found in more recent works like Edmund Bergler's *The Writer and Psychoanalysis* (1950) and Arthur Wormhoudt's *The Demon Lover* (1949). However, Edmund Wilson's collection of essays, *The Wound and the Bow* (1941) demonstrates that the psychoanalytical approach in the hands of a balanced and skilled critic

43. Floyd Dell, *Love in the Machine Age* (New York, 1930), p. 384.

can yield rich fruits. The analysis of Kipling and particularly "The Two Scrooges," a study of Dickens, are landmarks in the use of a method which has seldom been well employed in American criticism. Fred W. Boege is probably correct in saying, "In spite of its points of vulnerability, 'The Two Scrooges' is the best single piece of criticism of Dickens that has yet been written, and the most influential of recent years."[44] Several recent studies in the new American Men of Letters Series also demonstrate the value of the psychoanalytical method when it is employed with subtlety and discretion, notably Irving Howe's *Sherwood Anderson* (1951), John Berryman's *Stephen Crane* (1950), Newton Arvin's *Herman Melville* (1950), and Perry Miller's *Jonathan Edwards* (1949).

But Freudianism has other and more basic uses for the critic than those of biography, for it can be used to illuminate form, imagery, and symbolism. Its view of man has value for artist and critic alike. As Herbert J. Muller says, "Freudian man . . . has a genuine dignity and force. He is always torn by conflict, threatened by the powers of darkness; his victories are compromises, invitations to further battle; yet he continues to aspire, he is worthy of the struggle, and his virtues emerge from it."[45] Such aspects of Freudian psychology have supplied sensitive critics with valuable tools for examining the work of art both in terms of its creation and the creating forces and in terms of its own content and the laws that govern the universe which it portrays.

In 1922 Frederick Clarke Prescott, in *The Poetic Mind*, produced one of the best studies of the application of Freudian principles to literary creation, and applied them with skill to the examination of individual works. As Frederick J. Hoffman says, "Prescott's application of Freud to aesthetic theory is a far cry from what is known as 'psychoanalytic criticism': the latter makes out of literature a source for clinical reports; the former has contributed a study of much significance to one of the most

44. Fred W. Boege, "Recent Criticism of Dickens," *Nineteenth-Century Fiction*, VIII (1953), 176.

45. Herbert J. Muller, *Science and Criticism* (New Haven, 1943), pp. 156-157.

puzzling aspects of literary aesthetics [that of the imagination]."[46] This difficult critical task has been accomplished in America rather infrequently. Edmund Wilson, Kenneth Burke, and Roy P. Basler have practiced it with distinction; although Burke's use is always instrumental to the development of another method and, therefore, hardly deserves extended comment here.

Edmund Wilson has used Freud's principles with subtlety and grace in the examination of the inner meaning and the structural integrity of works of art. Particularly noteworthy in this field is his provocative treatment of Henry James's "The Turn of the Screw."[47] This essay makes a skillful reading of the story on the basis of the governess' being "a neurotic case of sex repression." Although by no means unchallenged, the interpretation illustrates how effectively Freudian concepts may be used in the interior examination of fiction. Wilson's early interpretation of *Finnegans Wake*[48] is an impressive demonstration of the use of such a method. Roy P. Basler's *Sex, Symbolism, and Psychology in Literature* (1948), after a judicious statement of the value of psychological methods in criticism, examines specific works by Coleridge, Tennyson, Poe, and T. S. Eliot in terms of their "psychological symbolism." Charles Neider's study of Kafka's symbolism in Freudian terms, *The Frozen Sea* (1948), may honorably be listed with this small but distinguished group.

Certainly such a restricted listing as this does not do justice to the casual and widely pervasive tendency of much recent criticism to employ a Freudian analysis of symbol and structure to works of art. Yet, useful as such a method is and common as its incidental use is, few critics have made it a primary method of analysis. In some respects it is surprising that this is true, but the fact remains that Prescott's *The Poetic Mind* from the early twenties shares with Frederick J. Hoffman's *Freudianism*

46. Hoffman, *Freudianism and the Literary Mind*, pp. 98-99.
47. Edmund Wilson, "The Ambiguity of Henry James," *The Triple Thinkers* (New York, 1938), pp. 122-164. An earlier version of this essay appeared in *Hound & Horn* (April-June, 1934). A Postscript was added in the 1948 edition of *Triple Thinkers*.
48. Edmund Wilson, *The Wound and the Bow* (New York, 1947), pp. 243-271.

and the Literary Mind in the middle forties the honor of being one of the two noteworthy attempts to examine with rigor and patience the importance of Freudian concepts for artistic criticism. Hoffman's book, although it examines the work of Joyce, D. H. Lawrence, Kafka, Mann, Anderson, and Waldo Frank with often illuminating results, centers its attention more upon the history of the use of Freudianism in literature than in the interpretation of literature in Freudian terms.

Another psychological theory, that of the Gestalt or "configuration," has attained widespread currency in literary circles without producing any sizeable corresponding criticism. Its outlines make it appear well adapted to critical use. Wolfgang Köhler's statement of its nature sounds almost like an expression of aesthetic theory: "It is precisely the original organization and segregation of circumscribed wholes which make it possible for the sensory world to appear so utterly imbued with meaning to the adult because, in its gradual entry into the sensory field, meaning follows the lines drawn by natural organization."[49] This emphasis upon "wholes" and patterns, upon unity and synthesis appears almost to beg for critical exploitation of a sort which it has not received. As Herbert J. Muller, perhaps its most effective advocate, says,

... it is a congenial psychology for all art lovers because it restores to intellectual respectability our concrete experience, the immediate, naive sensory impression that precedes logical analysis or verbal definition. . . . Yet nothing is more difficult in practice than a clear, full, steady awareness of the principle implied here: that all elements in art are variables whose value depends on their position in a configuration, their functional relation to the whole intention of the artist and the total effect of his work.[50]

In *Modern Fiction* (1937) Muller used Gestalt psychology effectively in the examination of "impressionistic" novelists, such as Conrad, Proust, Lawrence, Gide, and Virginia Woolf; and in *Science and Criticism* he made a cogent plea for its wider usage. Susanne K. Langer, in *Philosophy in a New Key* (1942)

49. Wolfgang Köhler, *Gestalt Psychology* (New York, 1929), p. 208.
50. Muller, *Science and Criticism*, pp. 164-165.

and *Feeling and Form* (1953), has employed the Gestalt psychology in the construction of her theory of symbol and form, fusing it with material drawn from a great many other sources, notably Jung and the anthropologists. However, anything that could properly be called a Gestalt criticism has not yet emerged, perhaps because recent critical interest in form has tended to have its origin in theories of the "collective unconscious" or in a return to classical principles.

In the forties and fifties, the modifications in Freud's theory that Carl Jung made, coupled with the anthropological discoveries of men like Frazer and Malinowski, have resulted in a richer view of the artist than the strictly Freudian method usually gives. Many critics, like many writers, share Thomas Mann's feeling:

The primitive foundations of the human soul . . . are those profound time-sources where the myth has its home and shapes the primeval norms and forms of life. For the myth is the foundation of life; it is the timeless schema, the pious formula into which life flows when it reproduces its traits out of the unconscious.[51]

Such critics have developed a theory of the "Myth" that has been peculiarly pervasive in recent criticism.[52] Perhaps the most important of these studies is that of the British critic Maud Bodkin, *Archetypal Patterns in Poetry*, although it would be a mistake to minimize the importance both of T. S. Eliot's poetic practice in the use of mythic materials (notably in "The Waste Land")[53] and his early illuminating comments on Joyce's *Ulysses*, where he says:

In using the myth . . . Mr. Joyce is pursuing a method which others must pursue after him. . . . It is simply a way of controlling, of ordering, of giving a shape and a significance to the immense panorama of futility and anarchy which is contemporary history. . . . Psychology . . .

51. As quoted in Muller, *Science and Criticism*, p. 156.

52. See the informative, though unfriendly article by Wallace W. Douglas, "The Meaning of 'Myth' in Modern Criticism," *Modern Philology*, L (1953), 232-242, both for its picture of the impact of the idea and for an iconoclastic summary of the major critics in the school.

53. See particularly Eliot's "Notes on 'The Wasteland,' " *Collected Poems* (New York, 1936), pp. 91-98.

ethnology, and *The Golden Bough* have concurred to make possible what was impossible even a few years ago. Instead of narrative method, we may now use the mythical method.[54]

Richard Chase has been one of the most persistent and diligent users of this method. His *Quest for Myth* (1949) traces the changing concept of myth in the history of modern thought and concludes with the idea that modern anthropologists (in his case, notably Malinowski) give justification for myth as an expression of "The terrific forces of the human emotions [that] cannot for long be trifled with."[55] Chase has applied his theory that myth is literature "functioning in a special way, achieving special modes of expression,"[56] to Melville, a writer peculiarly susceptible to mythic treatment, in *Herman Melville: A Critical Study* (1949), and to other writers such as the Brontës and Faulkner in articles in the *Partisan Review* and the *Kenyon Review*.

Francis Fergusson in *The Idea of the Theatre* (1949) applied the method of various modern schools to the nature of tragedy, in the belief that the anthropologists "have given us a new understanding of Greek tragedy by demonstrating its roots in myth and ritual, its implication in the whole culture of its time."[57] The result is probably the best American example of this school of criticism. Fergusson has recently applied the same method to Dante in *Dante's Drama of the Mind* (1953) and in a number of articles has written perceptive criticism of Joyce, D. H. Lawrence, T. S. Eliot, Shaw, and Shakespeare. William Troy, in articles in the *Partisan Review* and the *Kenyon Review*, has made extensive use of myth and ritual in examining the work of Proust, D. H. Lawrence, Thomas Mann, Balzac, Stendhal, and Scott Fitzgerald. Philip Wheelwright, in scattered essays, has studied the aesthetic and philosophical implications of

54. T. S. Eliot, *"Ulysses,* Order, and Myth," in *Critiques and Essays on Modern Fiction 1920-1951,* edited by John W. Aldridge (New York, 1952), pp. 424-426. This essay originally appeared in *Dial,* November, 1923.

55. Richard Chase, *Quest for Myth* (Baton Rouge, 1949), p. 21.

56. Richard Chase, "Myth as Literature," *English Institute Essays, 1947* (New York, 1948), p. 11.

57. Francis Fergusson, *The Idea of a Theater* (Anchor Ed.; Garden City, 1953), p. 22.

such ideas for literary criticism. Both Mark Schorer and North-rop Frye have found William Blake a fruitful subject for study in these terms, Schorer in *William Blake: The Politics of Vision* (1946) and Frye in *Fearful Symmetry: A Study of Blake* (1947). Schorer has pursued this interest into the field of fiction, notably in two significant studies, "Technique as Discovery,"[58] and "Fiction and the 'Analogical Matrix.'"[59] Frye's interests are directed toward archetypal patterns in literature, particularly dramatic works.

The determining of appropriate boundaries for modern critical movements is nowhere more difficult than it is between psychological critics and analytical critics; the greater portion of those mentioned as belonging to the "School of the Myth" might almost as effectively be categorized as "New Critics." In general, however, they do deserve a separate classification, for they stand on the bridge between intrinsic and extrinsic value, and they usually emphasize a larger structural pattern than the New Critics. Myth is associated with story, ritual with sequence of action, archetypal pattern with something closely akin to plot; and in the extent to which these critics see fundamental messages being conveyed through these larger devices they differ from their fellows who look analytically within the poem, there to find in its inner being and in its imagery the secret of its meaning.

The contribution of the psychological critics, and particularly of those interested in the "collective unconscious," to the defense of literature in the modern world is, however, indisputably great. In their hands the author becomes once more the prophet, the seer, and the sayer—a role which science appeared for a while to have rendered impossible for him.

IV
THE NEW CRITICS

Among the various critics commonly called "New" or Analytical or Formalist or Aesthetic it is easy to demonstrate almost

58. Mark Schorer, "Technique as Discovery," *Hudson Review*, I (1948), 67-87.
59. Mark Schorer, "Fiction and the 'Analogical Matrix,'" *Kenyon Review*, XI (1949), 539-560.

as many points of division as points of agreement. We can fruitfully follow Frederick Pottle's lead and say that "While remaining aware of real differences between the significant critics of the present day, [we] grant that they are a distinguishable group—even a party."[60] This group has had a pervasive and revivifying influence on American criticism since the middle thirties. In fact, it has developed a theory of criticism, advanced a method of critical attack, invented a vocabulary (often to the exasperation of its readers), and called forth much of that body of excellent writing about literature which entitles us to look with pride upon the critical accomplishment of America in the last quarter of a century.

The primary concern of the men in the group has been to discover the intrinsic worth of literature, to demonstrate that worth to intelligent readers, and to defend that worth against the types of attack inherent in much contemporary thought. The tendency of the twentieth century American to seek practical and immediate value, his desire to submit everything to the judgment of social significance, his habit of extending the methods and premises of science to every area of human affairs—all of these raise fundamental questions about the value of literature as anything other than tool or toy. The New Critics have consistently asserted the intrinsic value of literature against these attitudes, and it is this insistence on intrinsic worth that has set the group apart from other critical movements. As Alfred Kazin says, "The typical Marxist who persistently subordinated esthetic values to a rigid social doctrine and the Formalist who subordinated everything to his esthetic values were as far removed as the poles and at times did not even seem to occupy the same universe."[61] Another general characteristic of the group has been a keen sensitivity to implicit and explicit attack upon literature, so that, viewed in the perspective which we are allowed today, the early stages of the analytical movement tend to look like gallant and sometimes foolhardy defenses of the fortress of

60. Pottle, "The New Critics and the Historical Method," *loc. cit.*, p. 15.
61. Kazin, *On Native Grounds*, p. 407.

Art—defenses based upon the principle of attack and confusion, and justified primarily by the pragmatic proof of their success.

The New Criticism was called into being by a pattern of reaction to many features of the modern world. Alfred Kazin accurately though unsympathetically observes, "Their preciosity was not an 'escape' from anything; it was a social pressure, subtle and enraged and militant in its despair, working against the positivism of the age and sustained by a high contempt for it; a despair in the face of contemporary dissolution and material- ism and irreligion."[62] The New Critics were protesting against the mechanistic and positivistic nature of our modern world; and their protest was framed in terms of a cultural tradition, a religious order, and sometimes an Agrarian aristocratic social system. They were protesting against a view of life and knowl- edge that rested on fact and inference from fact alone; and their protest took the form of an insistence on literature as a valid form of knowledge and as a communicator not of the truths of other languages but of the truths incommunicable in other terms than those of the language of literature. They were protesting against Romanticism with its doctrines of self-expression and its philosophy of perfectibility; and their protest took the form of a theory of impersonal art and of neo-classic restraint. They were protesting against impressionism in criticism; and their protest took the form of intense methodological concern and sometimes of semantic analysis. They were protesting against the New Humanism of Babbitt and More; and their protest took the form of an insistence that the morality and value of a work of art is a function of its inner qualities and that literature can- not be evaluated in general terms or terms not directly related to the work itself. They were protesting against the kind of literary scholarship current in the thirties, a positivistic scholarship that looked in biography and social milieu for the meaning of litera- ture; and their protest aimed at substituting texual examination and analysis for bibliographical data and historical classification. In general, these critics worked on the assumption that, as Ray West expresses it, "our age is the victim of what has been called

62. *Ibid.*, p. 426.

a 'dissociation of sensibility'; that is, in its simplest sense, that the background myth or established moral order within which writers of other ages have worked is almost totally (certainly relatively) lacking in our time."[63] In the absence of such a moral order, each writer presents a "private vision" which requires interpretation. It becomes the peculiar function of the critic so to train himself that he may properly interpret these "private" visions to equally "private" readers, and he even has the added function of explaining the earlier moral order or tradition to a generation of readers ignorant of it or insensitive to its value.

The sources out of which this type of criticism came are as various and as contradictory as the movements against which it was protesting. Among the writers basically influencing the American New Critic are the influential French impressionist Remy de Gourmont, and the short-lived and seminal British classicist T. E. Hulme, one of the formulators of the anti-romanticism of our age. These two men were virtual tutors to Ezra Pound and T. S. Eliot—who share with I. A. Richards the distinction of having shaped the frame within which the New Criticism operates. Certainly Pound's long and ardent insistence on the active study of the text and his belief in criticism as a necessary means of winnowing the chaff from the wheat of art—the function of what he called "excernment"—taught modern criticism much. From Eliot the New Criticism learned by precept and superb example the high virtues of erudition, a sense of fact, comparison, and particularly a sense of tradition and order in the realm of art. From the British semanticist and psychologist I. A. Richards it gained a positivitistic and semantic scalpel for dissecting the language and the imagery of poetry. From the "new" psychologies it gained fresh insights into the nature of the imagination and the quality and significance of image and form. From the development of political and social movements, like that of the Southern Agrarians, it gained not only slogans and heat but also direction and force. From the New Humanists, and in particular from Irving Babbitt, it gained

63. Ray B. West, Jr., *Essays in Modern Literary Criticism* (New York, 1952), p. 324.

a sense of a moral and ethical order opposed to the mechanistic and pragmatic world of the twentieth century. From the Catholic Renascence, the Calvinistic Neo-Orthodoxy, and the development of both Christian and atheistic Existentialism it gained philosophical strength with which to oppose the presumed completeness of the assumptions by which a scientific materialism evaluates man and experience.

But multitudinous and conflicting as these various mentors are, they probably would have produced a less effective—and perhaps less extravagant—body of critical theory and practice had the seeds they cast not fallen upon the rich soil of a group of lyric poets of a high order of ability—Pound, Eliot, John Crowe Ransom, Allen Tate, Yvor Winters. These poets began under the strong influence of the French symbolists Baudelaire, Laforgue, Mallarmé, Verlaine, and Rimbaud; and when they looked back in the past it was not to the popular English Romantics but to the almost forgotten seventeenth century metaphysicals, Donne, Herbert, and Marvell. Their poetic talent gave to the older *explication de texte* method a richness and subtlety that it could not otherwise have had.

American analytical criticism was a direct outgrowth of I. A. Richards' *The Principles of Literary Criticism* (1924), William Empson's *Seven Types of Ambiguity* (1930), and the critical writings of Pound and Eliot, the significant bulk of which had been produced before the depression. All the New Critics draw in some degree upon I. A. Richards' psychological studies of literary methods and his positivistic approach to literary evaluation; yet most of them repudiate Richards' early psychological emphasis and trace with pleasure the shift from psychology to philosophy which occurred in his thinking at the time of his *Coleridge on the Imagination* (1934). Allen Tate, introducing a critical symposium in which Richards participated, expressed it in this way:

At present we may see a shift, in talking about poetry, from psychology to philosophy—from poetry as emotion and response to poetry as a kind of knowledge.

[229]

It is always proper to ask Mr. Richards to join a critical symposium; we asked him on this occasion because we may observe in his own intellectual history the shift that I refer to; and we wished to acknowledge him as the pioneer of our age in this field of study.[64]

The American analytical movement has sometimes been dated from the publication of *I'll Take My Stand* by Twelve Southerners in 1930, a collection of articles which, according to the Introduction, "all tend to support a Southern way of life against what may be called the American or prevailing way; and all as much as agree that the best terms in which to represent the distinction are contained in the phrase, Agrarian *versus* Industrial."[65] This volume announced an attitude and presented examples of a method which were fruitfully to be employed by the New Critics in the middle thirties and the forties.

In the frenetic early thirties, when the New Criticism was getting underway in America, it was attacking quite specifically historical scholarship, Marxism, and New Humanism. The positive qualities which fused the attackers into a coherent movement were initially very broad—a distrust of Romanticism, a passionate faith in the value of literature, and a common agreement that that value could best be arrived at by looking within the work itself. They developed too a common interest in a religious tradition and in a firm social order, although they have no common agreement about which religion or which social order they support. Some of them seem, in an American tradition that stretches back as far as Fenimore Cooper, to think in terms of hierarchy and to vote Jacksonian. Although they may

64. Allen Tate in *The Language of Poetry* (Princeton, 1942), pp. vii-viii.
65. *I'll Take My Stand* (New York, 1930), p. ix. It is important here to take cognizance of Allen Tate's caveat: "The Old South perpetuated many of the virtues of such an order [a unified Christendom]; but to try to 'revive' the Old South, and to build a wall around it, would be a kind of idolatry; it would prefer the accident to the substance. . . . . We are told by our Northern friends that the greatest menace to the South is ignorance; but there is the even greater ignorance of the delusion of progressive enlightenment." *Shenandoah*, III (1952), 29. This issue of *Shenandoah* presents a reappraisal of the Agrarian Movement twenty years after, and is a significant entry in its history. The recent critical anthology *Southern Renascence*, edited by Robert Jacobs and Louis Rubin, Jr. (Baltimore, 1953), both in its theme and in the assumptions of its criticism gives a clear proof of the continuing vitality of the Agrarian Movement.

be said to have started in Southern Agrarianism, they have not remained there, nor have they taken any single common road away. They have all been impressed forcefully, almost painfully, by semantic approaches to language, and they are emphatic about the value of close reading, but in general they can best be described by a word they despise, "eclectic." They are a definite group almost as an act of faith in literature.[66]

It is difficult to decide just which critics may properly be classified as members of the group, and almost everyone writing on the subject nominates a somewhat different group. An examination of eight treatments of contemporary criticism[67] revealed no single figure who appeared as a New Critic on all eight lists. Those who appeared most often were John Crowe Ransom and R. P. Blackmur (seven times each), Allen Tate, Yvor Winters, and Cleanth Brooks (six times each). Kenneth Burke was listed four times, Robert Penn Warren three times, and Edmund Wilson twice. The first five are certainly worthy of being called a distinctive critical school. Kenneth Burke is important as a theorist about art and language, but hardly as a major practicing critic. He is primarily an epistemologist and semanticist, interested in applying all knowledge to the problem of expressing the complexity of the modern world. He himself agreed with Malcolm Cowley's statement that "he was a side influence on all of them without being affiliated even loosely with them."[68] Robert Penn Warren has, with Cleanth Brooks, made an enormous impact on the academic critical method through the textbooks

66. Robert Wooster Stallman's commonplace book *The Critic's Notebook* (Minneapolis, 1950) is a useful compendium of critical statements by most of the members of the school, and its section headings reflect the major interests of the group: "The Nature and Function of Criticism," "Life and Art," "Form," "The Problem of Meaning," "The Concept of the 'Objective Correlative,'" "The Problem of the Personal Element," "The Problem of Belief in Poetry," "The Problem of Intentions."

67. The eight works are: Zabel, *Literary Opinion in America; Literary History of the United States*, edited by Robert Spiller *et al.* (New York, 1948), III, 61-62; O'Connor, *An Age of Criticism; Kazin, On Native Grounds;* John Crowe Ransom, *The New Criticism* (Norfolk, Conn., 1941); Robert W. Stallman, "The New Critics," *Critiques and Essays in Criticism 1920-1948,* edited by R. W. Stallman (New York, 1949), 488-506; Ray B. West, Jr., *Modern Literary Criticism;* William Elton, *A Guide to the New Criticism* (Revised ed.; Chicago, 1953).

68. Symposium on "The New Criticism," Act II, *American Scholar,* XX (1951), 220.

Understanding Poetry and *Understanding Fiction*, and has himself written perceptive criticism, particularly on Faulkner, Hemingway, and Coleridge's *Rime of the Ancient Mariner*. Edmund Wilson has used certain of the analytical methods brilliantly, but he has remained always historically and sociologically oriented and certainly should not be listed as a New Critic. There are dozens of good critics following in the paths which these leaders have blazed, and hundreds of mediocre and poor critics are stretching their legs across the pages of our reviews and journals in an effort to follow in the giants' footsteps. So vast has the movement been in sheer numbers of critics that it is not possible here to do more than examine sketchily the leaders.

John Crowe Ransom, because of the position as philosopher of the movement which he shares with Allen Tate, because his book *The New Criticism* (1941) attached a name to the group and defined it, perhaps too specifically, and because the magazine he edits, *The Kenyon Review*, is almost an official organ of the group, stands at the head of the American analytical movement in criticism. A practicing poet, associated with the academic world for the past forty years, and a leader in the Southern Agrarian Movement, Ransom has fostered and practiced a criticism that is philosophically oriented, precise and detailed, and "difficult" both in method and terminology. Perhaps the key idea of his criticism is:

The critic should regard the poem as nothing short of a desperate ontological or metaphysical manoeuvre. . . . The poet perpetuates in his poem an order of existence which in actual life is constantly crumbling beneath his touch. His poem celebrates the object which is real, individual, and qualitatively infinite. . . . The critic should find in the poem a total poetic or individual object which tends to be universalized, but is not permitted to suffer this fate. His identification of the poetic object is in terms of the universal or commonplace object to which it tends, and of the tissue, or totality of connotation, which holds it secure. . . . It is the prose object, which any forthright prosy reader can discover to him by an immediate paraphrase; it is a kind of story, character, thing, scene, or moral principle. And where is the tissue that keeps it from coming out of the poetic object? That is, for the laws of prose logic, its superfluity; and I think I would even say, its irrelevance.[69]

Given an object, and a poet burning to utter himself upon it, he must take into account a third item, the form into which he must cast his utterance. (If we like, we may call it the *body* which he must give to his passion.) It delays and hinders him. In the process of "composition" the burning passion is submitted to cool and scarcely relevant considerations. . . . The thing expressed there is not the hundred-per cent passion at all.[70]

This concept of art is, of course, an inorganic one; and it is this inorganicism that is Ransom's most distinguishing personal mark as a critic. He studies the meaning, the paraphrasable content, and the structure and texture, confident that the poem exists in its own right and as a cognitive fact. He strongly opposes what he calls Platonic poetry, where the objects in the poem are capable of translation into ideas or serve as ornamental properties in the representation of ideas. In *The World's Body* (1938) and *The New Criticism* (1941) and in numerous articles in the *Kenyon Review*, he has practiced the aesthetic and critical system everywhere implicit and often explicit in his work.

Allen Tate, eleven years Ransom's junior, has participated in almost all the movements that Ransom has and probably deserves Alfred Kazin's label, "the only philosophical mind among these critics."[71] He is distinctive for the firmness with which he has insisted on a religious and an aristocratic tradition, seeing that tradition best embodied in the ideals of the Old South, and for the intellectual vigor with which he has attacked all attempts, and particularly those of the positivistic logicians, to reduce the language of poetry to a vehicle for communication alone. Of poetry he declares, "It is neither the world of verifiable science nor a projection of ourselves; yet it is *complete*. And because it is complete knowledge we may, I think, claim for it a unique kind of responsibility, and see in it at times an irresponsibility equally distinct."[72] But the idea which is most distinctively his

69. John Crowe Ransom, *The World's Body* (New York, 1938), pp. 347-348.
70. *Ibid.*, p. 40.   71. Kazin, *On Native Grounds*, p. 437.
72. Allen Tate, *On the Limits of Poetry* (New York, 1948), p. 47.

is "tension," which he defines thus:

We return to the inquiry set for this discussion: to find out whether there is not a more central achievement in poetry than that represented by either of the extreme examples [the fallacy of communication and the fallacy of denotation]. I proposed as descriptive of that achievement, the term *tension*. I am using the term not as a general metaphor, but as a special one, derived from lopping the prefixes off the logical terms *ex*tension and *in*tension. What I am saying, of course, is that the meaning of poetry is its "tension," the full organized body of all the extension and intension that we can find in it.[73]

Using these terms, Tate defines good poetry as "a unity of all the meanings from the furtherest extremes of intension and extension. Yet our recognition of the action of this unified meaning is the gift of experience, of culture, of, if you will, our humanism."[74] Allied to these ideas is also Tate's high evaluation of the historical imagination (as sharply opposed to literary history). He expresses this idea in the paradoxical statement:

I take the somewhat naive view that the literature of the past began somewhere a few minutes ago and that the literature of the present begins, say, with Homer. . . . We must judge the past and keep it alive by being alive ourselves; and that is to say that we must judge the past . . . with as much of the present as our poets have succeeded in elevating to the objectivity of form.[75]

Tate's sharply logical and profoundly philosophical mind makes him unpleasantly aware of the truth of Frederick A. Pottle's judgment that the New Critic "insists on a starkly positivistic perception of the world, but . . . demands that this perception adumbrate nonpositivistic values."[76] Tate's criticism and aesthetic theory appear in *Reactionary Essays* (1936), *Reason in Madness* (1941), the collected essays in *On the Limits of Poetry* (1948), and *The Forlorn Demon* (1953). One awaits the later development of his theories with the expectation that his grap-

73. *Ibid.*, pp. 82-83.
74. *Ibid.*, p. 82.
75. *Reason in Madness*, pp. 114-115.
76. Pottle, "The New Critics and the Historical Method," *loc cit.*, p. 17.

pling with the problems of art seems more richly promising than any other single prospect that the New Criticism offers.

Yvor Winters brings to bear upon poetry an even more rigorously orthodox tradition than Tate's or Ransom's, and, although persistently analytical in his method, avoids either the fact or the appearance of positivism. The moral and ethical rectitude of the New Humanists and particularly of Irving Babbitt finds in Winters' criticism a continuing and effective voice. Almost bitterly opposed to Romanticism, rebelling against both didactic and hedonistic views of art, and impatient with determinism of all sorts, Winters views art through a confident belief in Absolutes that are frankly theistic and Christian. To the criticism of literature he brings an intense concern with the objective truth which it communicates (its paraphrasable content) and an inquiring interest in the methods by which this content is given form. Perhaps his key word is "morality," a term which evaluates both the content and the integrity with which the form presents it. He is corruscating in the effectiveness with which he has submitted many accepted works of art to such tests as those of "pseudo-reference"—a method by which explicit or implicit reference is made to "non-existent plot" or "non-existent symbolic value"—and "grammatical coherence" as opposed to "rational coherence" (the two should, in Winters' system, be equivalent). The highly classical tenor of his thought comes out in one of his definitions of poetry:

I believe that the work of literature, in so far as it is valuable, approximates a real apprehension and communication of a particular kind of objective truth. . . . The poem is a statement in words about a human experience. Words are primarily conceptual, but through use and because human experience is not purely conceptual, they have acquired connotations of feeling. The poet makes his statement in such a way as to employ both concept and connotation as efficiently as possible. The poem is good in so far as it makes a defensible rational statement about a given human experience (the experience need not be real but must be in some sense possible) and at the same time com-

[235]

municates the emotion which ought to be motivated by that rational understanding of that experience.[77]

Winters has devoted the greater portion of his practical criticism to a series of attacks on Romantic and obscurantist tendencies in American literature. *Primitivism and Decadence* (1937) was a series of studies in American poetry. *Maule's Curse* (1938) attacked Romantic obscurantism in nineteenth century American prose and poetry and discovered in Emerson the villain of American literature. *The Anatomy of Nonsense* (1943) dealt with critics and their theories. These essays were collected in 1947 in *In Defense of Reason*, with an illuminating Foreword.

For R. P. Blackmur, "Criticism . . . is the formal discourse of an amateur."[78] To the "Critic's Job of Work" he brings a total love that has made him employ with endless patience and painstaking care every tool that he can bring to hand in the meticulous examination of the linguistic, structural, and imaginative aspects of a poem. He is broadly contextual in his approach: ideas are important as they are embedded in the work, not as they are abstracted from it. His theory of art is fundamentally organic. As Stanley Hyman has pointed out about the title of Blackmur's first volume of critical essays, *The Double Agent* (1935):

Poetry is a double agent (content and form, the raw material of life and the shaping imagination), criticism is a double agent (analysis and appreciation, intimacy with particulars and evaluation of achievement), and poetry and criticism together are a double agent (keyed in the subtitle [of Blackmur's book, *Essays in Craft and Elucidation*]— craft and elucidation). The double agent is in fact any pair of critical terms—form and content, structure and texture, writer and reader, static and dynamic, tradition and revolt, expression and communication —and out of their interaction arises a third thing, the poem, the essay, or, in this case, Blackmur's book.[79]

77. Yvor Winters, *In Defense of Reason* (New York, 1947), p. 11.
78. R. P. Blackmur, "A Critic's Job of Work," in *American Literary Criticism*, p. 380.
79. Stanley Edgar Hyman, *The Armed Vision: A Study in the Methods of Modern Literary Criticism* (New York, 1948), p. 249.

Perhaps the greatest weakness of Blackmur's method is an excess of its virtue—hard work. In the thoroughness with which every possible means of approach to the poem is made, there appears to be a failure to develop an overall method or theory, and he remains an amateur. Analysis is his forte; at synthesis he is not always successful; and his final views often appear indecisive. No one, however, has set the American critic a finer example of persistence, catholic knowledge and method, and courageous labor than Blackmur has. In addition to *The Double Agent*, there are two other volumes of collected essays by him, *The Expense of Greatness* (1940) and *Language as Gesture* (1952).

Of the New Critics, Frederick Pottle has said, "Let us assign them representatives. My choices . . . would be, for theory, Mr. Allen Tate; and, for applied criticism, Mr. Cleanth Brooks."[80] That honored but secondary position appears more firmly to be Brooks's with each passing year. Perhaps his idea of paradox in poetry, coupled with his thorough pursuit of the meaning of metaphor, his earnest rejection of the heresy of the paraphrase, and the rigor with which he has excluded from consideration "The Intentional Fallacy" and "The Affective Fallacy,"[81] make into false modesty his statement that "such credit as I may legitimately claim, I must claim primarily on the grounds of having possibly made a successful synthesis of other men's ideas rather than on the originality of my own."[82] Yet in works like *Modern Poetry and the Tradition* (1939) and *The Well Wrought Urn* (1947), as well as in his many uncollected essays, Brooks has made a splendid and richly useful synthesis. In *Understanding Fiction* (edited with Robert Penn Warren in 1943), *Understanding Drama* (edited with Robert Heilman in 1945), as well as in the epoch-making *Understanding Poetry* (edited with Warren in 1938), Brooks has made negotiable for the classroom and the seminar hall a method that has gone far in a single genera-

80. Pottle, "The New Critics and the Historical Method," *loc. cit.*, p. 15.

81. Two ideas advanced by W. K. Wimsatt, Jr., and M. C. Beardsley in articles by those titles in, respectively, *Sewanee Review*, LIV (1946), 468-488, and *Ibid.*, LIX (1949), 31-55.

82. Cleanth Brooks, *Modern Poetry and the Tradition* (Chapel Hill, 1939), p. x.

tion toward revolutionizing the teaching of literature in our colleges and universities.

To this list of the leaders of the New Criticism many other honorable names might be added, yet these leaders set the patterns, shaped the thought, and issued the challenges that constituted the movement. While today the New Criticism has passed beyond the stage of armed truculence, the ideals of an autonomous art, of an inherent value in literature, and of a concern with methodology which are its particular earmarks have permeated most of the sensitive areas of American critical thought; so that today the conflict is less obvious and the New Critics' triumph more real than ever before. In the *Sewanee Review*, the *Kenyon Review,* the *Partisan Review,* and the *Hudson Review,* along with *Accent* and many other University quarterlies, it has produced a cogent, and sometimes incoherent, group of critical organs. In its current common acceptance on college and university campuses, the magnitude of the victory it has won over the older concept of literary history is manifest, and in the increasing concern with contemporary writers and writing is to be found one measure of the influence it has exerted; for Professor Pottle is probably right when he says, "What the New Critics seem to me really to have done is to have discerned the defining characteristics of the best contemporary literature, and to have made those characteristics the standards for judging the literature of the past."[83]

With these merits and achievements, however, must be listed several limiting features of the New Criticism. Broadly, they are that it often loses sight of the edifice of art in minutely analyzing the carvings over the doorway; that it is more effective for intensive criticism than for extensive; that it grapples wonderfully well with certain types of lyric poetry, although not all, but has so far proved inadequate to deal with equal effectiveness with larger forms of poetry, with the novel, and with the drama. One of its finest practitioners has stated these weaknesses with love and vigor. R. P. Blackmur says:

83. Pottle, "The New Critics and the Historical Method," *loc cit.,* p. 16.

It is a criticism . . . which has dealt almost exclusively either with the executive technique of poetry (and only with a part of that) or with the general verbal techniques of language. Most of its practitioners have been men gifted in penetrating the private symbolisms and elucidating the language of all that part of modern poetry we have come to call the school of Donne. . . . It was a criticism created to cope with and develop the kind of poetry illustrated by Eliot's *Waste Land* and Yeats' *Tower*. . . . Eminently suited for the *initial* stages of criticism of this poetry, it has never been suited to the later stages of criticism; neither Eliot nor Yeats has been compared or judged because there has been no criticism able to take those burdens.[84]

V

MORE RECENT TENDENCIES

The last few years have seen several tendencies in criticism worthy of note, and the development of at least one new school of importance. Among the tendencies, perhaps the most obvious has been the establishment of friendly relations and a degree of mutual respect among the various schools which in the thirties had the air of armed camps. This lessening of the intensity of the critical antagonisms has resulted in a kind of cross fertilization which is producing new flowers of criticism which often show attitudes that two decades ago would have been considered incompatible. The more promising of the critics of the "younger generation"—men like Lionel Trilling, Mark Schorer, Randall Jarrell, and Robert Heilman—although they lean individually toward certain patterns in criticism, are, like Kenneth Burke in epistemology and Edmund Wilson in historical criticism, the users of a group of methods, various, varied, and multitudinous in their patterns and assumptions.

There has developed too an increasing concern with the aesthetic and philosophical assumptions behind criticism. This development, always implicit in the New Criticism, stands today as a separate concern to that of the practicing or even the theoretical critic. R. P. Blackmur has said of the distinction between him and Kenneth Burke:

84. R. P. Blackmur, "A Burden for Critics," *Lectures in Criticism* (New York, 1949), p. 200.

The difference between Mr. Burke and myself is that where he is predominantly concerned with setting up methods for analyzing the actions as they are expressed in the symbol, I choose to emphasize the created or dead-end symbol. He explores the puzzle of language in the process of becoming symbolic. I try to show in a series of varied and progressive examples how the symbol invests the actions in language with poetic actuality. Mr. Burke legislates; I would judge; the executive is between us.[85]

Among the noteworthy works of this type have been Burke's *The Philosophy of Literary Form* (1941), *A Grammar of Motives* (1945), and *A Rhetoric of Motives* (1950), works which focus a variety of types of thought on the epistemological and semantic problems of literature. The essays of W. K. Wimsatt, Jr., and Eliseo Vivas are contributions toward the analysis of literature in broadly similar terms, although not to the same conclusions always. Wayne Shumaker's recent inquiry into the nature of literary value, *Elements of Critical Theory* (1952), is another manifestation of this trend.

A similar tendency has placed increasing emphasis on the nature and history of criticism in recent years. Morton Dauwen Zabel's *Literary Opinion in America* (1937), with its good selections and admirable introduction surveying criticism in this century, stood for years as undisputed master of its field. When the expanded and revised edition appeared in 1951, it was soon surrounded by a host of competing and complementing works. In 1948 Stanley Edgar Hyman, in *The Armed Vision*, made an industrious and persevering "study in the method of modern literary criticism," examining twelve representative British and American critics in detail. In 1949 Robert Wooster Stallman edited *Critiques and Essays in Criticism 1920-1948*, a comprehensive anthology and a selected bibliography of contemporary British and American critical writing, with emphasis on the analytical critics. In 1951 Charles I. Glicksberg, in *American Literary Criticism 1900-1950*, presented a sizeable sketch of American criticism in this century and an anthology of representative writ-

85. R. P. Blackmur, "Language as Gesture," *Accent Anthology*, edited by Kerker Quinn and Charles Shattuck (New York, 1946), p. 467-468.

ings by critics of almost every school. In 1952 William Van O'Connor published *An Age of Criticism 1900-1950*, a brief, gracefully written historical summary of the major movements. And the same year Ray B. West, Jr., edited *Essays in Modern Literary Criticism*, an anthology of contemporary criticism with a noticeable leaning toward the analytical critics. The annual publication of critical papers presented at the English Institute, *English Institute Essays*, now in its twelfth year, is indicative of the continuing concern with critical history and problems. And the new "Perspectives in Criticism" series, published by the University of California Press, three volumes of which—Shumaker's *Elements of Critical Theory* (1952), Solomon Fishman's *The Disinherited of Art* (1953), and Robert Humphrey's *Stream of Consciousness in the Modern Novel* (1954)—have appeared, reflects this growing interest.

There has developed, too, an increasing concern with fiction as a subject for intensive critical examination. The literary historian has usually been interested in literary movements broadly independent of forms. The sociologically oriented critic has usually been interested in ideas rather than forms. The Marxist critic has been interested in the novel, but usually as a mirror of social states and forces, seldom as a literary form. The psychological critics have often examined drama and novels with serious concern, but the more truly analytic critic has generally centered his attention on the briefer forms of poetry. In 1945 Allen Tate called for an application to fiction of certain methods which had been successfully applied to poetry;[86] and he edited, with Caroline Gordon, a critically sensitive anthology of the short story, *The House of Fiction* (1950). In 1948 William Van O'Connor edited a collection of essays on the novel by various critics, *Forms of Modern Fiction*, presented in honor of Joseph Warren Beach, whose *The Twentieth Century Novel: Studies in Technique* (1932) and *American Fiction, 1920-1940* (1941) were early landmarks in the critical examination of fiction in terms of form and structure. John W. Aldridge's comprehensive

---

86. Allen Tate, "Techniques of Fiction," in *The Hovering Fly and other Essays* (Cummington Press, 1948), pp. 35-51; also in *On the Limits of Poetry*.

anthology *Critiques and Essays on Modern Fiction 1920-1951* (1952), with its extensive bibliography by R. W. Stallman, gives convincing evidence that the serious examination of modern fiction, using the methods of the psychological and the analytical critics, is an established and fruitful aspect of contemporary criticism. This trend in modern criticism is probably a result of and at the same time a partial cause for the revival of interest in the works and the theories of Henry James.

There is a further tendency, as the contemporary critic looks back into the American past, to re-evaluate the writers of the nineteenth century. The great transcendentalists of New England have given place before an intensive interest in Herman Melville and Nathaniel Hawthorne. Jonathan Edwards has begun to challenge Benjamin Franklin's eighteenth century supremacy. Henry James has gained an unquestioned ascendency over William Dean Howells. Whitman has been partially eclipsed by interest in figures like Emily Dickinson and Stephen Crane, while the revival of interest in Poe, particularly as a critic, is rapidly restoring him to a preeminent position as the artist of the nineteenth century in America.

The new major critical movement is neo-Aristotelianism. It is new primarily as an organized "school"; for many of its methods and assumptions are centuries old, and their particular combination within a broadly neo-Thomist philosophical framework has ramifications throughout this period and certainly seems to have been adumbrated in the New Humanists. In fact the neo-Aristotelian School has points of contact with most of the recent tendencies in criticism, although it is most obviously associated with the growing interest in the larger forms of literature. It is an attempt to unite the functions of critic and scholar under the methodological aegis of Aristotle. Richard McKeon and Ronald S. Crane have led the movement at the University of Chicago, a fact which accounts for its popular name as the "Chicago School." In 1952 Crane edited an impressively large volume of neo-Aristotelian essays on theory and practice, with an extended introduction, *Critics and Criticism.*

The volume contains five essays each by Richard McKeon, upon whose interpretations of Aristotle the School appears to build, Crane, and Elder Olson, two each by W. R. Keast, Bernard Weinberg, and Norman Maclean. Following Crane's introduction, an essay in the definition of the neo-Aristotelian method, is a group of studies pointing out the inadequacies of the New Criticism. Then follow a section examining classical and other theories of art and criticism, a section on the bases of contemporary Aristotelian criticism, and finally two essays demonstrating the method by applying it to specific works—*Lear* and *Tom Jones*.[87]

The basic concern of these critics appears to be the creation for modern literary forms, notably the novel and the drama, of critical standards and procedures similar to those which Aristotle created for the drama and epic of his day in the *Poetics*. As Elder Olson expresses it in an instructive essay on "The Poetic Method of Aristotle: Its Powers and Limitations":

> The definition on which everything centers, thus, is no mere statement of the meaning of a term or name . . . it is a statement of the nature of a whole produced by a certain art; and it is introduced, not merely to clarify meanings a little but much more importantly, to serve as the principle of the art and hence as the basis of all reasoning. . . .
>
> The argument leading to the definition may be stated as follows. Assuming that certain arts are imitative . . . specific forms of these arts must be specific forms of imitation. To imitate implies a matter or medium (means) in which one imitates, some form (object) which one imitates, and a certain way (manner) in which one imitates.[88]

It is this concern with the "wholeness" of the art object, with the arriving at a definition that is critically useful in terms of the form of the object, defining that form in terms of a unified

---

87. *Critics and Criticism* has been the recipient of several extended review essays, which should be consulted by the serious student of the movement; notably, W. K. Wimsatt, Jr., "The Chicago Critics," *Comparative Literature*, V (1953), 50-74; Eliseo Vivas, "The Neo-Aristotelians of Chicago," *Sewanee Review*, LXI (1953), 136-149; S. F. Johnson and R. S. Crane, " 'Critics and Criticism,' A Discussion," *Journal of Aesthetics and Art Criticism*, XII (1953), 248-267.

88. Elder Olson, "The Poetic Method of Aristotle: Its Powers and Limitations," *English Institute Essays, 1951*, pp. 70-94; the quotation is from pp. 79-81.

combination of means, object, and manner, and employing the general inductive-deductive method of Aristotle which represents the program of the neo-Aristotelians. As Crane states this ideal:

> It is the merit of Aristotle . . . that he grasped the distinctive nature of poetic works as *synola,* or concrete artistic wholes, and made available, though only in outline sketch, hypotheses and analytical devices for defining literally and inductively, and with a maximum degree of differentiation, the multiple causes operative in the construction of poetic wholes of various kinds and the criteria of excellence appropriate to each. . . . The important thing in Aristotle for the present essayist, however, is not so much the statements of doctrine and history contained in the *Poetics* itself as the method through which these statements are derived and validated.[89]

While the group has so far talked about a more pluralistic method than its practices seem to indicate that it is willing to employ, and while it has been ungracious and unfriendly to other critical schools, its concern with form in terms of a demonstrably efficient method and its interest in basic critical concerns, together with the good criticism which it produces from time to time in *Modern Philology*, a journal which is becoming its unofficial organ, all make it a movement of importance for our day. There is one major direction in which its assumptions have so far not been explored, however; that is the application of modern psychology of the "unconscious" and of Gestalten and of modern anthropology to the problems which the Aristotelian method both poses and attempts to solve. That as yet unexplored path looks rich with promise. Paul Goodman's *The Structure of Literature* (1954), with its explanation of "inductive formal analysis" and its illustrations of such analyses, is an important and promising formulation of neo-Aristotelian method that seems to move broadly in this direction.

But whatever one may judge to be the most promising present school of criticism, he is certain to find the average literary critic and student of literature in the middle of the twentieth century the inheritor of the fruits of a series of victories over the anti-literary forces that beset art in the earlier part of the century.

89. *Critics and Criticism,* edited by R. S. Crane (Chicago, 1952), p. 17.

His task of defending art from continuing attacks from all quarters is no easy one, but out of the struggle and bitterness of the pitched battles of the thirties there has been forged for him a set of critical tools of a precision and accuracy never before seen in American literary history. And since they have been forged in the smithy of groups that have often derided the accepted values, been critical of the pragmatism of our culture, looked with contempt upon the optimism of our literary childhood, and decried the perfectibilitarianism of our adolescence, both the tools and their forgers have often been condemned for being either out of the mainstream of American thought or antagonistic to it. And yet these men—radical and reactionary alike—belong to the mainstream of our national life and letters; and only a view of American literature which shuts out all but the cheerful optimism of the idealistic tradition and disposes in some manner of Edwards, Hawthorne, Melville, Poe, Henry James, Crane, Dreiser, Robinson, Faulkner, and Hemingway can deny their protest and their frequent pessimism its proper place in the American tradition.

Allen Tate has said:

Literary criticism, like the Kingdom of God on earth, is perpetually necessary and, in the very nature of its middle position between imagination and philosophy, perpetually impossible. Like man, literary criticism is nothing in itself; criticism, like man, embraces pure experience or exalts pure rationality at the price of abdication from its dual nature. It is of the nature of man and of criticism to occupy the intolerable position. Like man's, the intolerable position of criticism has its own glory. It is the only position that it is very likely to have.[90]

The glory of criticism in our time is that it has consistently met its challenges and has occupied its intolerable position with honor. Although it has sometimes appeared to speak primarily in magazines of limited circulation, issued from some recess in an ivory tower, still to the shifting and confused sensibility of a significant segment of modern America it has spoken often as an aesthetic, sometimes as a philosophical, frequently as a sociological, but always as an American conscience and guide.

90. Tate, *The Forlorn Demon*, p. 111.

SELECTED READING
LIST

Among the titles listed below the reader of this book will find useful supplementary works on the history of literary criticism in America. The collections contain representative essays which will suffice for an introduction to the field. The student who desires to read more widely should consult the bibliographies named, some of which are extensive. He will find additional bibliographical references in the notes of this volume.

BIBLIOGRAPHIES

Useful bibliographies will be found in the following works:

Aldridge, John W. *Critiques and Essays on Modern Fiction, 1920-1951.* New York, 1952. Extensive bibliographies of the criticism of fiction compiled by R. W. Stallman.

American Writers Series. Selected bibliographies of individual authors.

Brown, Clarence Arthur, Editor. *The Achievement of American Criticism.* New York, 1954. A full bibliography, classified and arranged by periods.

Charvat, William. *The Origins of American Critical Thought, 1810-1835.* Philadelphia, 1936. Bibliography particularly useful for the early period.

Gayley, C. M. and Scott, F. N. *An Introduction to the Methods and Materials of Literary Criticism.* New York, 1899. Topically arranged, handbook style, with excerpts and full index.

Glicksberg, Charles I., Editor. *American Literary Criticism, 1900-1950*. New York, 1951. A list of critical works by and about each author represented appears immediately before the essay by him in the text. There is no general bibliography.

Grattan, C. Hartley. "The Present Situation in American Criticism," *Sewanee Review*, XL (1932), 11-23. Has a brief bibliography.

Hyman, Stanley Edgar. *The Armed Vision: A Study in the Methods of Modern Literary Criticism*. New York, 1948.

Ransom, John Crowe, Editor. *The Kenyon Critics*. New York, 1951. A brief bibliography is included.

Spiller, Robert E. and Others, Editors. *Literary History of the United States*. New York, 1948. Vol. III.

Stafford, John. *The Literary Criticism of "Young America."* Berkeley, 1952. Has a limited and specialized bibliography.

Stallman, Robert W. *The Critic's Handbook*. Minneapolis, 1950. Bibliography covers the period 1920-1950 and is arranged by topics.

Stallman, Robert W., Editor. *Critiques and Essays in Criticism: 1920-1948*. New York, 1949. Extensive bibliography covering the years 1920-1948.

Taylor, Walter F. *History of American Letters*. New York, 1936. Bibliography compiled by Harry Hartwick.

Zabel, Morton D., Editor. *Literary Opinion in America*. New York, 1937; revised edition, 1951. Bibliography covers the twentieth century to 1950. Appendix III has a useful list of the magazines which have published essays in literary criticism.

COLLECTIONS

Aldridge, John W., Editor. *Critiques and Essays on Modern Fiction, 1920-1951*. New York, 1952. Contains essays by British and American critics on the technique, meaning, and mode of the novel.

Bowman, James Cloyd, Editor. *Contemporary American Criticism*. New York, 1926. Contains Lowell's "Nationality in

Literature" and extracts from Whitman's *Democratic Vistas* in addition to essays by twentieth century critics.

Brown, Clarence Arthur, Editor. *The Achievement of American Criticism*. New York, 1954. The larger part of the selections are drawn from the nineteenth century, though a few have been taken from the seventeenth and eighteenth centuries, and representative essays are included from the twentieth century.

Burgum, Edwin B., Editor. *The New Criticism: an Anthology of Modern Aesthetics and Literary Criticism*. New York, 1930. Contains only a few selections from American authors.

Crane, Ronald S., Editor. *Critics and Criticism, Ancient and Modern*. Chicago, 1952. This collection contains six new essays and fourteen reprinted, with revisions, from earlier publications since 1936.

Drake, William A., Editor. *American Criticism: 1926*. New York, 1926. This was the first issue of what was apparently intended to be an annual publication, but no other issue was published.

Foerster, Norman, Editor. *American Critical Essays, XIXth and XXth Centuries*. World's Classics Series. London, 1930.

Glicksberg, Charles I., Editor. *American Literary Criticism, 1900-1950*. New York, 1951. Includes several essays in sociological criticism. Biographical sketch of the author accompanies each selection.

Moulton, Charles W., Editor. *The Library of Literary Criticism of English and American Authors*, 8 vols. Buffalo, 1901-1905. Most of the American materials are contained in Volumes V-VIII.

Payne, William Morton, Editor. *American Literary Criticism*. New York, 1904. Contains essays by R. H. Dana, George Ripley, Whipple, Stedman, Howells, Lanier, and James.

Ransom, John Crowe, Editor. *The Kenyon Critics*. New York, 1951. Contains essays by Rahv, R. P. Warren, Austin Warren, Blackmur, Trilling, and others; also fifteen book reviews.

Spingarn, Joel E., Editor. *Criticism in America: Its Function and Status.* New York, 1924. Contains essays by Babbitt, V. W. Brooks, Brownell, Boyd, Eliot, Mencken, Sherman, Spingarn, and Woodberry.

Stallman, Robert W., Editor. *The Critic's Notebook.* Minneapolis, 1950. Consists of short quotations from more than fifty critics arranged topically.

Stallman, Robert W., Editor. *Critiques and Essays in Criticism: 1920-1948.* New York, 1949. Consists of essays by and about critics, American and British chiefly, arranged topically.

Stauffer, Donald, Editor. *The Intent of the Critic.* Princeton, 1941. Contains essays by Stauffer, Wilson, Foerster, Ransom, and Auden.

Tate, Allen, Editor. *A Southern Vanguard.* New York, 1947. An anthology of critical essays, poems, and stories published as a memorial to John Peale Bishop (1892-1944). Includes "William Faulkner's Legend of the South," by Malcolm Cowley and "The New Criticism and the Southern Critics," by Robert W. Stallman, and seven other critical essays.

Tate, Allen, Editor. *The Language of Poetry.* Princeton, 1942. Contains essays by Philip Wheelwright, Cleanth Brooks, I. A. Richards, and Wallace Stevens, read at Princeton University in the spring of 1941 under the auspices of the Creative Arts Program.

West, Ray Benedict, Jr., Editor. *Essays in Modern Literary Criticism.* New York and Toronto, 1952. Contains 43 essays, including one each from Coleridge, Arnold, James, De Gourmont, Croce, and Santayana, and the rest from the chief British and American critics of the present century.

Wilson, Edmund, Editor. *The Shock of Recognition: the Development of Literature in the United States Recorded by the Men Who Made It.* New York, 1943. Contains essays, chiefly on their own contemporaries, by Lowell, Poe, Melville, James, Howells, Eliot, Mencken, and others.

Zabel, Morton D., Editor. *Literary Opinion in America.* New York, 1937; revised edition, 1951. Contains essays by James and Howells and by the principal American critics of the twentieth century, arranged topically. Includes quite a number of essays in analytical criticism.

WORKS ON THE HISTORY OF LITERARY CRITICISM

Boyd, Ernest. "Marxian Literary Critics," *Scribner's,* XCVIII (1935), 342-46.

Brown, Clarence Arthur. *The Achievement of American Criticism.* New York, 1954. Essays are arranged in five chronological periods, and the editor has provided an extended historical introduction to each period. The five introductions amount to about 120 pages of the history of criticism.

Brown, E. K. "The National Idea in American Criticism," *Dalhousie Review,* XIV (1934), 133-47.

Charvat, William. *The Origins of American Critical Thought: 1810-1835.* Philadelphia, 1936.

Clark, Harry H. "Literary Criticism in the *North American Review,* 1815-1835," *Transactions of the Wisconsin Academy of Sciences, Arts, and Letters,* XXXII (1940), 299-350. Contains brief summaries of 231 articles.

Clark, Harry H. "Nationalism in American Literature," *University of Toronto Quarterly,* II (1933), 492-519.

Clark, Harry H., Editor. *Transitions in American Literary History.* Durham, N. C., 1954. *Passim.*

De Mille, George E. *Literary Criticism in America.* New York, 1931. Contains a chapter on the *North American Review* and one each on Lowell, Poe, Emerson and Margaret Fuller, Stedman, James, Howells, Huneker, and Sherman.

Denny, Margaret, and Gilman, William H., Editors. *The American Writer and the European Tradition.* Minneapolis, 1950. Twelve essays from twelve lectures delivered in the winter of 1948-49 at the University of Rochester.

Fishman, Solomon. *The Disinherited of Art* (No. 2 in the series, Perspectives in Criticism), Berkeley, 1952.

Foerster, Norman. *American Criticism.* Boston, 1928. Extended essays on the criticism of Poe, Emerson, Lowell, and

Whitman, and a summary essay on criticism in the twentieth century.

Foerster, Norman, Editor. *Humanism and America.* New York, 1930. Contains essays by More, Babbitt, Eliot, Shafer, H. H. Clark, Munson, and others.

Frierson, W. C., and Edwards, Herbert. "Impact of French Naturalism on American Critical Opinion, 1877-1892," *PMLA,* LXIII (1948), 1007-16.

Glicksberg, Charles I., Editor. *American Literary Criticism, 1900-1950.* New York, 1951. Introduction, pp. 3-59.

Glicksberg, Charles I. "Two Decades of American Criticism," *Dalhousie Review,* XVI (1936), 229-42.

Grattan, C. Hartley. "The Present Situation in American Criticism," *Sewanee Review,* XL (1932), 11-23.

Hyman, Stanley Edgar. *The Armed Vision: A Study in the Methods of Modern Literary Criticism.* New York, 1948.

Kazin, Alfred. *On Native Ground.* New York, 1942.

McWilliams, Cary. "Localism in American Criticism," *Southwest Review,* XIX (1934), 410-28.

O'Connor, William Van. *An Age of Criticism: 1900-1950.* Chicago, 1952.

Pritchard, John Paul. *Return to the Fountains.* Durham, N. C., 1942.

Quinn, Arthur Hobson, Editor. *The Literature of the American People.* New York, 1951. Pp. 384-422 and 628-984 *passim.*

Ransom, John Crowe. *The New Criticism.* New York, 1941. Discusses I. A. Richards as the Psychological Critic, T. S. Eliot as the Historical Critic, and Yvor Winters as the Logical Critic. Points out the need of an Ontological Critic.

Shafer, Robert. *Paul Elmer More and American Criticism.* New Haven, 1935. Literary criticism in general is discussed in the first part.

Shumaker, Wayne. *Elements of Critical Theory* (No. 1 in the series, Perspectives in Criticism), Berkeley, 1952.

Smith, Bernard. *Forces in American Criticism.* New York, 1939.

Interpretations, in general, are made from the Marxian point of view.

Spencer, Benjamin T. "A National Literature, 1837-1855," *American Literature*, VIII (1936), 125-59.

Spiller, Robert E., and Others, Editors. *Literary History of the United States*. New York, 1948. Vols. I and II *passim*; Vol. III, pp. 54-64.

Stafford, John. *The Literary Criticism of "Young America."* Berkeley, 1952.

Zabel, Morton D., Editor. *Literary Opinion in America*. New York, 1937; revised edition, 1951. In the Introduction, revised edition, pp. 1-43, the editor discusses briefly Poe, Emerson, James, and Howells, and in more detail the critics of the twentieth century.

INDEX

INDEX

INDEX

INDEX

INDEX

INDEX

INDEX

INDEX

Twain, Mark, 4, 8, 118, 122, 123, 127, 128, 131, 147, 219
Twentieth Century Novel: Studies in Technique, The (Beach), 241
Two Years Before the Mast (Dana), 79, 80
Tyler, M. C., 193
Typee (Melville), 38, 39, 105

Ulysses (Joyce), 224n
Understanding Drama (Brooks and Heilman), 237
Understanding Fiction (Brooks and Warren), 232, 237
Understanding Poetry (Brooks and Warren), 232, 237
United States Catholic Magazine, 39
Use of Poetry and the Use of Criticism, The (Eliot), 187

Véron, Eugène, 140
Verplanck, G. C., 37, 46, 60
Very, Jones, 23, 37, 61

Walden (Thoreau), 24, 96
Walker, Timothy, 67
Walsh, Robert, 19, 43
Walt Whitman, an American (Canby), 211
Ward, S. G., 23, 35, 51, 52
Warner, C. D., 131, 146
Warren, Austin, 205
Warren, R. P., 208, 231, 237
Washington Square (James), 128
Week on the Concord and Merrimack Rivers, A (Thoreau), 24
Weigand, Wilhelm, 56
Weinberg, Bernard, 243
Wellek, René, 205, 208
Well Wrought Urn, The (Cleanth Brooks), 237
West, Ray, 227, 241
Westfall, A. W., 36
Westminster Review, 7, 64
Wharton, Edith, 163
What Maisie Knew (James), 147

Wheaton, Henry, 62
Wheelwright, Philip, 224
Whelpley, J. D., 75, 80, 81
When Knighthood Was in Flower (Major), 146
Whig Review, 5, 47, 75, 77, 82
Whipple, E. P., 37, 64, 65, 75, 80, 88, 106, 107, 108, 111, 120
White Jacket (Melville), 105
Whitman, Walt, 4, 7, 8, 9, 10, 11, 59, 72, 75, 87, 88, 90, 91, 92, 93, 94, 95, 96, 102, 103, 105, 111, 116, 120, 121, 129, 138, 140, 145, 149, 152, 154, 164, 176, 177, 179, 242
Whittier, J. G., 23, 39, 44, 71, 119, 127
Wilde, Richard, 62
Wilhelm Meister (Goethe), 50
Wilkins, Mary, 147, 148
Willis, N. P., 50, 52
Wilmer, L. A., 45
Wilson, Edmund, 168, 170, 173n, 177, 180, 192, 194, 205, 206, 209, 213, 214, 219, 221, 231, 232, 239
Wilson, Woodrow, 69, 168
Wine of the Puritans (Brooks), 167
Winters, Yvor, 10, 229, 231, 235, 236
Wirt, William, 25
Woodberry, G. W., 115, 132, 136, 154, 175
Woolf, Virginia, 222
Woolson, C. F., 128
Wordsworth, William, 23, 43, 47, 48, 66, 76, 81, 94, 102, 110, 111, 187, 188
World of Fiction, The (De Voto), 213
World's Body, The (Ransom), 233
Wormhout, Arthur, 219
Wound and the Bow, The (Wilson), 219
Writers in Crisis: The American Novel, 1925-1940 (Geismar), 212

Yeats, W. B., 84, 194
Youth and Life (Bourne), 167

Zabel, M. D., 203, 240
Zola, Emile, 119, 126, 129, 130, 146, 147, 150